# The $10 Trillion Opportunity

■

## Designing Successful Exit Strategies
## for Middle Market Business Owners

*A Guide for Professional Advisors*

# The $10 Trillion Opportunity

■

## Designing Successful Exit Strategies for Middle Market Business Owners

*A Guide for Professional Advisors*

■

**Richard E. Jackim, JD, MBA**

*with*

**Peter G. Christman**

Published by the

Exit Planning Institute

An R. Jackim & Company Publication

Published by Exit Planning Institute, LLC
www.exit-planning-institute.org

Printed in the United States of America

Book design and typesetting by JustYourType.biz

Discount pricing is available for bulk orders of this book.

For additional information contact Book Sales at
booksales@exit-planning-institute.org

Second Hardcover Edition 2005 Library of Congress Catalog Number: 2005922716

Jackim, Richard E., 1961 -

The Ten Trillion Dollar Opportunity: Designing Successful Exit Strategies for Middle Market Business Owners

p. cm.

ISBN 0-9776023-0-3 (previously ISBN 0-9766603-0-X)

1. Business Enterprise – United States. 2. Business Enterprise, Sale of – United States. 3. Business Enterprise, Planning – United States. 4. Business Enterprise – Consulting. 5. Business Enterprises – Taxation – United States.

Although the case studies presented in this book are based on real clients and real situations, the names and facts in each case study have been changed to protect the privacy of the individuals or clients involved.

This book is designed to provide readers with accurate and authoritative information regarding the subject matter covered. It is sold with the understanding that although one of the authors is an attorney, neither he, his investment banking firm, nor the publisher are engaged by the reader to provide or render legal, accounting, or other professional advice. If legal, tax, or other expert advice is sought or required by the reader, the services of competent professionals licensed to perform those services should be retained. The purpose of this book is to educate readers. The authors and the Exit Planning Institute shall not have any liability or responsibility to any person or entity with respect to any loss or damage caused, or alleged to be caused, directly or indirectly by reliance on information contained in this book.

# Acknowledgements

This book was written with the support, guidance, and inspiration of Peter G. Christman, my friend and former partner.

In addition, I would like to thank the literally dozens of people behind the scenes who reviewed, edited, and provided valuable comments and feedback on this book. In particular, I wish to thank Anneke Chamy, Jack Emmons, Mike Nall, Perry Phillips, Ward Rantala, and Jim Bates, for their insightful contributions to this book and their comments on multiple drafts of this book in manuscript form. Thanks to Art Fox for his creative input and ideas when this book was only a concept.

I am also deeply indebted to Ward Rantala for his careful and insightful editing of this book. Ward's unique ability to change a word here and there made a tremendous difference in the quality of my writing.

Finally, I must thank the hundreds of clients and former clients as well as their advisors from whom I have learned so much.

Richard E. Jackim

## Richard E. Jackim, JD, MBA

Richard Jackim is an experienced attorney and investment banker. During his career as an investment banker, Mr. Jackim has been involved in more than 60 mergers or acquisitions of middle market companies with a combined market value of over $1 billion.

Mr. Jackim is a respected expert on the topic of exit planning and middle market investment banking. He has been quoted in or written articles for *Business Week, The Chicago Tribune, The Counselor, The Business Ledger, Injection Molding Magazine, Transport Topics*, and other regional and national publications.

Rich received his law degree with honors from Cornell Law School. He began his career with the New York law firm of White & Case.

Rich later received an MBA from The Kellogg Graduate School of Management.

After business school, Rich worked as an investment banker for Prudential Capital, one of the investment units of The Prudential Insurance Company. Mr. Jackim was recruited to become President of a national middle market mergers and acquisitions firm with 14 offices around the country. Rich left to co-found The Christman Group with Peter G. Christman.

Rich is now a managing director with MidCap Advisors, LLC, a middle market investment banking firm, based in New York, with offices across the United States. MidCap Advisors provides business owners with comprehensive exit planning and investment banking services.

## Peter G. Christman

Peter Christman is an experienced entrepreneur, corporate executive and investment banker. After spending 25 years as an investment banker with other firms, Peter Christman co-founded The Christman Group to provide middle market business owners with a comprehensive and integrated suite of services that simplify the exit process while maximizing the value of the client's business.

During his 25-year career Pete has successfully sold more than 200 companies in a wide variety of industries. Transactions have ranged in size from several million dollars to over one hundred million dollars.

This book is dedicated to my wife, Susan Bush, whose love and support helped me tackle this project, and to my daughter, Skyler, and my son, Parker, for their enthusiastic love of life and all its adventures.

For the last 20 years, I've been working with business owners, attorneys, CPAs, and other highly, qualified, financial advisors in the challenging and rewarding field of middle market mergers and acquisitions. The many transaction successes and failures I've observed over this time have made me a life long believer that independent professionals must collaborate effectively in order to deliver superior results to clients. Nowhere is this more true than in the complicated, high-stakes arena of exit planning.

*The Ten Trillion Dollar Opportunity* is, without a doubt, the most comprehensive and integrated approach to exit planning available. This book is a pioneering work on the important topic of exit planning addressing important topics such as understanding an owner's goals, the importance of a good business valuation, the role of financial planning, how to maximize value, and how to open up channels of communication. It also tackles topics such as the roles of each of the professional advisors, the return on investment that exit planning delivers, and how to market your exit planning expertise. As a result, this book is an essential guide for practitioners representing middle-market, private business owners.

*The Ten Trillion Dollar Opportunity* does a masterful job summarizing this complex, multidisciplinary topic. Rich Jackim's experience, as an investment banker, entrepreneur, and Wall Street attorney, gives him the unique ability to write about the business, marketing, and technical issues of exit planning with equal authority. *The Ten Trillion Dollar Opportunity* is sure to become one of the most important resources for professional advisors who want to learn how to successfully design and implement successful exit plans for their clients. It also takes a very practical "how-to" approach to help you integrate exit planning into your practice. Using illustrative examples and case studies the author has distilled over 15 years of insight into a wise, down-to-earth, and eminently practical guide on exit planning.

As someone who spent nearly my entire career selling professional services, I was fascinated by the fundamental business proposition featured in *The Ten Trillion Dollar Opportunity*. Rich Jackim and Peter Christman make a very convincing argument for using an exit planning context or framework to help you more effectively position your professional services and products. Using exit planning as a contextual framework puts consultative selling in an entirely new and more practical light. Anyone needing to build their professional practice (and who doesn't) will appreciate, use, and benefit from the lessons of this book!

In *The Ten Trillion Dollar Opportunity*, Jackim and Christman weave together professional disciplines, ideas, and marketing techniques with a single goal in mind, maximizing business value and the personal wealth of private business owners. The author makes a very persuasive case that by building a multi-disciplinary team of advisors you can deliver best-of-the-best service and results to your clients. Jackim also points out that this approach has the added benefit of creating a new business referral machine to significantly grow your business. However, Jackim constantly reminds us that exit planning is all about focusing on the client's goals, and that by using the tools and techniques offered in this book to do just that, your professional practice will grow by leaps and bounds.

If you are just entering your professional life, *The Ten Trillion Dollar Opportunity* will chop years off your learning curve. If you are an old pro, Jackim's observations will elevate your professional practice to new levels. *The Ten Trillion Dollar Opportunity* is not simply about becoming a better business advisor; it is about positioning yourself so your services sell themselves while making you, your clients' "most trusted advisor."

In summation, the multidisciplinary approach Jackim advocates offers an attractive alternative to the "one stop" shopping model offered by many professional firms. Jackim encourages independent business advisors to collaborate with other professionals to bring clients the additional expertise needed for more complex client engagements. With global access to intellectual capital, proven resources, and other "world class" experts, clients (and their advisors) can now exercise enormous "free choice" to best satisfy any specific need.

The Gartner Group forecasts that by 2005, 80% of all global knowledge work will be delivered by virtual project teams. Virtual teams are groups of people who work together but are physically apart. Their activities are often time-bound – they come together to accomplish a specific task and when their objective is met, they disband, with members joining other newly formed project teams.

I strongly encourage you to read and re-read this book and then incorporate its concepts into your professional practice. You and your clients will be glad you did.

Michael R. Nall, CPA, CM&A

*Founder*

*The Alliance of Merger & Acquisition Advisors (AMAA)*

*and The Alliance for Corporate Wealth (ACW)*

# TABLE OF CONTENTS

# Chapter 1

# An Introduction to Exit Planning

## Case Study: The Beginning

Jim Unger sat across a table from me at the University Club in Chicago. His hand trembled slightly as he placed a wire transfer confirmation in front of me. My firm and I just spent 12 months creating and implementing Jim's strategic exit plan. As a result, Jim just sold his business and he was pleased; $12 million had just been deposited in his bank account.

Jim was smiling from ear to ear, but his eyes were brimming with tears. This had been a very emotional process for him. He admitted, as we spoke, that the process of exiting his business had been exhilarating and terrifying at the same time. When he said this, he added he could not have done it without our help. The exit process we helped Jim design ensured that Jim and his family would be able to accomplish all their personal and financial goals.

We toasted Jim's success with a bottle of champagne he ordered for the occasion. As we were leaving that night, Jim gave me a big hug and told me a few business owners from his country club were curious about how he had been so successful selling his business. When Jim asked if I'd be willing to talk them, I smiled. That is how it started.

Our success with Jim and other business owners like him pointed out a real and growing need in the business community. The day after my dinner with Jim, I began reflecting on some of the not-so-successful exits many business owners have experienced.

## Case Study: Not So Fortunate

Terry Burns contacted us to sell his company. Terry was in his forties, but was burned out and wanted to spend more time with his family. The company he built was one of the finest in his industry and generating approximately $3 million in cash flow each year. In the end, Terry decided to use another firm to help sell his company. I was disappointed our firm did not get the engagement, but even more disappointed when I learned who Terry had chosen instead of us. Despite our repeated efforts, Terry went ahead with his decision.

We did not hear from Terry for two and a half years. Then, out of the blue, Terry called and asked if I had time to talk. When we sat down,

Terry shared the experience he had in trying to sell his business.

Terry's story is one commonly heard in investment banking circles. The intermediary Terry selected did not do any advance planning or develop a comprehensive road map for the investment banking process. The intermediary was focused on taking Terry's company to market as quickly as possible. Because Terry and his advisors did not have a well thought out marketing program for the company, the intermediary only came up with two potential buyers for Terry's business. This was astonishing given the reputation and financial performance of Terry's company. It turned out the intermediary had not proactively marketed the company or run an investment banking auction process. Instead, the intermediary worked on finding one buyer at a time.

The first buyer was an individual who owned a similar company in Terry's industry. The buyer and seller entered into due diligence and documentation before anyone thought to determine if the buyer was financially qualified to purchase Terry's company. In the end he was not. By that time, Terry had spent over $40,000 in legal and accounting fees

After this deal fell through, Terry's intermediary arranged meetings with another buyer and Terry went down the due diligence track again. While the second buyer was financially qualified, and the purchase price was right, but the terms the buyer proposed were unacceptable. At this point, Terry was so frustrated he terminated the sale process and took his company off the market after spending nearly 20 hours a week for 12 months on these two transactions.

To add insult to injury, the intermediary sued Terry claiming he was owed a success fee since he delivered a "ready, willing, and able buyer." The judge threw the lawsuit out, but it cost Terry $35,000 in legal fees to defend himself.

In the meantime, because Terry was not able to remain focused on his business during the sales process, his company's financial performance deteriorated. By the end of the sales process, the company had lost 30% of its revenues and was in the red. As a result, the company was no longer saleable. Terry had to commit himself to rebuild his business, realign his management team, and get the company back on track.

Terry called us to admit he made a mistake and that it cost him dearly. The good news, and there is good news here, is that Terry did not lose his business or sell his company only to discover it did not accomplish any of his personal goals. The good news is Terry got a second chance many business owners do not. In a few years, when the company is back at its peak, Terry will be in a position to avoid his past mistakes and exit his business the right way.

Reflecting on the very different experiences of Jim Unger and Terry Burns, led me to believe there was a better way to provide investment banking services to middle market business owners.  I began thinking about how to change the way we do business so we could consistently deliver success stories for all of our clients.

We began by redefining our investment banking practice, narrowing and refining our focus from that of a traditional, middle market investment banking firm, to an investment bank specializing in developing and executing successful exit plans for private business owners.

Our focus on exit planning is one of the reasons we no longer make cold calls.  It is the reason that clients and their advisors seek us out.  It is the reason clients do not negotiate our fees.  It is the reason why virtually all our clients are referrals from other professionals and former clients.  *The $10 Trillion Dollar Opportunity* shows you how you can reposition your professional practice and enjoy the same success.

*The $10 Trillion Dollar Opportunity* is designed specifically for investment bankers, business brokers, lawyers, accountants, estate planners, financial advisors, wealth managers, real estate professionals, commercial bankers, and virtually any other professional who advises owners of privately held businesses.

It will show you how to help your clients achieve these three key goals:

1. Commit to developing and implementing a good exit plan
2. Create a comprehensive exit plan custom-tailored to meet each business owner's individual needs
3. Successfully execute the plan

## Why this Book Is the Most Important Business Development Tool You'll Use for the Next 20 Years

This book shows you how to tap into a new source of business opportunities that will let you grow your professional practice in dynamic and rewarding new ways.

Within a few months you'll be bringing in new clients, larger clients, and better clients.  You'll be generating more revenues than ever before.

*The $10 Trillion Dollar Opportunity* takes you step by step through a process that enables you to gain instant credibility with business owners and other professional advisors.  It teaches you how to differentiate yourself from every other professional with whom you compete.  It will turn you into a client magnet that regularly attracts leads and prospects.

And, the best part is that these new opportunities will become more and more plentiful over the next 20 years.  Why?  Because they are driven by needs of the maturing Baby Boomer generation.

## What Is an Exit Plan?

An exit plan is a comprehensive road map to successfully exit a privately held business.  *An exit plan asks and answers all the business, personal, financial, legal, and tax questions involved in selling a privately owned business.*  It includes contingencies for illness, burnout, divorce, and even the owner's death.  Its purpose is to maximize the value of the business at the time of exit, minimize the amount of taxes paid, and ensure that the business owner is able to accomplish all his or her personal and financial goals in the process.

An exit plan can be complex and usually requires advice from a number of different specialties.  But, the failure to create a well-defined exit plan virtually guarantees that business owners will:

- Exit their companies as a result of pressure from outside circumstances, not as a result of their own desires
- Exit their companies on a timetable that's forced on them instead of one that meets their needs
- Undervalue their companies and leave hard-earned wealth on the table
- Pay too much in taxes
- Lose control over the process by being reactive and limiting their exit options
- Fail to realize all their business and personal goals
- Suffer unnecessary psychological stress
- Watch a lifetime of work disintegrate as a result of poor business continuity planning
- Lose confidentiality during the sale or exit process

On the other hand, a well-designed and implemented exit plan enables business owners to:

- Control how and when they exit
- Maximize company value in good times and bad
- Minimize, defer, or eliminate capital gains taxes
- Retain control by generating a number of strategic exit options
- Ensure they achieve all their business and personal goals

- Reduce their stress and that of their employees and families
- Ensure continuity of the business

A recent survey showed the number one reason private business sales fail or only partially succeed is a lack of planning on the seller's part.[1] However, in spite of the importance of exit planning, most business owners spend more time planning a family vacation, than when and how to exit their businesses.

## Your Role in the $10 Trillion Opportunity

Within the next 20 years, more than 90 million people in the United States and Canada will be retiring. These are the "baby boomers," the generation born between 1946 and 1964.

Baby boomers' needs and wants dominate and drive the marketplace, and the marketplace has bent over backward to meet their desires. For example, as the boomers passed from birth through infancy, sales in the prepared baby food industry skyrocketed from 270 million jars per year to 1.5 billion jars. As they enjoyed early childhood, the baby boomers were greeted with Frisbees®, Hula Hoops®, skateboards, and Tinker Toys®. Toy companies made billions by providing tens of thousands of brand-new playthings to educate and entertain the boomers. As the boomers hit their teenage years, companies such as McDonald's®, Burger King®, and Kentucky Fried Chicken®, earned billions. They became part of a brand-new industry specifically designed to cater to the first generation spending a good deal of its social life in a car.

Community infrastructures also were defined by the boomers' needs. Architects, engineers, and builders saw their businesses jump as roads, housing developments, and schools were built at breakneck speed to accommodate this unprecedented growth. Social programs were implemented to cope with the huge numbers of new problems and opportunities created by this massive group, while the number of universities and vocational schools more than doubled to accommodate the enormous influx of students.

Baby boomers have been the most affluent and influential population group in the history of mankind, and now they're getting ready to retire. Economist and demographic expert Robert Avery, at Cornell University, predicts baby boomers will transfer $10 trillion to later generations—the largest generational transfer of

---

1  Source: PriceWaterhouseCoopers, *Whose Business Is It Anyway? Smart Strategies for Ownership Succession, and* University of Connecticut Family Business Program, *Family Business Survey*

wealth in the history of humankind. The vast majority of this wealth is held as stock in more than 12 million privately owned businesses, and during the next 10–15 years, more than 70 percent of these companies are expected to change hands.

This unprecedented transfer of wealth presents a unique opportunity for you to add tremendous value, enhance your clients' lives, and take your practice to the next level. Baby boomers are charging toward retirement with the same unstoppable single-mindedness with which they've approached the rest of their lives. If you want to ride this trend to greater success, you must have an understanding of exit planning and the important role that you can play in the process.

## Why Exit Planning Is a Win-Win Solution

You are in a position to help your clients do more than simply exit from their business; you have the power to help them realize the American dream. You can help your clients redefine themselves in exciting and meaningful ways as they move into a retirement free from worries about money—and by helping your clients realize their dreams, you will be doing the same thing for yourself.

An advisor who is trained in exit planning, and who approaches the exit-planning process in a client-centered holistic way can provide value-added services that will almost certainly have a dramatic and positive effect on his or her client's lives while simultaneously boosting the advisor's businesses—a true win-win outcome. Some of the benefits of successful exit planning for the professional advisor include:

- Build deeper and stronger relationships with existing clients
- Create clear differentiation between a skilled exit-planning professional and the advisor who focuses merely on exercising his or her traditional skills
- Generate additional revenues for you as you provide value-added solutions to clients
- Identify opportunities to provide new value-added services or products to your clients
- Build a collaborative network with other professionals that fosters mutual business referrals in an exit-planning environment
- Generate a high degree of personal self-actualization by expanding individual and professional skills

## The Secret to Success Is Easing a Business Owner's Pain

In spite of overwhelming evidence that exit planning is a vital part of business ownership, most business owners don't create an exit plan. There are a number of reasons why they avoid it, ranging from the deeply psychological to the purely practical.

First, just as most of us don't like to talk about our own deaths, business owners don't want to talk about the end of their businesses. Even if the business goes on after they exit, they are losing a part of themselves that has provided extraordinary value and meaning to their lives. They're afraid to talk about the subject, just as some of us put off making out a will or buying life insurance. Dealing with these subjects somehow makes them more real, which means we have to acknowledge the pain they might cause. It's basic human nature to avoid the unpleasant, and no matter how smart or successful a business owner is, he or she will almost always avoid painful situations even if they're necessary for future health.

Second, exit planning is time consuming. Most business owners are swamped with work on a day-to-day basis. Some spend 60-80 hours per week keeping things running, putting out fires, and trying to balance the demands of the business with family and social obligations. It's no wonder they don't feel they have time to create a comprehensive exit plan.

Third, exit planning is complex and very few resources exist to guide a business owner step by step through the process. Ignorance of the process, combined with the knowledge it must be done sooner or later, can create a lot of tension for a business owner. If a business owner lacks the means to attack the problem head-on, he or she usually will sidestep it as long as possible.

Finally, studies show that most business owners do not understand the tremendous returns investment exit planning can provide them. A lack of understanding prevents them from weighing the benefits of doing something versus the costs of doing nothing. As a result, they favor the status quo and inertia.

The combination of an intense need for exit planning and an equally intense resistance to doing so creates a powerful and painful tension in your clients' minds. At first glance, these problems might suggest that any sensible advisor should run, not walk, away from any exit planning engagement. Why would anyone in his right mind want to tackle a task loaded with so much client resistance?

The important thing to remember is that whenever change is imminent and unavoidable, as it is for retiring baby boomers, the advisor who can help clients make that change smoothly and painlessly becomes invaluable.

In Chapter 4 we discuss each of these issues in more detail and provide you with ways to help business owners resolve these problems.

As a skilled exit planner, you will have the power to relieve your clients' tension. You will not only provide enormous value to your clients, but also move way beyond being just a knowledgeable resource - you will become a trusted and indispensable advisor.

## What You Will Learn from This Book

The *$10 Trillion Dollar Opportunity* shows you how to help business owners articulate and crystallize their business, personal, and family/estate goals, which will become the foundation the rest of the exit plan is built upon. You'll learn:

- How to build a team of advisors to help you prepare a detailed business appraisal establishing a baseline value for the business
- Methods for enhancing the value of the client's business prior to an exit
- Pros and cons of various exit alternatives, such as a third-party sale, ESOP, management buy-out, family succession, refinancing, or liquidation
- Ways to identify sound strategies for minimizing taxes related to the exit, including capital gains, ordinary income, and estate taxes
- How important it is for clients to develop a wealth management plan before the liquidity event, rather than afterward, so the exit accomplishes their personal and financial goals
- Finally, how to create an action plan that spells out the specific steps owners and their advisory team must take to prepare for an exit

This book contains real-world examples of the different steps involved in creating and implementing a successful exit plan and the benefits they provide to the business owner. We also point out each step's importance to you, as a professional advisor, and how each contributes to your success.

As you will see, a variety of skill sets is necessary to design a comprehensive and integrated exit plan. Because no single professional advisor has all the expertise required, exit planning is a multidisciplinary endeavor. The best exit plans are developed by a team that includes a:

- Business attorney with mergers and acquisitions experience
- Financial advisor or wealth-management professional who does planning work
- Tax specialist well-versed in the latest personal and business tax issues
- Insurance professional
- Investment banking firm that specializes in exit planning

Depending on each individual business owner's circumstances, additional professionals might also be involved, such as a real estate broker, a family psychologist, or a business consultant.

In addition to covering the details of an exit plan, *The $10 Trillion Dollar Opportunity* shows you how to assemble the right team of professionals to help your clients, how to quarterback the team, and how to make these professionals become your biggest source of new clients.

Finally, we show you how to keep the exit planning and execution process on track, and how to ensure that all the different players are working together to produce the best possible outcome for you and your clients.

Let's get started.

# Chapter 2

# The Benefits of Exit Planning for Business Owners

Exit planning is one of those unique win-win propositions. In this book we demonstrate the significant benefits a well-designed exit plan can deliver for a business owner. At the same time, we explore the significant benefits professional advisors stand to gain by helping business owners design and implement successful exit plans.

## The Benefits to Business Owners

A well-designed and implemented exit plan is a powerful and valuable business and personal planning tool. It enables business owners to:

- Achieve their business and personal goals
- Facilitate their retirement
- Control how and when they exit
- Ensure survival and growth of their business
- Preserve family harmony
- Reduce employee and family uncertainty
- Maximize company value in good times and bad
- Minimize, defer, or eliminate capital gains, estate, and income taxes
- Have strategic options from which to choose

On the other side of the equation, the failure to have a well-defined exit plan results in real costs to business owners. Without a comprehensive plan, business owners typically:

- Undervalue their companies leaving hard-earned wealth on the table
- Pay too much in capital gains and estate taxes
- Lose control over the exit process
- Fail to realize their personal, financial, or business goals during the exit process

Experience has shown that a business owner who sells his business without an exit plan, typically sells it for too little. Worse yet, if they do nothing and the business is sold after they die, its value usually falls dramatically and it becomes a burden to their family. That's not the legacy most business owners want to leave behind.

Despite the tremendous value of exit planning, most business owners do not have an exit plan. In fact, only an estimated 28 percent of private businesses have done any exit planning. Due to a lack of good planning, only 30 percent of family-owned businesses survive through the second generation. A study of 300 former business owners who sold their companies within the last 12 months showed that 75 percent of the respondents felt the sale did not accomplish their personal or financial objectives. These statistics suggest too few business owners are proactively planning for the inevitable exit process.

## Case Studies

The following case studies are based on our real-world experience with two family businesses. Each family handled the exit planning process in a dramatically different way. These case studies illustrate the importance of goal setting, communication, and a holistic or comprehensive approach to succession planning.

### Case Study: The Keil Family

**The Situation:** Ronald Keil is a business owner in his late sixties. Mr. Keil has two children, Duke and Sarah. Duke is interested in playing a more active role in the business but does not have much experience. Sarah does not currently work in the family business and has expressed little interest in doing so. Mary, Ronald Keil's wife, owns stock in the company but is not active in the company. Mary has been asking Ronald to scale back his involvement in the business so the two of them can enjoy their retirement years together. Mary would like to move to Florida and be able to travel freely without the demands of the business.

**The Keil Exit Plan:** Ron Keil met with his attorney to create an estate plan— one that included family partnerships and trusts that hold insurance and company stock. Ronald Keil did not completely understand what had been done but felt there would be large estate tax benefits. To train the next generation to take over the company, Duke was brought into the family business and made its president while Ron took on the CEO role. The family believed the business succession plan was "complete."

**A Year Later:** Ronald Keil was ready to scale back his involvement in the business but found he was not able to do so. The business under Duke's leadership began to flounder, due in part to Duke's lack of experience and focus. As a result, Ron relied more and more on two key employees (who were not family members or shareholders in the company) to get things done. Duke began to recognize this, and an unspoken resentment began to build between Duke and the key employees. Meanwhile, Sarah, Ron's daughter and Duke's sister, began to feel unappreciated. She saw Duke drawing a significant salary, driving a company car, and living at the perceived expense of Sarah's year-end distribution. Sarah also saw how the company was performing under Duke's leadership and felt her birthright or inheritance was at risk. Sarah became increasingly resentful of other family members who had rallied behind her brother.

Ron now began to feel pressure at work and at home—and, not surprisingly, began developing health complications. His doctor recommended Ron reduce time spent in the office. Ron's absence left a vacuum Duke had to fill—a role for which he was not adequately prepared. As a result, the company's two key employees left, taking several of the company's key customers with them. Sales dropped dramatically and the company's top salespeople began to leave for the competition.

Sarah saw the market value of the company dropping and demanded Duke either be demoted or fired. Ron and Mary worried the poor results from the company would affect their retirement cash flow and long-awaited travel plans. This additional stress contributed to Ron's continuing health issues.

**Two Years Later:** Ron Keil's health was the same and the company continued to suffer. The children no longer spoke with each other and the annual Keil family get-togethers were cancelled. Sensing Ron would not replace or demote Duke, Sarah lobbied that her father sell the company to a third party for cash.

The company was ultimately sold to a third party, but the value received was a fraction of the value used in the estate plan prepared several years earlier. The company's corporate structure and the terms of sale left the family with only about 50 percent of what it had originally expected. In addition, because no capital gains tax planning was done, Ron paid more capital gains taxes than he should have, further eroding the proceeds of the sale.

**Postscript:** Unfortunately, Duke was not prepared to find a similar job elsewhere and struggled professionally for many years. Ron and Mary's retirement plans had to be revised given the lower-than-expected sale proceeds. In fact, their updated financial plan showed they would need to use a large portion of the sale proceeds to fund their retirement needs. This situation dramatically reduced the inheritance Duke and Sarah would ultimately receive. As a result, both siblings were resentful. They silently blamed their father for the reduction in their inheritance. This was certainly not the legacy Ron Keil hoped to leave his family.

Ron Keil used sophisticated estate planning advisors, but didn't realize a succession plan is different from an estate plan, and that he also must consider other issues that can have a dramatic affect on the success or failure of an owner's ultimate exit from business.    Unfortunately, this is how the vast majority of business owners go about the process of exiting from their businesses.

Now let's look at a different business owner and a different approach.

### Case Study: The Bacas Family

Andrew Bacas was a privately held business owner in his late sixties. Mr. Bacas had two children, Regina and Virginia. Regina had worked in the family business for almost 15 years and was VP of Operations. Virginia was a practicing nurse not actively involved in the family business. Andrew Bacas' wife, Kathy, owned stock but did not participate actively in company management. Kathy and Andy had many interests outside the business, including the desire to live overseas. Andy wanted to scale back his involvement in the business so he and Kathy could enjoy these interests together while they remained active and in good health.

**The Bacas Exit Plan:** Andy Bacas began his succession planning by using the multidisciplinary approach advocated in this book. The process is designed to encourage the input and participation of all key stakeholders affected by the plan (in this case, Andrew Bacas, Kathy Bacas, Regina Bacas, Virginia Bacas, and two key employees).

Guided by an experienced professional and using proven methods and assessment tools, each stakeholder was able to communicate his or her goals, expectations, and feelings in an open and non-threatening way. The net result? A concise statement about these feelings was compiled and presented to the owner and the other stakeholders. Strategic meetings with stakeholders were conducted and a multidisciplinary blueprint for success was developed. Everyone became focused *as a team* on the important strategic decisions ahead.

Andrew Bacas discovered his daughter Regina was very concerned she might be expected to play a role in the company at some point in the future. She was not interested and she was afraid saying so would hurt their father's feelings. In addition, both daughters were afraid that if their father's exit were handled poorly, it would have a significant impact on the financial legacy they expected from the business. This possibility was an unspoken source of stress for both girls because they had made a number of life style decisions counting on a significant legacy from their father at the time of his death.

In addition, Andrew discovered a key employee was concerned about Andrew's future plans and had been privately exploring his options with a competitor. This individual had been offered an attractive compensation package but preferred his current position if his future with the company was secure. He did not have any ownership expectations, but did express a desire for a greater share of the expected success the company would enjoy over the next few years, based on his contributions.

The information collected during the first phase of the exit planning process helped Andrew organize and prioritize issues that could have an impact on the exit process. Lines of communication between stakeholders were opened, and a new understanding of everyone's perspectives helped the individual family members coordinate their respective goals and expectations with those of the entire family.

This goal formulation and communication process enabled Andrew Bacas to effectively represent the interests of the other stakeholders and to act in everyone's best interest.

Andrew also was made aware of the significant capital gains tax exposure he had. In addition, his advisors estimated the estate tax liability, based on Andrew's current estate plan, would be several million dollars causing the family and the business serious liquidity problems.

Finally, Andrew and Kathy had done no retirement planning to quantify their ability to fund the retirement lifestyle they desired. Complicating matters, Andrew had always been a do-it-yourself investor without a strategic plan. He tended to buy the hottest investment and follow industry trends. As a result, his investment performance had been somewhat erratic and his portfolio had a significantly higher risk profile than he was comfortable with while at the same time underperforming the market.

As a result, Andrew Bacas and the other stakeholders discussed all the critical issues presented to them and collectively agreed to an action plan that spelled out short-term objectives as well as long-term goals. The action plan identified what specific steps needed to be taken, which professional or stakeholder was in charge of that step, and when each step needed to be completed.

All the stakeholders agreed to this blueprint, and Andrew Bacas began to take steps to implement this plan with the full support of the other stakeholders. Responsibility for monitoring and periodic review during the succession planning process was assigned to Andrew and Kathy. All other stakeholders were kept apprised of progress during regular updated meetings.

**18 Months Later:** Andrew completed implementing most of the suggestions made during the exit planning process. He sold his company to a financial buyer on his terms and at a price that represented the fair market value of this company. The company was sold in eight months and no surprises appeared along the way. Andrew was able to reduce his capital gains taxes by more than 50 percent, saving more than $2 million.

**Postscript:** Andrew continued to work at the company in a transitional role for six months after the sale. One of his key employees was promoted to president of the company when Andrew stepped down. The company continues to do well, and Andrew does not regret his decision to retire.

Andrew invested the proceeds of the sale with an experienced money manager in accordance with a detailed wealth-management plan. The plan showed they could live very comfortably with conservative returns and not invade their principal. Andrew and his wife were able to retire on their terms and do everything they had hoped. Andrew and his wife used a portion of the proceeds to make gifts to trusts they established for their daughters. Each year now, Andrew hosts a family retreat in the U.S. Virgin Islands that includes his immediate family plus his daughters' husbands and children. Andrew left a family legacy of which he can be very proud.

## Understanding the Benefits of Exit Planning

As you consider the case studies presented previously, ask yourself the following questions:

Q. Which approach was most rational?

Q. Which approach was most cost effective for the client in the long run?

Q. Which case study resulted in the greatest tax savings?

Q. Which approach created the most harmony among the stakeholders and ensured their cooperation and support?

Q. Which approach delivered the goals and objectives of the various stakeholders?

Q. Which set of stakeholders enjoyed greater piece of mind and confidence in the process?

Q. As a professional advisor, which client would you have preferred working with?

Q. Which approach delivered more value to the client and, at the same time, resulted in the largest financial reward to the advisor?

Q. Which client would be likely to provide you with future referrals?

Q. Which engagement afforded you an opportunity to work with other professionals and create a value-added referral network?

## Summary

As the previous discussion showed, every business owner, regardless of age, should have a strategic exit plan. An exit plan is the only way to ensure the business owner is consistently building a company that will ultimately achieve the owner's long-term goals.

At the same time, this chapter demonstrates that every business advisor should be involved in helping business owners with this important process. The next chapter provides more important information about why this involvement is so important for advisors.

# Chapter 3

# The Benefits of Exit Planning for Advisors

As the case studies in the previous chapter illustrate, exit planning delivers tremendous value to the client. It also creates significant value for the professional advisors involved in the process. Exit planning:

- Deepens and strengthens an advisor's relationship with his or her client
- Creates an opportunity to identify additional value-added services the client may need and the advisor can provide
- Enables professionals to earn the role of "most trusted advisor"
- Creates a framework in which you work with other professional advisors in a complimentary and mutually supportive way
- Creates a new source of revenues for your practice
- Differentiates you from all other professionals who provide similar types of services
- Enables you to charge for your services based on value, not cost
- Positions you to serve the client and the client's heirs after the exit
- Creates a client who is a "raving fan" and a good source of referrals

As many business experts say (and as you probably know from personal experience), existing clients are far more profitable than new clients. Many experts believe it costs 5 times as much to generate business from a new client as it does to generate the same business from an existing client.

Everyone enjoys landing a big new client or a nice new piece of business, but professionals often forget the huge hidden costs of developing new clients. These costs include the unpaid time spent on:

- Researching, networking, and prospecting
- Drafting proposals
- Marketing
- Meetings
- Follow-ups and so on

Let's look at a few case studies to illustrate this point.

## Case Study: Lawyer Brings New Life to Established Practice

Marybeth is a senior partner in a 100-lawyer firm in Michigan. She is a business attorney and primarily works with owners of small and mid-sized private companies in the Detroit suburbs. She has been practicing law for 20 years and has a nice list of long-term clients. She works with over 200 small to mid sized businesses. Her typical client owns a successful private business and is approximately 50 years old. Most of these clients have a personal net worth of $1 million or more.

Marybeth's clients, as is true of the clients of most attorneys, are not active users of her firm's services. They use Marybeth and her firm to periodically review contracts or handle minor commercial disputes. A few of them used her firm to draft wills and trusts when they first got married or had children, but most are not active trust and estates clients. Marybeth estimates her average business client in "maintenance mode" generates $5,000 in annual billable fees.

Marybeth has a nice legal practice, but admits she has hit a wall. She needs to continue to expand her practice, but her current clients keep her so busy she does not have time to do all the leg work, entertaining, networking, and so forth that developing new clients requires.

What is the answer? Marybeth is not alone. Her story is repeated by CPAs, financial advisors, business consultants, bankers, wealth managers, and other professional service providers. One answer is that Marybeth, and anyone in her shoes, needs to get more business from existing clients. How does she do this? She must become her client's "most trusted advisor." To earn this position, Marybeth must be able to show her clients that she:

- Understands the client's big picture (not just his or her legal needs)
- Is pro-active and responsive
- Delivers solutions that add value

In this respect, exit planning can play an important role.

By discussing the importance of exit planning with her existing clients, Marybeth was able to get many of them to examine all the business, personal, legal, financial, tax, and insurance issues involved in exiting a privately owned business. As a result of Marybeth's new focus on exit planning, several of her existing clients have engaged her firm to provide:

- Exit planning services
- General corporate "housekeeping" services
- Estate planning services

- Merger and acquisition advice when they sell
- A pre-transaction due diligence review
- A capital gains tax strategy

The following is a hypothetical example of how Marybeth's time is spent on a typical exit planning engagement.

Table 3-1.

| Task | Time (Approximate) |
|------|--------------------|
| Extensive data collection, including interviews with the client and family members: | 10 hours |
| Assembling the client and the team of professional advisors and conducting the first meeting: | 8 hours |
| Drafting the exit plan to circulate to the client's other advisors: | 10 hours once a basic template is created |
| Assembling the input from the various advisors and incorporating it into a draft of an exit plan for the client and other advisors to review: | 10 hours |
| Meeting with the client and collecting comments from the other advisors: | 3 hours |
| Finalizing exit plan: | 4 hours |
| Arranging and coordinating annual follow up meetings (Annual Strategic Reviews) with the client and the advisory team: | 6 hours each year |
| Total | 51 hours |

As shown above, a typical exit planning engagement involves approximately 51 hours of professional time. Let us assume Marybeth's firm charges a blended billable rate of $250 per hour. In this case, the exit planning engagement represents approximately $12,750 in fees or an increase in billable revenues of 155 percent over the value of a typical "maintenance" relationship with a client.

You also should note that this analysis does not include the other value-added legal services the exit planning process may indicate are required. These services often include a pre-transaction due diligence review of the company (see Chapter 17, "The Important Role of the Attorney," to learn more about this review). Fees for this type of engagement range anywhere from approximately $5,000 and up, depending on the scope of the project and the problems that need fixing.

If your law firm also provides sophisticated tax planning advice, there is an opportunity to provide clients with services addressing that portion of the exit plan as well. Fees for this type of engagement start from around $3,500 for a general outline of a tax strategy, but could be significantly higher if you are asked to implement the tax strategy.

So let us look at the total value of a hypothetical exit planning engagement from an attorney's perspective.

**Table 3-2.**

| Exit planning review and recommendations: | $12,000 and up |
|---|---|
| Pre-transaction due diligence: | $5,000 and up |
| Tax planning: | $3,000 and up |
| Estate planning: | $3,000 and up |
| Total: | $23,000 and up |

The value of each of these engagements can range from approximately $20,000 to $60,000 or more, depending on scope of the assignment. As a result, Marybeth's billable revenues have more than doubled. In addition, now that she is becoming known for her exit planning approach, other business owners are seeking her out. She also now has a unique niche to talk about with potential new clients, a niche that enables her to differentiate herself from all the other good business attorneys in her area.

As a result, while the fees generated from preparing an exit plan, in and of themselves, can significantly enhance your practice, the exit planning process also puts you in a position to identify and provide additional legal services the client may need. Every attorney who works with privately held businesses and their owners should, therefore, be thinking about exit planning. Encouraging clients to begin the exit planning process should be part of every attorney's business development strategy.

Let's examine another case study involving a financial advisor.

### Case Study: Financial Advisor Finds New Focus

Susan is a financial advisor with a large, national brokerage firm. She currently has about $100 million in assets under management. She prides herself on being not a stockbroker, but a financial planner who works with clients to develop long-term, wealth management solutions. Susan is very good at what she does. While her book of business is smaller than many people with her level of seniority, she has put most of her clients into accounts that are managed by professional money managers. As a result, Susan has converted much of her book of business to a recurring revenue model. Now she spends her time helping clients with big-picture concerns and finding creative solutions to their problems.  These are aspects of her practice that her clients really value.

Because of Susan's unique approach, she has a number of clients who own successful businesses.  As a result, Susan has more than a dozen clients who have businesses with $5 million to $50 million in sales and net more than $500,000 per year.  Unfortunately, most of these businesses owners either reinvest a significant portion of their company's earnings into the company to help it grow or they spend a significant portion of what they take out of the business to support their lifestyles. This means these same clients typically have less than $500,000, on average, in their personal investment accounts.

Although these clients have much future potential, Susan reported that they required a great deal of maintenance and that each one generated less than $4,000 in annual fees for her firm.  Susan continued to work with them with the hope that when it came time to sell their company she would be given a chance to manage the proceeds of the sale.  Even then, she was not sure she would get the business.

However, like Marybeth, Susan has reached a point in her life where balance was important.  She needed to find a way to continue to add value for her existing clients, make those relationships more profitable, and expand her business all at the same time.

What was the solution?  Exit planning.

Susan began to incorporate an exit planning message into her conversations with these clients.  The net result was that by using an exit planning framework, Susan was able to talk with her clients about their financial situations in an entirely new light.

As a result, Susan was able to begin to get her clients to approach the financial planning process with a new discipline and enthusiasm.  As part of the clients' exit planning team, Susan was able to:

- Get her clients to begin using her financial planning services
- Understand what other financial assets the clients had
- More effectively manage her clients' existing portfolio
- Work with clients to define their financial legacy
- Review her clients' insurance needs
- Provide quotes on new insurance
- Develop a wealth-management strategy for the proceeds in advance of the sale to ensure that she will get that money when the liquidity event occurs

Each of these services enabled Susan to generate additional revenues for her firm. Perhaps more important, however, is that they helped Susan solidify her relationship with her clients, and created a road map so the proceeds of the sale would be brought to Susan to manage. Susan is no longer working with the hope that sometime in the future she may get a shot at managing her clients' liquid net worth. An actual plan is now in place to make that happen. In addition, Susan has built up such tremendous goodwill with the clients' spouses and heirs during this process that she has become their most trusted advisor. The likelihood of their shopping for another financial advisor after the sale is virtually eliminated.

## Summary

In this chapter we looked at two case studies involving an attorney and a financial advisor. However, the same benefits outlined apply to any professional who works with business owners. Insurance professionals, business consultants, real estate brokers, and commercial lenders can all benefit by incorporating exit planning into their professional practices.

As you continue to read this book you will learn specific steps and effective ways to incorporate exit planning into your practice.

# Chapter 4

# Helping Clients Take the First Step

An old Chinese proverb says "the longest journey begins with a single step." Taking the first step is often the hardest part. The same is true with exit planning. Getting business owners to start the exit planning process is often the most difficult part. In this chapter we discuss the most common reasons business owners give for delaying the exit planning process. We also explore the underlying reasons for this resistance. Finally, we discuss the question of timing and when a business owner should ideally start the exit planning process.

## Common Objections

The following reasons are offered most frequently as to why business owners delay the exit or succession planning process:

- They are not sure exactly how to start the process or whom to call for help
- They have difficulty discussing financial matters and personal goals with others (or outsiders) because it is too private, somehow unpleasant, or considered taboo
- They spend all their time "putting out fires" and do not have the time to focus on long-term planning.
- They believe the time is not right to start the process
- The entire process seems too daunting
- They are afraid of what life without their business would be like, so they do nothing

With all these anxieties, it is not surprising that fewer than 30 percent of private businesses have an actionable succession plan. By default, most business owners simply do nothing. For those business owners who believe they have an exit plan in place, we often find they have focused on just one element of a succession plan, such as an estate plan or management succession, and have ignored other equally important areas. This situation usually results in business owners making poor decisions and not achieving all of their personal and business goals in the process.

The exit planning process involves helping business owners wrestle with several issues, including their fear of letting go, their desire to avoid the stress and conflict it may cause in their family, and not knowing when they need to start. We explore each of these areas as the book goes on.

## Understanding Transition Satisfaction

Business owners view a business transition or "retirement" much differently than most Americans. For most business owners, retiring or making the transition out of a business does not mean slowing down or endless days of rest and relaxation. Rather, they see "retirement" as a new, active stage in their lives characterized by continued, personal growth, personal reinvention, and new beginnings in work and leisure. Nonetheless, this prospect creates a huge unspoken fear in the minds of many business owners. They fear "retirement" will not be as vital or satisfying as being the CEO of a thriving, private company.

Helping business owners identify and understand these issues is the first step. Helping them create a plan to ensure their retirement is fulfilling and exciting is what exit planning is all about. A recent survey conducted by Harris Interactive revealed that an entirely new paradigm for retirement is emerging. The good news is many people are experiencing long, fulfilling, and exciting retirements. The bad news is many business owners will not be satisfied fully with retirement because of inadequate personal planning.

The key findings are as follows:

1.  The concept of retirement as a "slowing down" is obsolete. Fewer than a quarter of those surveyed agreed with the idea of relaxing and doing nothing in their retirement years. Instead, respondents viewed retirement as a new chapter in life (38 percent) or a continuation of life as it is (40 percent).

2.  Approximately 95 percent of pre-retirees expect to work in some capacity during retirement, and money was not the sole motivator. Almost 50 percent said they intended to work in retirement, even if paid nothing at all.

3.  Satisfaction with retirement is directly related to how financially prepared the respondent was for retirement. More than 60 percent of those who said they had more than adequate resources to support themselves in retirement, reported they were extremely satisfied with retirement. However, only 46 percent of respondents who reported they had to cut corners in retirement, indicated they were satisfied with retirement.

It is important to realize that, historically, retirement was something relatively few people lived long enough to enjoy. Only one hundred years ago the average life expectancy was 47 years. As a result, most people worked until they became too weak to continue. Around the turn of the century, most adults spent about three years in retirement.

However, in the early twenty-first century, the average life expectancy is 76 years and the average age at which people choose to retire is 65. As a result, on average, you can expect to spend 11 years in retirement!

It is interesting to note that the modern concept of retirement as a time of leisure, travel, family activities, hobbies, and educational pursuits is the result of the passage of the Social Security Act in 1935. With the creation of Social Security, the United States government created a financial incentive for older workers to retire in order to enable younger workers to take their place. This was considered good national policy at the time because it stimulated economic growth and progress.

## Deciding to Retire

Ever since 1935, retirement has become a stage of life people look forward to, plan for, and experience after many years of work. Although eligibility for Social Security is one factor that contributes to the retirement decision, it is a relatively small one for most business owners. Other contributing factors are discussed in the following sections.

### *Financial Security*

Evaluating one's financial ability to retire is often the first step taken when the retirement decision is being considered. For a business owner who has the vast majority of his net worth tied up in a privately owned business, this is an important first step.

### *Health Status*

Being diagnosed with a serious health problem or a debilitating illness can significantly influence one's decision to retire. For business owners this is particularly meaningful given the huge commitment of personal time and energy a privately owned business requires. At the same time, healthy, energetic business owners often decide to retire in order to enjoy the fruits of their hard work before they develop future health problems.

### *Family Responsibilities*

Sometimes the decision to retire is based on the needs of family members, for example, wanting to spend time with grandchildren or taking care of a sick spouse or aging parents.

### *Timing of a Partner's Retirement*

For business owners, retirement is more of a joint experience than it is for most people. Many business owners decide to time their retirement to coincide or coordinate with the retirement of a long-time business partner. Despite a potential difference in age, younger business owners are more likely to retire early so they retire at the same time as a senior business partner.

### Retirement Satisfaction

Frequently, people assume the transition to retirement is easy. For business owners, even more than for most working Americans, retirement is a significant change that triggers all sorts of conscious and subconscious reactions. Despite the freedom and excitement that retirement offers, a significant period of adjustment also is required to become fully comfortable with this new stage of life. This adjustment to retirement is influenced by a number of factors including the following:

1.  **Personal Identity:** For business owners, whether they are prepared to admit it or not, a great deal of their personal identity comes from their role in their business. Many business owners report that thinking about retiring is as stressful as going through a divorce or bankruptcy, and raises questions about self worth, personal fulfillment, self-actualization, and mortality. Identifying and wrestling with these issues before retiring is important; otherwise, they can taint a business owner's enjoyment of retirement.

2.  **Marital Status:** Being married in retirement can contribute to a successful adjustment to retirement and result in greater satisfaction. Men, typically, have greater difficulty with the loss of the work-related identity and have not developed alternative roles to depend on once retired. As a result, the social and emotional support of a wife is particularly important to a man's adjustment to retirement.

3.  **Financial Resources:** The financial status of business owners during retirement significantly influences satisfaction with retirement. First, those with more retirement resources are likely to pursue enjoyable recreational and leisure activities while retired. Second, being financially secure increases the likelihood the business owner will not have to change the lifestyle to which he and his family have become accustomed. Finally, receiving quality health care and support services is more likely for those with more financial resources. However, it is important to note that financial security does *not* guarantee satisfaction with retirement *and* is not required in order to enjoy one's retirement.

4.  **Involuntary vs. Voluntary Transition:** Business owners who make the transition out of a business involuntarily, that is, due to family responsibilities, financial difficulties, or poor health, report they have much greater difficulty adjusting to retirement. In contrast, business owners who plan

for retirement and voluntarily exit their businesses are three times more likely to be satisfied with the retirement experience and adjust more successfully to the role of retiree.

5.  **Contact with Others:**  Having a personal network of family, friends, and business contacts contributes to retirement satisfaction. Although many business owners view retirement with a sense of anticipation and excitement, business owners often fail to realize how much they depend on and enjoy the daily contact with work colleagues. It is important for both men and women to have a network of old friends as well as to make new friends in retirement.

6.  **Having a Plan:**  Adjusting to retirement, as with anything else in life, is more certain if one has a plan and a set of well-defined goals.  For business owners in particular, it is important to create a retirement lifestyle that is challenging, rewarding, and vital.  Developing a retirement plan, complete with personal goals, deadlines, and activities provides a sense of purpose and meaning to retirement.  Whether the plan involves working in the wood shop, getting involved in another business venture, volunteering in the community, or spending more time with grandchildren, the retiree needs to feel valued and productive.

I have worked with hundreds of business owners who were beginning to think about retirement. Based on those experiences and my independent research, I have distilled attitudes about retirement into six categories or groups:

1.  Perspectives about Work and Retirement
2.  Financial Preparation for Retirement
3.  Expectations about Retirement
4.  Friends, Family, and Community
5.  Health Concerns
6.  Involvement

Business owners' pre-retirement attitude on these issues is a good predictor of their subsequent satisfaction with retirement. I used our research to build a model to help predict a business owner's probable satisfaction with retirement.

## The Transition Satisfaction Predictor

In our exit planning practice we use a predictive model to help business owners determine whether they are psychologically prepared to exit their businesses and make the transition into a new stage of life.  This model uses 36 questions to gauge a business owner's attitudes, beliefs, and values about making a transition out of a business or retiring.  The questions are based on research performed by a wide variety of experts in the field of entrepreneurship, aging, and retirement.[2]

Helping business owners understand how they feel about retirement on both a conscious and subconscious level is important before you help them make any important decisions about exiting or retiring from their business.

### Conflicting Value Systems

The second, most common reason business owners put off exit planning involves wrestling with deep, subconscious issues that can create stress and anxiety for the business owner.

Despite the benefits exit planning delivers to business owners, the decision-making process is not a rational one.  Exit planning involves business, personal, family, and financial issues that trigger questions about mortality, identity, family closeness, competence, financial security, and vitality.  As a result, exit planning can be an emotional process for a business owner and his or her family.

Because no clear line exists between where personal or family concerns begin and business concerns end, an advisor must consider exit planning issues from both perspectives. Without this sensitivity, the decision-making process can become confused and inconsistent, family relationships can suffer, a business can lose focus, and the exit plan can get derailed.

Why do business owners put off exit planning?  The answer has to do in part with the conflicting value systems in which most private business owners work. The following analysis is intended to help the reader understand the complex context in which exit planning takes place.

Business owners work in an environment in which they are torn between three different and conflicting value systems:  the Family Value System, the Management Value System, and the Owner Value System.  Family business experts believe most family business problems can be traced to situations that cause these three value systems to conflict.

**The Family Value System.** A key purpose of the family is to nurture and develop self-esteem in younger people so they grow into emotionally mature and responsible adults. Emotion and love are the basis for the family system. Admittance and acceptance in the family are unconditional and based on a

---

2 Sonnefeld, Jeffery A. (1989) "The Parting Patriarch of a Family Firm" *Family Business Review*, Vol. 12, Nov. 4. Atchley, R.C. (2000). *Social Forces and Aging (9th Ed.).* Belmont, CA: Wadsworth.    Connidis, I.A. (2001)  *Family Ties & Aging.* Thousand Oaks, CA: Sage.    Christine A. Price, Ph.D., OSU State Extension Specialist, Gerontology, The Ohio State University.    "Re-Visioning Retirement Survey" sponsored by AIG SunAmerica and conducted by Harris Interactive and Dr. Ken Dychtwald, the nation's foremost expert on aging and retirement.    Grace, Richard E. (2004) *When Every Day is Saturday, The Retirement Guide for Boomers,* San Jose CA: Writer's Showcase.

"birthright" or love alone. In the family setting, while successes are certainly celebrated and encouraged, failures often elicit an equally loving and supportive response (for example, the child who cannot run as fast as the other kids will often be encouraged even more than the child who consistently wins each race). Family members who are not owners or managers in the business may see the business only through this value system.

**The Management Value System.** The goal of management in a business is to generate profits, increase shareholder wealth, and develop organizational depth so the business can function and grow. Business issues are typically addressed in a rational, analytical, and pragmatic fashion. Acceptance and reward in a managed business environment depend on skill and performance (for example, the kid who consistently loses races will be cut from the team, while the kid who consistently wins races will receive trophies and special treatment). Those family members who have a management stake in the business will have different motivations than those who are uninvolved or are passively involved.

**The Owner Value System.** The principal concerns of owners or investors in a business are with wealth creation, balancing risks and rewards, and liquidity. The value of a business to them is based on meeting wealth creation goals in light of a specific risk/reward trade-off (for example, the kid may not be allowed to run in any races if he or she consumes too much of the family's time and resources). Those family members who have ownership in the company will have different motivations than family members who do not own stock.

The following table demonstrates the three value systems mentioned above and the values that are inherent in each.

Table 4-1.

| Family | Management | Ownership |
|---|---|---|
| Needs Based | Performance Based | Financially Based |
| Unconditional Loyalty | Conditional Loyalty | Return on Investment |
| Equality | Unequal | Risk Management |
| Cooperation | Competition | Control |
| Wealth Consumption | Wealth Management | Wealth Creation |

These three value systems are very different from each other. To make matters particularly difficult, the three value systems overlap in the family business as shown in Figure 4-1:

## Classic Interference Patterns
## Affect Exit Planning

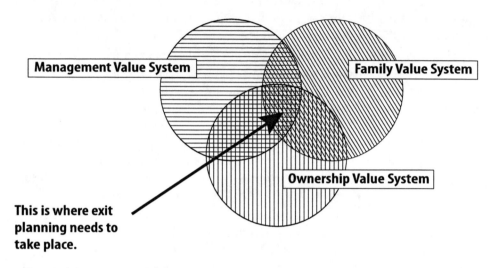

Figure 4-1

Family issues, tasks, or motivations are placed in the family circle. Business issues, tasks, or motivations are placed in the management circle. Shareholder issues are placed in the ownership circle. The overlap of the three circles illustrates the difficulty that emerges when the competing systems collide. Unfortunately, exit planning needs to take place where the three value systems overlap and where the conflict and related stress is the greatest.

Identifying this inherent conflict—what may be positive in the family system but negative in the business system—is the first step in helping family-business owners face difficult decisions that affect all three systems. After the issues are sorted out, a solution addressing the family issues, business concerns, and ownership issues can be devised.

A full discussion about how to manage these conflicts and help a family business prosper in spite of these difficulties is beyond the scope of this book. However, in the exit planning context, it is important to recognize that all three value systems are equally important to the long-term success and prosperity of a family business. In order to devise a successful exit plan, all three must be granted equal respect and consideration.

The ultimate challenge business owners face in exit planning is dealing effectively with business and financial issues (i.e., ownership transition, management training, retirement planning, tax planning, and strategic direction), while simultaneously managing the emotional condition of all the stakeholders, including the owners themselves during the process. The emotional aspect can be the most difficult aspect of exit planning. Most of the difficulties associated with exit planning can be traced to inadequate communication between key stakeholders in the business.  As a result, one of the goals of the exit planning process is to enhance understanding among the stakeholders, to promote empathy and trust, and to lead to compromise and resolution, which ultimately improves each stakeholder's ability to achieve his or her respective goals in the process.

Many of these difficulties can be addressed through the use of formalized structures to open lines of communications between relevant stakeholders (see Chapter 7, "Communicating with Stakeholders").

But on a personal front, when you are working one-on-one with the business owner, asking questions is the best way to overcome many of the conscious and subconscious obstacles that prevent business owners from starting the exit planning process.

Gentle but focused probing is an important tool to help business owners reach the conclusion that they could really benefit from the exit planning process. Consultative selling is all about identifying a client's issues and showing the client you have an effective solution for these problems.

Following are some examples of the types of open-ended questions that can lead to some productive discussions with business owners.  The client here is a typical 55-year old business owner who came in to visit his business attorney (although the same dialogue could easily have taken place with his estate planner, his financial advisor, his CPA, his banker, or any other trusted advisor).

> Q: Have you thought about what you'd like to do when you retire?
>
> Q: How much longer do you want to continue to work in your business?
>
> Q: Do any of your children work in the business with you?  If so, in what roles?
>
> Q: Do you have an exit plan in place for the time when you want to retire?

Be warned: Most business owners are very private and do not open up easily unless you are a trusted advisor.  Therefore, the first response you get to these types of questions is often flippant and not thought out.  For example, the following exchange is typical but demonstrates how each question needs to be followed up with focused, gentle probing.

---

*Advisor:* Have you thought about what you'd like to do when you retire?

*Client:* Play golf! (He laughs.)

*Advisor:* That sound's great. I love golf too, but I can't see myself playing golf every day for the rest of my life. Have you thought about what you'd like to do when you're not out on the links?

*Client:* Well, actually my wife and I thought we'd like to travel a bit. Maybe take a cruise around the world. Do something kind of fun to celebrate 30 years of hard work.

*Advisor:* Now you're talking. That sounds like fun. Do you think there'd be room for me in your suitcase? How would your company be managed while you're gone? Do you have a successor in mind, or are you thinking of selling the company when it comes time to retire?

*Client:* I've got several key people who work for me but none of them is really ready to take on the role of CEO and run the company. Our kids are all happily pursuing their own careers and none of them has expressed any interest in the business. I'm guessing I would probably just sell it when the time is right.

*Advisor:* That's a very viable option. Any idea of what your company might be worth?

*Client:* Not really. I've got some industry rules of thumb in my files. Several years ago my accountant gave me an informal estimate, so I have a rough idea, but I'm not sure. Maybe $7 million?

*Advisor:* Okay, good. Now, you obviously want to maximize the price of your company when you decide to sell, but do you know how much money you would need to net from the sale of your company to fund your retirement and do all the fun things you want to do?

*Client:* Well, I know how much money I spend each year now, and we would like to maintain the same lifestyle. But we would also like to take some fun trips. Some of these cruises we would like to take are pretty expensive. We have also been thinking about buying a second home in Arizona so we would need money to do that. I guess I have a rough idea, but I'm not sure.

---

You can see where this is going. In this brief exchange, the advisor learned the business owner is beginning to think about his exit options but really doesn't have the information he needs to make informed decisions. The advisor learned that his client needs a business valuation and a retirement needs analysis, two of the basic components of an exit plan. This conversation leads naturally into a discussion about the need for and importance of exit planning.

Despite the need for your services, many business owners take the "do-it-yourself" approach. This decision usually is driven by their desire to save professional fees or an often unacknowledged need to maintain absolute control. In some circumstances, such as when the business is relatively small and the complexity limited, this approach may work. But, in the case of a larger business system (involving a considerable amount of wealth, multiple stakeholders, significant income, compensation issues, complex insurance needs, business valuation, and communication issues), the task becomes too complicated to accomplish without expert assistance.

To help a client understand the importance of developing a responsible exit plan you may want to consider enlisting the assistance of some of the client's other advisors. Investment bankers experienced in exit planning can often be a valuable resource to call in because they are able to offer the client a "carrot" while most advisors use a "stick." A credible investment banker with exit planning experience can provide the client with real-world examples of businesses that developed actionable exit plans, and the dramatic results, both in terms of additional wealth at closing and the business owner's peace of mind and satisfaction. Using this approach, business owners can see the "value" and are more likely to make the investment of time, money, and energy necessary to develop a good exit plan.

## Timing Is Everything

One final reason that business owners put off exit planning is they honestly do not know when to start. That said, having sufficient time to design and then implement an exit plan is one of the most important factors in its success.

We believe every business owner should have a strategic exit plan regardless of his or her age or the stage in the life cycle of the company. Venture capitalists who fund start-up companies will not invest in a business unless they believe the founders have a good exit plan. Private equity groups will not buy or invest in a successful middle-market company without developing a detailed exit plan for themselves prior to investing.

Why do sophisticated investors such as these believe in exit plans? They know firsthand that unless a well-defined exit plan is in place, no strategic road map exists for all stakeholders to follow and ensure everyone's short- and long-term goals are met. They know that without a detailed strategic exit plan, they are less likely to achieve their objectives.

Exit plans are not just for pre-retirement business owners. Today's entrepreneurs, unlike their parents, who typically stayed in one business for their entire lives, are comfortable with the idea of buying and selling businesses. These younger entrepreneurs need exit plans as much as their parents do.

Unfortunately, however, most business owners do not have an exit plan. They tend to put off this process for as long as possible, but there is some truth to the old saying "better late than never."

The more time a business owner has to design and implement an exit plan, the better. In an ideal world, business owners would develop their exit plan when they start their businesses. If that hasn't been done, we suggest, if possible, that the exit planning process begin at least three years before the business owner ultimately wants to exit. To demonstrate why such a long lead time is advisable, let us start at the owner's final departure from the company and work backward to understand when he would need to start.

First, let's assume the owner's ultimate exit strategy is to sell the company to a third-party buyer (approximately 70 percent of business owners elect this strategy). In contrast to selling publicly traded securities, no liquid market exists for the shares of privately held companies. While the market for private companies is active, a great deal of time and effort is needed to package the company for sale, identify and contact the right buyers, and then negotiate and close the transaction.

Depending on the type of investment banking firm engaged to sell the company, and the process that firm uses, it typically takes anywhere from 6 to 18 months to sell a privately owned company. This period can be significantly longer if the client has unique structuring requirements or other issues that limit the universe of potential buyers.

However, even after the transaction is closed, buyers usually want the former business owner to continue to play a role in the company as an employee, consultant, or advisor. This transition period can last anywhere from several months to as long as several years. We, therefore, advise clients to think of the actual exit occurring between 12 and 24 months after the closing depending on the length of the transition period.

Remember that one of the goals of the exit plan is to position the company so it can maximize its value at the time of sale. Many value-enhancement projects take time to implement and show results. Although this work can and should continue during the sales process, it is important to be able to demonstrate concrete results to buyers when the company is taken to market. Consequently, we advise business owners begin the exit planning process at least three years before they want to completely exit the business.

## Exit Planning Timetable (in Reverse Order)

| | |
|---|---|
| 1. Transition process | 1 year or more |
| 2. Investment banking/sales process | 1 year |
| 3. Implementation of value enhancement and tax planning | 1 year or more |
| **4. Prepare exit plan** | **6 months – 1 year** |
| Total Time | 3.5  years or more |

Figure 4-2 :  Exit Planning Timetable (in Reverse Order)

## Summary

As this chapter pointed out, getting a business owner to start the exit planning process is often the hardest part.  To help overcome the business owner's natural reluctance to start the process, you need to help the owner understand and come to grips with his or her perceptions about retirement.  In addition, we discussed the importance of understanding the three conflicting value systems that govern the lives of most business owners, and the stress this conflict causes.

Helping business owners understand these issues and successfully navigate this conflict is a great way to help them take that important first step.  Finally, this chapter pointed out that to be most effective, business owners should begin the exit process approximately three to four years before they would like to fully exit or retire from the business.

# Chapter 5

# The Exit Planning Process

Exit planning is a highly personal process. There is no off-the-shelf solution that is right for everyone. Helping an owner exit a business must be handled in a methodical, logical, and rational manner. Because there are so many moving pieces and different parties involved, successful exit planning must follow a rigorous process in order to ensure each engagement is handled in a consistent manner and the client receives the best possible results.

It is important to note that most owners do not invest much thought or planning in ownership transition. In fact, our research shows most business owners spend more time planning a family vacation than how to exit from their business. This is not due to a lack of desire or lack of intelligence. It is simply because they do not know where or how to begin. The vast majority of business owners are unaware there is a specific planning and implementation process that can help ensure they achieve their objectives.

In our practice we have developed, "The Exit Planning Coach Process," to help clients exit from their businesses on their timetables and on their terms. The following diagram (Figure 5-1) illustrates the steps involved in our exit planning practice.

## The Exit Planning Process:

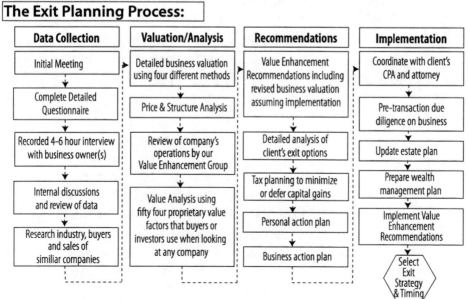

| Data Collection | Valuation/Analysis | Recommendations | Implementation |
|---|---|---|---|
| Initial Meeting | Detailed business valuation using four different methods | Value Enhancement Recommendations including revised business valuation assuming implementation | Coordinate with client's CPA and attorney |
| Complete Detailed Questionnaire | Price & Structure Analysis | | Pre-transaction due diligence on business |
| Recorded 4-6 hour interview with business owner(s) | Review of company's operations by our Value Enhancement Group | Detailed analysis of client's exit options | Update estate plan |
| Internal discussions and review of data | Value Analysis using fifty four proprietary value factors that buyers or investors use when looking at any company | Tax planning to minimize or defer capital gains | Prepare wealth management plan |
| Research industry, buyers and sales of similiar companies | | Personal action plan | Implement Value Enhancement Recommendations |
| | | Business action plan | Select Exit Strategy & Timing |

Figure 5-1: The Exit Planning Process

However, simply knowing and understanding these four basic steps is not enough. As the old saying goes, "The devil is in the details." In the following text, we describe each of the exit planning steps in general, and the remainder of this book covers these steps in much more detail.

## Step One: Data Collection

1. **Initial Meeting.** This meeting is intended to get the client and the other members of the exit planning team excited about the exit planning process and to educate them about what to expect (and what is expected of them) along the way.

2. **Complete Detailed Questionnaire.** The client completes a detailed questionnaire covering personal, business, financial, family, and estate goals. The questionnaire also collects operating and financial information about the client's company.

3. **Interview with Business Owner.** After the questionnaire has been completed and reviewed by an exit planning professional, we sit down with the client for a 4 to 6 hour interview to discuss the client's answers in the questionnaire and additional questions that occurred to us while reading it.

4. **Review of Data.** At the end of the interview, we summarize the session and the answers to the questionnaire, and condense them into a concise format we can use for subsequent steps. This data is then shared with all the members of the exit planning team to help them begin the work required as part of the exit planning process.

5. **Research.** Often, additional industry research is required to fill in the blanks or to provide information the client did not have during the interview process.

## Step Two: Valuation/Analysis

6. **Business Valuation.** We use the operational and financial data about the client's company to prepare a detailed baseline business valuation for the client. This valuation lets the client know what the fair market value of the business is today, as well as providing some indication of how marketable the company is based on current market conditions.

7. **Personal Financial Plan and Analysis.** We use personal financial information supplied by the client to figure out how much the client needs to net after taxes from the sale of the business to support his/her desired lifestyle. This financial plan explores not only the client's anticipated lifestyle needs, but also the type of financial legacy he/she wants to

leave to respective family members or the community. Chapter 14 covers more about this legacy.

8. **Price and Structure Analysis.** Using the baseline business valuation, we examine the impact transaction structuring could have on both the total sales price for the client's company and the net proceeds the client receives at closing.

9. **Analysis of Ways to Maximize Value.** We also examine the client's company to identify the company's strengths and weaknesses in order to recommend specific ways the owner can improve the value or salability of her company. You will read out more about this in Chapter 12.

10. **Tax Strategies.** The last step of the Valuation/Analysis phase is to show the client what the likely tax impact of a transaction would be if the client does nothing. In most cases, business owners have done little or no tax planning, so showing them how much of the sales proceeds would go to Uncle Sam can be a huge motivation to begin the tax planning process. You will read more about this in Chapter 17.

## Step Three: Recommendations

11. **Fair Market Value and Salability of the Business.** After informing the client about the fair market value and salability of his/her business, we make recommendations about what the client should do based on current facts and the client's personal goals.

12. **Financial Terms/Structure.** Based on the financial planning performed in a previous step, we recommend how to structure an exit in order to meet the client's financial goals.

13. **Exit Options.** We review all the exit options available to the business owner and present a "pros and cons" analysis of each option relative to the owner's personal goals and objectives. You will read more about this in Chapter 10.

14. **Ways to Maximize Value.** We make specific suggestions to the client regarding how to maximize the value of the owner's company.

15. **Ways to Minimize Taxes.** If the taxes the client would pay are inconsistent with the client's stated goals, we provide suggestions about tax structures the owner may want to explore with his/her attorney and CPA.

16. **Legal Options.** Based on our understanding of the company and the client's personal situation, we recommend specific actions the client

should discuss with her attorney to prepare for an eventual exit. These are formulated in conjunction with the client's attorney, or they motivate the client to seek a good attorney.

17. **Specific Action Plans.**    The last step in the Recommendations phase is to develop specific action plans detailing who needs to do what, and when.    These action plans detail each task that needs to be accomplished prior to the exit, who is responsible for doing it, and when it needs to be done.    This becomes the basis for the next phase.

## Step Four: Implementation

18. **Pre-transaction due diligence.**    The client engages his/her attorney to perform a legal due diligence on his/her company as if the attorney was representing a buyer.  See more about this in Chapter 16.

19. **Tax plan.**  The client meets with his/her tax attorney and CPA to review the current tax situation, and to develop an appropriate strategy to minimize taxes at the time of exit.  See Chapter 17.

20. **Estate Plan.**  The client meets with his/her estate planner to develop an estate plan that is dovetailed with the tax plan and reflects the estimated net proceeds from the eventual sale of the company.  See Chapter 15.

21. **Maximizing Value.**  If the client decides doing this is appropriate, then he/she begins to work on the value maximizing recommendations made in the Exit Planning Report.  See Chapter 12.

22. **Wealth Management Plan.**    The client begins to develop a working relationship with a personal financial advisor or wealth-management professional in advance of the exit to determine how the net proceeds from the sale will be invested and managed so the client effectively achieves her goals.  See Chapter 14

23. **Investment Banking Process.**  When the owner decides the time is right, he/she instructs us to implement the appropriate exit option.  More about this in Chapter 19.

## Summary

According to the Small Business Administration, most business owners who begin the exit planning process do not follow through. To succeed, you and your clients need a <u>written</u> plan that:

1. Sets out your client's exit objectives, including the client's personal, business, and financial goals as well as any other factors to be considered
2. Documents the specific tasks required to achieve those objectives
3. Assigns responsibility for each task to be completed during the exit planning process
4. Sets a date for the task to be completed
5. Designates one person to be responsible for managing or quarterbacking the process and making sure everything gets done

# Chapter 6

# Understanding Goals and Objectives

The goals of the business owner and the other stakeholders are the foundation upon which the exit planning process is based. Achieving these goals is the fundamental purpose of exit planning. As a result, a great deal of time and effort must be expended to ensure everyone involved in the process understands and can articulate exactly what their goals are for an exit.

In this chapter we explore who the stakeholders are in a privately held company and how to most effectively include them in the exit planning process. We also discuss how to help stakeholders articulate, evaluate, and revise their goals in a constructive and mutually supportive way.

### Case Study: I Trust You, But Not That Much!

In common with many business owners, Ben dreamed of selling his business to his son, and then retiring after spending 30 years building his business. When the time came to retire, Ben discovered his two exit objectives were inconsistent. First, if he sold his business to his son he would not get much money up front. His son did not have any cash to buy Ben out, and no bank would lend him anything close to what Ben needed to retire comfortably. As a result, his son would have to pay him over the course of 10 years from the company's earnings. This meant Ben would still have to depend on the company to support him in retirement. Although Ben trusted his son to run the company, Ben wasn't comfortable with the market risk the company faced, particularly now that he was 63 and needed a dependable source of retirement income.

Ben realized that if he wanted to sell now, receive cash at the closing, and achieve financial security, he would need to sell to an outside third party with cash to invest. Ben's situation illustrates why setting *consistent* objectives early in the exit planning process are so critical.

The three principal issues nearly all business owners wrestle with are the following:

1. **Leaving the business on their timetable.** How much longer do they want to remain active in the business?

2. **Creating financially security for themselves and their family.** Think of financial security as a stream of after-tax income, adjusted for inflation. How much money is needed (not *wanted*) to support the owner's lifestyle after leaving the business? Does the owner want to be cashed out when he leaves the business or is he willing to receive the purchase price over many years if it will maximize the proceeds he receives?

3. **Who should get the business?** To whom does the owner want to transfer the business? A child? A key employee? A co-owner? Or, perhaps an outside party who can pay top dollar for the company?

The first step is to help your clients answer these questions and define their basic exit objectives. If they do not do so, they will end up like Ben. The only way for an owner to leave his business on his terms is to make sure the owner has formulated specific, consistent, and attainable goals and objectives. These exit objectives become the foundation for all subsequent work you and your client will do.

## The Stakeholders

Exit planning is a complex undertaking when you are dealing with one business owner. The process becomes even more complicated when other stakeholders are involved. But bringing these other stakeholders into the process is important, nonetheless.

Business owners often forget that although they may own 100 percent of the stock in their private company, the business actually has a number of stakeholders or constituents in addition to its owner and their involvement in the exit planning process can be either a tremendous help or an impediment to the exit plan's success.

The following groups are the primary stakeholders or constituents in a private company:

- Shareholders (the owners)
- Spouse (or significant other)
- Children
- In-laws (spouses of children)
- Key management/employees

In addition to important stakeholders, companies have a number of secondary stakeholders, including:

- Non-essential employees

- Customers/clients
- Vendors/suppliers
- The local community

Understanding and addressing the goals of each stakeholder (at least the important stakeholders) is the best way to ensure the exit planning process is successful.

What may appear to be a relatively straight forward task becomes much more complex when you introduce stakeholder concerns. As we discussed in the previous chapter, this is because the goals of the business from the owner's perspective may be in direct conflict with the recognized (and unrecognized) goals of the other stakeholders.

It is important to understand that none of the decision-making authority of the owner is diluted by the involvement of other stakeholders. Even if these stakeholders do not have voting rights, they still have important views and opinions that need to be integrated into the exit planning process. Therefore the exit planning process must provide all stakeholders with a formal mechanism to express their goals, expectations, and desires while supplying the business owner with a complete understanding of everyone's positions so he/she can make informed decisions. In the next chapter we look at some of the ways to include stakeholders in the communication process.

By allowing stakeholders a voice in the process, all parties feel a sense of ownership in the exit plan which greatly improves the likelihood of its ultimate success. Exit plans unilaterally implemented without communicating or fully understanding the issues of the people affected by them typically waste time and money, and, not surprisingly, fall apart. Even the best exit-planning techniques fail, if assumptions are made regarding the desires of the other stakeholders.

## Evaluating Goals

At its simplest, a goal is just something you aim for. But goals are powerful contributors to successful business growth in several ways. To begin with, the process of setting goals forces a business owner to think through what he or she wants from the business. The goal formulation process helps suggest directions for accomplishing those goals, which greatly improve the business owner's chances of achieving those goals in the first place.

Goals also give the exit planning team a framework within which to work. Having a framework tends to focus the team's efforts by helping its members rule out actions that will not contribute to achieving the owner's goals.

A very important part of creating a clear statement of goals is defining a timetable. Any good goal must have a timetable and that timetable influences everyone's actions profoundly. For instance, if the client's goal is to be fully exited from his business by age 60, everyone knows that the action plan must work backward from that date.

It is not enough to simply have goals. Goals need to be appropriate, realistic, and achievable. When helping a client define his or her goals, make sure goals are:

- **Specific.** You stand a better chance of achieving a goal if it is specific or quantified. "Maximizing my company's value when I exit" is not a specific goal; "netting $5,000,000 or more after taxes when I exit" is much better.

- **Optimistic.** Goals must be positive and uplifting. "Being able to retire" is not exactly an inspirational goal. "Having $10 million in the bank so I never need to worry about money again" rephrases the same goal in a more specific, positive manner.

- **Realistic.** Goals that are too aggressive are never met. It is better to begin with smaller, achievable steps, such as increasing the company's earnings by 20 percent. After the first goal is met, the owner can reach for larger ones.

- **Short- and long-term.** Short-term goals are attainable in a period of weeks or months. Long-term goals are achieved in one year, five years, or even 10 years. Every plan needs a good balance of short-term and long-term goals.

- **Measurable.** Many entrepreneurs want their companies to provide them with financial security. Try to translate a goal such as this into a measurable goal. That means determining how much money the business owner needs to make each year (or some other criteria) so you can help the owner define and then measure whether the company is meeting his/her goal.

- **Lifestyle-based.** This includes helping owners define their goals in areas such as travel, hours of work, investment of personal assets, and geographic location. How many hours is the owner willing to work? How much risk does the client feel comfortable with?

- **Consistent.** Let's be honest. As Mom always told us, "You can't have your cake and eat it too." Some goals, even though sincere, may be inconsistent with other equally sincere goals. Very often a business owner is too close to the issues involved to see that his or her goals may be inconsistent. Help your clients understand which goals are consistent and which are not. If goals are not consistent, help your clients prioritize them.

■   **Honest.** The most important rule of goal setting is honesty. Help your clients be honest about their strengths and weaknesses, their likes and dislikes, and their ultimate ambitions. This clarity enables them to confront dilemmas with greater confidence and a greater chance of success.

## Summary

As this chapter points out, the goals of the business owner and other stakeholders are the foundation upon which the entire exit planning process is based. Helping stakeholders achieve these goals is the fundamental purpose of exit planning. To that end, having a well-thought-out and clearly defined set of goals for each stakeholder is the first step in the exit planning process.

The next chapter helps you help your clients develop formal communication mechanisms to facilitate the exit planning process, build family harmony, and improve stakeholder teamwork and focus.

# Chapter 7

# Communicating with Stockholders

As previously discussed, every business has several groups of important stakeholders in addition to its owners. Creating formal avenues of communication with these stakeholders is vital to the success of any exit plan as well as to the long-term success of any business or family unit. In this chapter we look at two ways to foster impartial, constructive dialog between and among the different stakeholders. These include using:

- An Outside Board of Advisors
- A Family Council

Both of these vehicles have been used successfully by hundreds of middle-market businesses that have navigated difficult management succession and exit planning issues. Although each can be implemented individually, the true power of open communication is released when they are used in tandem.

## Outside Board of Advisors

As companies grow, their circumstances become more complex. Continued business success means more employees to manage, more processes to oversee, more relationships to cultivate, and more financial information to track and evaluate. As the company begins to outgrow some of the old ways of doing things, the owner's roles begin to change with that growth. More and more of the owner's time is spent performing high-level planning and management issues, and less time is spent "in the shop" or "in the field." This success and growth may lead the owner to consider creating an outside board of advisors.

Many owners of privately held businesses do not take full advantage of the benefits provided by formalized governance structures. If a company has an outside board of advisors, many owners treat the board of advisors as a mere "rubber stamp." Others see it as nothing more than an administrative nuisance. Still, others use the board as a way to channel fees to family members who are not otherwise on the business payroll. None of these are good uses for a board of advisors.

Businesses that do not have a functioning outside board of advisors are missing out on a tremendous opportunity to improve the management and profitability of their company, especially during a period following the owner's exit. An outside board provides the business owner with valuable advice from individuals with years of business experience. These board members make recommendations on what they believe represents the best interests of the shareholders and the company.

An outside board of advisors plays an important role in the implementation of a management-exit plan. These advisors help the owner(s) sort out possible successors from the pool of candidates. They help with the implementation and monitoring of the management talent assessment and the management-grooming plan (see Chapter 8, "Defining a Legacy").

When the management-development plan is in place, the board provides oversight of the plan, ensuring the process remains untainted by family issues and bias. Further, the directors serve as mentors for successor candidates, help them to deal with their concerns, and make suggestions for their development. Finally, the board lends credibility and authority to the management-succession process through its ratification of the final choices for future executive-management positions.

In addition to serving as a sounding board and providing guidance during the implementation of an exit plan, the board helps monitor and improve business management by:

- Reviewing financial statements and audits
- Reviewing corporate mission and strategy
- Reviewing and approving budgets
- Monitoring business performance
- Monitoring business goals
- Making recommendations regarding major capital expenditures
- Assessing organizational structure and policies
- Approving acquisitions and mergers
- Approving major debt transactions

Assembling an outside board of advisors is often one of the suggestions an exit planning team makes to a business owner in the course of working with him on his exit plan. In some cases, the exit planning team itself may become a good substitute for a board, if no one else can be found.

Initially, owners may resist taking the plunge and involving an outside board in what always have been private business affairs. The owner may fear the interference of outsiders or the involvement of strangers in the "family business." Even if an outside board is created, the worried owner may not allow the board to function in a meaningful way. The owner may be inclined to select long-time friends, advisors, or subordinate employees to serve on the board. Unfortunately, these folks do not have the independence needed to provide the owner with the objective advice he or she needs to hear. Alternatively, the owner may create a board but not hold board meetings at regular intervals, or consult board members on trivial matters only. In such cases, the board of advisors can rarely, if ever, provide anything of value, and might as well not exist.

## Creating an Outside Board of Advisors

If you intend to help your clients assemble an outside board as part of their exit or succession planning efforts, you may find the following discussion helpful. Although a detailed explanation of how to set up and run an outside board of advisors is beyond the scope of this book, the following overview gives you an idea of how the process works.

- **Develop a statement of purpose for the board.** The business owners meet and decide what role the board will play vis-à-vis company management and ownership. The end result is a written, overarching statement of purpose for the board.

- **Decide on characteristics of the ideal board members/advisors.** Spend some time deciding on what sorts of individuals you may want on your board. Some owners decide that experience in the company's industry or a similar industry is a prerequisite. The owners also may decide to include someone older and someone younger to represent the values of more than one generation. The owner may decide each of the members should have a different professional background (lawyer, business operations, accounting, and business sales.)  Also, consider strategic criteria (for example, a company that is planning to expand sales or operations into a new market may want a board member who successfully ran a business in that market).

- **Prepare a Member Prospectus.** Some businesses prepare a document referred to as an "Advisory Board Prospectus," used to help screen and recruit board candidates. The prospectus explains the purpose and goals of the board. It also lays out the details such as the board structure, the time demands, the fees board members receive, and the meeting schedules. Finally, it describes the capabilities, qualifications, and characteristics the company is seeking in board members. The prospectus need not be long; one or two pages is usually sufficient.

- **Identify possible board candidates.** The business owner's first instinct usually is to invite close friends and trusted advisors (i.e., the company's lawyer, CPA, and banker) to serve on the board. However, business owners should resist this urge whenever possible. The best board members are usually fellow business owners, entrepreneurs, business peers, and retired CEOs or CFOs.  You may be surprised to learn that a large number of these folks are eager to serve on advisory boards.  Many former business owners and retired executives will even do it for free, simply to stay involved in the business world. These outside advisors already may have faced some of the hurdles that lie ahead for the company and can offer advice from an owner's perspective. The company's exit planning and other trusted advisors often serve as an excellent source of referrals to potential board members. If a prospectus is prepared, include a copy with your request for a referral.

- **Meet with candidates.** The business owner(s) and his or her exit planning team meet with and interview the board candidates. The owners explain the company's needs and ask about the candidate's qualifications to meet those needs. Always be certain to check references. Seek out people who know the candidates, and find out about their character, personality, and professional history.

- **Ensure support from owners and managers.** Before an offer is made to a candidate, have the candidate meet all shareholders and key managers to make sure the stakeholders are comfortable with the candidate. Owners and managers of the company need a forum to express their opinions about the candidate—both positive and negative—but the business owner has veto power.

## Family Councils

As discussed in previous chapters, one of the biggest challenges in managing a family business is managing the collision of family issues and business issues. This is especially true in the area of exit planning. As discussed earlier in more detail, families in business contend with three different worlds: "the family world," "the management or business world," and "the owner's world." Each of these worlds is equally important, but are often at odds.

A traditional board of advisors can be a very effective tool in addressing management and ownership issues, but it may not be as useful in handling the family dynamics described above. Through the creation of a family council, family members—in conjunction with the advisory board—are able to improve communication, accountability, and family harmony. By participating in a family council, stakeholders may consider themselves part of the family/management/ownership system. Family issues are addressed separately from business issues rather than being exposed in front of employees or managers. Lines of communication remain open, interpersonal relationships are improved, and the quality of life for everyone is enhanced.

## What Is a Family Council?

A family council serves as a sort of board of directors for the family. Just as an outside board acts as a sounding board to protect the financial and business health of the company, a family council protects the growth, development, and welfare of the family itself. A family council provides family members with a regular, structured forum to communicate voice concerns, have input, and participate in determining how to deal with business issues.

Just as the protocol followed in a corporate board meeting is determined by the corporation's articles of incorporation, by-laws, and shareholder agreements, the purpose and procedures of a family council are determined by the family charter, its by-laws, and its vision/mission statement.

A family council operates separately from, but in coordination with, a board of advisors. The family council deals with the "business of the family," while the board of advisors deals with the "business of the business." There should be at least one liaison between the outside board and the family council. This liaison is responsible for coordinating and managing the family goals and expectations with the company's strategic plan. The use of a family council helps keep family issues out of the boardroom and business management issues out of family functions. The overlapping issues are managed or communicated by the board of advisors. With this structure, the family does not feel obliged to pack the corporate board with family members, which prevents the involvement of objective, experienced outside directors who bring new perspectives to the business. The family council also provides a regular time and place for dialogue concerning the interests of the family in the business. By following the family council protocol, issues are presented, information is shared, misunderstandings are cleared up, and matters can be resolved without escalating them to involve the whole business.

But, perhaps the most important benefit provided by the family council is improved family relations. The council provides family members with a support system for each other during difficult times. The council meetings may serve to help maintain the communication between family members, foster family involvement in giving back to the community, help educate family members on financial and other issues, teach the younger generation about family history and values, and provide an excellent backdrop for people to get together and enjoy each other's company. Our clients tell us that one of the more unexpected outcomes of this family-business governance structure is a new sense of family identity and togetherness.

## Setting Up a Family Council

A trusted advisor, such as an exit-planning specialist, usually helps organize the family council. Sometimes the organization of the family council is accomplished in conjunction with the establishment of an outside corporate board of advisors, described earlier. The whole notion of a family council may be foreign to business owners, so seeking outside help to set up and run a family council is a good idea. The advisor should attend the first few family council meetings to observe and make recommendations. After the family governance structures are in place and operating, the advisor usually is not needed on an ongoing basis. The established family governance structure (outside board of advisors and family council) operates fully with family members and business owners controlling all its activities.

Although a detailed description of how to set up a family council is outside the scope of this book, the following general steps provide an overview of the process.

1.  **Explain the Family Council Concept**

    We recommend the family leaders (mother and father) send written invitations to each family member to attend a family meeting. Some choose to conduct this initial meeting in a retreat setting to help put family members at ease and make the event feel special, as well as to set the tone for the event. The exit planning advisor who helps set up the family council also should be present to help facilitate the meeting, educate the group, gain family "buy-in," and help develop the schedule going forward.

2.  **Develop a Statement of Family Vision and Core Values**

    The first order of business is to draft the family's mission and vision statements. A family council should have a clear statement of its purpose, intent, and goals. Under the leadership of the senior family members, the entire family participates in drafting and then ratifying these important statements. The family vision statement is a strong, cohesive message to the outside world that sets the tone for the family culture. The vision statement is intended to help family members develop a common sense of purpose and motivation in their lives. The family mission statement defines the purpose of the family and describes the family's most important core values.

3.  **Develop Family By-Laws**

    The council also should have a statement containing the family council's rules of procedure. The family by-laws or charter fills this purpose. The family by-laws are the "Constitution and Bill of Rights for the Family." The by-laws contain the rules and formalities to be followed by the council. A provision for making amendments to the original by-laws is included.  Developing a set of family by-laws takes several family meetings and should be viewed as an evolutionary process.  They will and should change over time.  It is usually helpful to get the assistance of an outside advisor to facilitate the process. Nonetheless, this is an important and meaningful step in creating a sense of ownership, empowerment, and participation for all family members.

## 4. Schedule Family Council Meetings

Family council meetings are held regularly and scheduled a year in advance.  All family members have the dates reserved for family council meetings for the upcoming year.  We recommend family council meetings be held not more often than quarterly but at least semi-annually.  It is important that meetings not be spaced too closely together.  Enough time must elapse between meetings so family members have time to take action on agreed-upon items and have results to discuss. If families meet too frequently, the meetings can feel unproductive.  At the same time, if families meet only annually, family members may not believe they have an effective forum to be heard and may resort to other means of expressing themselves.  This is counterproductive.

Many clients find that holding a meeting three times a year is perfect. This schedule doesn't interfere with the traditional quarterly business calendar.  Spacing meetings four months apart gives everyone enough time to tackle big projects and make significant headway so they can report back to the group.  This schedule also fits well into the family vacation schedules so meetings can be coordinated around spring break, summer vacation, and the late fall/early winter holidays.

## 5. Elect Family Council Officers

Officers are entrusted with conducting the business of the council. A president, vice president, and recording secretary are examples of family council officer positions. The president generally plans the agenda and conducts the business at the general council meetings. The vice president assists the president in this regard, and presides over meetings when the president is absent. The secretary records and reads the minutes, and distributes copies of general meeting agendas.  We recommend that the family business founder or CEO not be the president of the family council.  Giving another family member this responsibility is good training, can open the channels of communication, and ensures the family council does not become simply another vehicle to continue existing family dynamics.

### 6. Assign Responsibility for Council Subcommittees

Each family council member is afforded the opportunity to serve on a council subcommittee designated to address a specific family issue of personal interest. Examples of subcommittees might include: corporate liaison committee, charitable/philanthropic committee, family health and welfare committee, family information committee, and/or community relations committee. In some cases, special task forces are formed to tackle specific objectives such as the development of a family employment policy or dividend policy. The subcommittees report their activities in general family council meetings.

### 7. Conduct Regular Family Council Meetings

Family council meetings are conducted with all the formalities and respect typical in formal business meetings. Meeting reminder notes and agendas are distributed before the meeting date. Quorum requirements must be respected. People should be reminded of the meeting ground rules, and a copy of the by-laws should be available at every meeting. Minutes are kept, recorded, and reread at the beginning of each meeting. Old business items are revisited and resolved first. Subcommittee reports follow. New-business items are introduced next. Motions for council action are nominated and subjected to an oral vote by the family members. Motions without unanimous consent are discussed again, and, if necessary, referred to the subcommittee for further examination. Subcommittees then examine the motion in detail and prepare a formal policy for presentation at a general council meeting. During this presentation the "edict" is examined in light of the family vision/mission statement and family charter. Arguments for both sides are presented and the family members vote again. If the edict passes, it becomes family policy. If the edict fails to pass as written, the issue may be abandoned or returned to the subcommittee for redrafting and reconsideration.

### 8. Participating in the Family Council

Family members should earn the privilege to have a voice on the family council. This does not mean younger family members should be prohibited from attending general family council meetings, but they must be old enough to conduct themselves in a mature manner. We recommend that young family members be permitted to attend family council meetings as soon as they are able to sit through a meeting without being disruptive. This is a great way to teach younger family members to understand, respect, and work with each other. It also helps educate younger family members about the family's history, traditions, and values. In this sense, the very existence of a family council helps to instill a family's core values in the next generation from a very early age.

That said, younger family members, nevertheless, must understand they need to meet certain criteria before they can participate on the family council with older family members. The family determines what these qualifications are when drafting the family charter. Qualifications may include quantitative criteria such as reaching a certain age or completing a degree, or qualitative criteria such as demonstrating a commitment in one's chosen vocation (for example, working in the family business, managing a household, or academic studies); demonstrating financial responsibility; showing an understanding of business including the ability to interpret financial statements; demonstrating trust and respect for other family members; and demonstrating they can handle disputes in a mature manner. Whatever the standard, some performance-based criteria is important so participation in the family council is not viewed as a birthright.

## Summary

As discussed in Chapter 5, "The Exit Planning Process," one of the most common reasons business owners put off exit planning is that it involves discussing difficult issues with family members, other shareholders, key managers, and outside advisors. Knowing these issues need to be addressed, and lacking the tools to do so, effectively creates a great deal of anxiety for business owners. Helping them create an environment in which these issues can be addressed in a constructive and proactive manner is the first step in the exit planning relationship.

# Chapter 8

# Defining a Legacy

As the previous chapter discussed, setting goals is an important first step in the process of designing an exit plan for a business owner and the other stakeholders in the business.

One way to help a business owner think about goals is to couch the process in terms of defining a legacy. Leaving a legacy is often a subconscious goal business owners have during the exit planning process. This is especially true for family-owned businesses whose founder may express a strong desire to have sons or daughters assume control of the family business and preserve the company for future generations. Other business owners and their children may be just as comfortable converting the family business into a more liquid asset and then passing a financial legacy to subsequent generations. Helping a business owner define what that legacy should be and how it should be achieved is a crucial part of the exit planning process.

An exit plan for a business owner needs to consider all the owner's exit options including a transfer or sale to a family member (an intra-family transfer). When an intra-family transfer is the business owner's goal, the exit plan needs to address topics other than those relating to selling to a third party.

In this chapter we explore how to help a business owner identify and develop a successor. We also explore what needs to be done to groom a successor for success rather than failure. Finally, we discuss how to help a business owner gracefully exit his or her company so the successor can assume the role and mantle held by the business owner.

## Developing a Successor

If the most appropriate legacy is to keep the business in the family, a good exit plan requires more than the business owner's selecting a son or daughter to be his successor. Careful thought and attention must be given to a range of issues, especially during the critical "transition period" when the successor and owner's roles in the company are evolving into something new. Too many business owners overlook the need to train, coach, and develop a successor, and they forget how important it is to work out the mechanics and formalities of the transition period in advance. When company owners do not act proactively and simply hope the pieces will magically fall into place, the business suffers and family discord results.  Remember the Case Study involving the Keil Family in Chapter 1.

If this process is not addressed up front, other issues are likely to surface at a less opportune time, including:

- Does the chosen successor even want the job?
- Is the chosen successor competent and willing to do everything it takes to succeed?
- Is the parent willing to relinquish the amount of control necessary for the successor to assume the parent's role?
- Are there other family members who feel that this position was really their birthright?
- What about dealing with non-family key employees who are currently more experienced than family-member successors?

Because most family business owners are natural entrepreneurs, they are take-charge people who find it difficult to delegate responsibility.  As a result, many family business owners do very little to select and groom a potential successor.

Frequently, formal training or developing a successor is deferred. The irony in this is that, of all the types of businesses in our economy, private businesses are actually the ones that have the greatest need to design and implement a formal management-training program. If the business owner waits too long to address management succession, the ability to teach and assert values also diminishes, due to advanced age or failing health. It is better to deal with these issues while the owner still exerts strong leadership over the business and family.

## Dealing with More Than One Potential Successor

Ultimately, the senior business owner must name the next president or CEO of the company and, if there is more than one possible successor, the process is even more complicated. Not surprisingly, fallout can ensue from the nomination of one family member or employee over another. Family members may not accept the selection of the most *qualified* candidate and their views may be clouded by feelings of loyalty, acceptance, or comparative love. Other "personal" issues are likely to further complicate the situation, such as an oldest child who feels that company leadership is part of a "birthright" (even if he or she does not possess the right combination of competency, character, and chemistry to succeed).

To preserve family harmony and promote sound decisions, family-business owners must separate family issues from business issues when deciding on the next business leader. This can be done in a variety of ways. For example, the company may appoint an outside, unrelated advisory board to consider various candidates, monitor their progress, and keep the owner apprised of their development. Another option is an impartial outside consultant who develops and monitors management grooming and incentive compensation plans. Some family businesses form "family councils," which function as a board of directors for the family to help separate family issues from business ones (as discussed in Chapter 7, "Communicating with Stakeholders").

By not being appointed as successor, a candidate may feel deprived of a birthright. When this happens, it is important to quickly evaluate possible alternatives suitable for the disgruntled family member. For example, the company may decide to spin off a division into a separate, new corporation for the "displaced" family member to run. Success in the management succession process often hinges on keeping all communication in the open and available to all stakeholders. Open honest communication and adequate feedback must be provided along the way to the successor(s).

Toward this end, the exit planning team may wish to consider the use of impartial consultants and other advisors (such as non-family mentors or outside advisory boards) in the development and monitoring of the successor-grooming plan. But clearly, the successor-development program must be coordinated with all other elements of the exit plan (for example, the stock transfer program, the estate and gift plan, or the retirement plan timetable) to be responsive and successful.

## Groom Successors, Not Failures

The younger generation is often reluctant to bring up the issue of exit planning and management succession because they do not want to appear pushy or greedy; or genuinely want to avoid the topic of a parent's mortality. The prospect of life without the presence of the founder can be very difficult and daunting for everyone. Many people prefer to operate under the illusion that a company founder or parent will always be around to help guide the company and protect the family legacy.

The responsibility to groom the next generation belongs to the business owners. The younger generation does not typically have the experience or the foresight to understand what leadership skills are required to run a business and are not in a position to create their own management-training program.

For these and many other reasons, the senior-generation owners must formulate and implement the successor-training program on behalf of the stakeholders. This is often a difficult concept for older business owners to grasp. They may not have benefited from a "successor-grooming" program when they took over control from their parent(s). Nonetheless, it is an important step as the business world becomes more complicated and as the stakes involved get larger and larger.

Although it is beyond the scope of this book to describe in detail how successful successor training or grooming programs should be implemented, the remainder of this chapter provides an overview of this important issue.

Many experts in the field of successor grooming believe that in a family business it is important for the successor to understand the business from the ground floor up.  As a result, many successor-training programs require the family member entering the business to start by working "on the shop floor" or "in the field".  The thought is that by spending time as a line employee, then line supervisor, middle manager, assistant to a corporate officer, and finally in an upper-management position, the successor will understand how the business works, including what is right and wrong with the current operation, and have developed the credibility with other employees and managers to implement changes.  To do this right takes years. The successor should be allowed to spend a meaningful amount of time in each role (often six months or more) and gradually afforded more and more responsibility. It should be understood that the successor will make mistakes, but it is important that he or she be treated like any other employee and face the same consequences. In fact, it is in the process of making these mistakes that the successor will learn some of life's most valuable lessons.

The point in time when the successor moves into an executive position is pivotal in the grooming process. Even though a successor may have worked for the company for years, he or she still may require additional development to step into a senior management role. An entirely new set of skills must be honed or acquired to understand strategic and financial planning, accounting fundamentals, relevant industries, crisis management, leadership, sales/marketing, communication, and critical interpersonal skills.

To encourage development of these skills, a responsible plan requires the successor take university-level courses in finance, accounting, marketing, and management.   Many organizations and local universities offer management-development programs and leadership training, which are valuable in developing a successor.   Other training programs require the successor to work outside the family business for a number of years to gain insight into the fair market value of his or her skills, and to understand how other professionally managed organizations function.

The successor also may be assigned a senior executive to work closely with as a personal mentor. When mentoring is used, the designated mentor will be someone in the organization who is not threatened by the successor. Otherwise, the mentor may not be committed fully to the successor's training and development, and subconsciously, feel the need to sabotage the process.

## The Continuing Role of the Business Founder

Planning an orderly transition, from the founder to the next generation or to a third-party owner, can be difficult. Even in situations where the successor or new owner has a high level of competence, some owners will have a difficult time "letting go." Many founders desire to remain active in company management because growing the business has been their life's work. Feelings of identity and self-worth also may be tied to the operation of the company. At work, the founder feels vital, comfortable, and useful. A great deal of his or her identity is tied up with the notion of being the captain of a great ship. Without work, the owner's perception of the quality of his or her life is likely to diminish. In such a situation, it is not reasonable to expect the founder to turn company control easily over to others, even a trusted family member.

In addition, if the founder is relying on the cash flow from the business to fund retirement needs, it is a further stretch to expect the owner to, either consciously or subconsciously, give up control.

At the same time, the owner's successor may have spent an extended amount of time in subordinate roles or obtaining advanced degrees and be anxious to make his or her mark on the company. Motivated by the need to establish independence from the older generation, the successor may want to implement his or her own business plans as soon as the founder relinquishes control.

The difference in the parent/owner's need to retain control in order to create retirement security and the next generation's desire to take over immediately, can create a significant expectations gap. In such cases, the involvement of other advisors serves as an important way to bridge this gap and avoid unnecessary conflicts.

## Keeping the Founder Involved

The keys to the successful transition of management are planning, communication, and balance. It is important for business owners to understand they have an important role to play in the ongoing success of the company, even if they are not at the helm. As the successor develops and accepts increasing amounts of responsibility, he or she must be given room to make increasingly important management decisions without interference from the founder. However, appropriate "checks and balances" can be instituted.

When the successor is able to assume management of the company, the founder should be prepared to continue to play an important role in the company during a transition period. This period may involve shared management responsibility or some other form of coaching that may include:

- Providing ongoing mentoring to assist the younger-generation management team
- Providing guidance in the formation of long-term strategic plans
- Maintaining long-time relationships with important clients, bankers, and others

- Helping with special projects, joint ventures, or expansion plans
- Handling customer problems and complaints

As described above, business owners can continue to be involved in the business in a variety of roles. The owner may decide to serve as an outside consultant to the business, play a role on the company's board of directors, or serve as the head of an advisory board that guides and advises the successor.

We believe it is vitally important that the owner's continuing role is spelled out in a memorandum of understanding. This helps ensure everyone understands each other's respective roles, and that boundaries are established so the retiring owner's responsibilities do not begin to unintentionally cross over into those reserved for the new successor. Such a document should address terms and conditions such as:

- Use of an office, a company car, or other company resources
- The founder's specific roles pertaining to defined tasks
- Availability of the founder for a defined transition period to work on defined tasks
- A policy about reimbursing the founder's fees and expenses
- A "chain of command" establishing how contact with company personnel will be handled

As this chapter shows, a good exit plan requires more than merely anointing a successor. Careful thought and attention must be given to a myriad of issues, especially during the critical "transition period," when the successor and founder's roles in the company are evolving into something new. Too many business owners overlook the need to develop mechanics and formalities to help through this often difficult transition period. When company owners are not proactive and merely hope that the pieces will somehow work themselves out, business difficulties and family discord are often the result.

## Summary

In this chapter you learned that an exit plan is just as important for business owners who are thinking of a generational transfer as it is for owners thinking of selling to a third party. In fact, we argue it is even more important to ensure the transition goes smoothly, everyone's interests are respected, and all goals are achieved.

Given that the exit planning process can take several years, in the next chapter we discuss how to deal with the one unexpected event most business owners never want to consider: their death or disability.

# Chapter 9

# The Contigency Plan

Most business owners are very good at contingency planning. They plan for every possibility imaginable, but surprisingly, few business owners plan for the one thing that is certain: their eventual death or disability.

In this chapter we explore the differences between a contingency plan and an exit plan. We also look at the important role a contingency plan plays in the overall exit planning process. Finally, we explore the key components of a good contingency plan, including concepts such as stay bonuses, disability buy-out insurance, and buy-sell agreements.

## Contingency Plan vs. Exit Plan

An exit plan is a comprehensive plan that shows a business owner how to exit a business on his or her terms. A contingency plan, however, shows the owner's heirs and advisors what the owner would like them to do with the business in the event the owner cannot do it himself. Think of it as a plan that deals with the least desirable exit option of all—the death or disability of the business owner.

Generally speaking, owners have more pleasant endings in mind when they think of exiting their businesses; nonetheless, we all know someone who died too soon. It is easy to put off or overlook this possibility during the exit planning process.

Without continuity of leadership, your client's business will probably fail. If ownership transition for a business is uncertain, business continuity is seriously threatened. Your client's death can have a significant effect upon the company's ability to maintain its financing, its relationships with key customers and vendors, its bonding status, and its relationships with other parties who are important to the ongoing success of the business.

Failing to understand the consequences the client's death can have on his or her business, can result in the unintended death of the business itself. A good exit plan requires you to help your clients develop a contingency plan for their business and update it every year. The plan should be updated to include a current value for the business and any changes in the client's exit plans.

Business owners who are contemplating exiting their businesses are often the most vulnerable. They are typically 55 years old or older and are usually several years away from a liquidity event (sale of the company). They have all the health issues that come with that stage of life.

Often forgotten is that a large part of the value of your client's company is based on the buyer's assumption that your client will be around for 6 to 12 months to facilitate the transition of ownership with the company's employees, vendors, and customers. If the business owner dies or becomes disabled and cannot play this vital role, the buyer will discount the value of the company dramatically.

Let's look at what can happen to a business when its owner dies or becomes disabled unexpectedly.

### Case Study:  Until Death Do Us Part

Stan Carpenter was the 55 year old sole owner of a successful software company. Stan had recently completed his formal exit plan, and was in the process of getting his business and personal affairs in order, so he could sell his company to a third party within the next 24–36 months.

Unfortunately, before Stan could put much of his exit plan into place, he was killed in a traffic accident while riding his 1974 Harley Davidson motorcycle. Stan's unexpected death sent a shock wave through the company. Uncertain about the future of the company after Stan's death, two of his key programmers left for jobs with more stable futures. These key employees feared the company might not continue without Stan's vision, leadership, and financial backing.

Their departure was another big blow to the company. A number of clients questioned the firm's future ability to deliver its projects on time, which resulted in a sharp drop in revenues. In addition, the firm missed a key delivery date on a project, exposing the company to significant liabilities. After six months of waiting and watching, Stan's bank grew uneasy and decided to call in his company's debt—debt that Stan had personally guaranteed.

Unfortunately, at this point the company had no value to a third party and was not salable.

As you can see, business continuity planning is vitally important to any company in which the owner plays an active role. Without a well-thought-out "survival plan," the consequences to employees, customers, and the owner's family and estate are dire.

Fortunately, there are a number of methods owners can use to avoid the type of business collapse Stan Carpenter experienced.

### 1. Written Instructions

First, the exit plan should be a written document that states: (1) who the business owner wants to run the business; (2) whether the business should be sold (and if so, to whom), continued, or liquidated; and (3) who the business owner's heirs should consult regarding the sale, continuation, or liquidation of the company. This plan should be as detailed as possible and provide names and contact information.

## 2. Communicate

Second, it is important that a business owner let his or her advisors know about the contingency plans. This includes meeting with the business owner's lender or banker to discuss these arrangements and confirm that insurance is in place to affect these plans. It is important to make sure the owner's lenders are comfortable with the contingency plan. If they have any reservations, they should be asked what arrangements they would suggest.

## 3. Stay Bonus

Third, to keep key employees on board after an owner's unexpected disability or death, it is important to provide them with an incentive to stay for a predetermined period. This incentive, called a "stay bonus," is a written, funded plan providing monthly or quarterly bonuses, usually over a 12 to 18 month period, for key employees who remain with the company during its transition to new ownership or while it is being liquidated in an orderly way. (New ownership may consist of a third party, employees, or family members.)

The bonus needs to be substantial, often twice an employee's salary. Alternatively, the incentive could be partial ownership in the company—using a buy and sell agreement. Regardless of the type of compensation, the bonus needs to be tied directly to company profitability and continued success.

Typically, the stay bonus is funded with life insurance in an amount sufficient to pay the bonuses over the specified time period. The plan should be communicated to the important employees when it is created so they know the plan and the money to fund it exists.

## 4. Life Insurance

Fourth, business owners and the exit planning team should work closely with a capable insurance professional to make certain the necessary insurance (such as funding the stay bonus) is purchased by the proper entity (the client, a trust, or the business) for the right reason and for the right amount. Owning the insurance policy in the wrong entity can have serious tax consequences.

## 5. Disability Insurance

Fifth, a contingency plan also should take into account the possibility that instead of dying, the business owner might suffer a serious disability that could impact the future operation and success of the business.

**Disability Overhead Protection Insurance.** This is an often overlooked type of disability insurance. In order to help manage the risk of cash flow problems associated with the extended disability of a business owner, many companies buy disability *overhead protection* insurance. Overhead protection insurance is for the benefit of the company, not the disabled owner's family. It is intended to keep the business viable until the disabled employee-owner is able to return to work or the company can be sold. The insurance benefits are used by the company to replace cash flow lost due to the absence of the key employee/owner. For example, the insurance proceeds may be used to pay debt, rent, and utilities and help make payroll until the disabled owner can return. This is especially comforting coverage if the owner has personally guaranteed bank debt and the owner is not at the helm.

**Personal Disability Coverage.** When it comes to disability planning, business owners have more responsibility than regular employees. If a regular employee with disability insurance is injured or becomes ill and is unable to work, the employee's family receives payments from the insurance company to replace the paychecks until the disabled earner can return to work. For business owners this is not as simple. Just like everyone else, business owners need disability insurance to provide income for their families in the event of a disabling injury or sickness. But business owners must also plan for the survival of the business in the event of diminished capacity.

Generally speaking, there are two types of disability coverage: short-term disability and long-term disability. A short-term disability is usually defined as 26 weeks or less. Long-term disability coverage normally includes a waiting or elimination period of 90 to 180 days before benefit payments begin.

Because the total risk of loss for the employer is less significant with short-term disability, some employers find it cost effective to "self-insure" the risk of short-term disability. The employers agree to make direct payments of disability benefits to employees rather than pay insurance premiums. For the same reason, long-term disability is usually not self-insured. Instead, employers may obtain a long-term group insurance policy covering all full-time employees. It is fairly typical for long-term group disability plans to provide benefits of between 60 to 70 percent of the employee's lost income due to disability.

There is a planning opportunity in arranging employee disability coverage for business owners. If properly structured, some self-funded disability plans (plans that agree to make direct payments to the disabled employees rather than use insurance to fund benefits) are not subject to the IRS rules requiring equal participation of all employees and annual reporting.

Accordingly, a properly structured, self-funded disability plan can discriminate in favor of highly paid executives of the company. A self-funded employee disability plan, without any employee contributions, is considered a "payroll practice" rather than a qualified plan. It is not subject to the IRS anti-discrimination and other ERISA restrictions as long as the plan pays a significant portion of the employee's salary from the company's general assets as a result of a disability (29 CFR Sec 2510.3-1(a)(2)). In this way, generous disability benefits can be afforded to the owner without interference by IRS.

Benefits paid to an owner under a self-funded disability plan are fully deductible by the company for income tax purposes, as are company-paid group disability insurance premiums. The disability benefits received by an owner under a self-funded plan or a typical group plan are usually taxable to the recipient/owner.

### 6. Shareholder Buy-Sell Agreement

Shareholder agreements or *buy-sell* agreements are legal and binding agreements between the individual shareholders of a corporation in order to provide restrictions on the transferability of closely held stock for the overall protection and benefit of all shareholders. Certain agreed upon events cause the corporation and/or other shareholders to redeem or cross purchase the stock from the shareholder who "triggered" the specified event. Most buy-sell agreements define the death of a shareholder as a triggering event and purchase life insurance in order to fund the redemption or cross-purchase of the deceased shareholder's stock.

## Reasons for Having a Buy-Sell Agreement

Unfortunately, many buy-sell agreements overlook long-term disability as a triggering event. The result can be the paralysis of the corporate board and senior management to take those strategic actions that would be in the best interest of the business. This can occur because the responsibilities and voting power of the disabled shareholder have been relegated to relatives or others not prepared to make informed business decisions.

For this reason, it makes sense to include a provision in the buy-sell agreement defining long-term disability as a triggering event for redemption or cross-purchase of the disabled shareholder's stock.

The company, or other shareholders, can acquire a long-term disability insurance policy on each of the owners in order to fund the buyout. The buy-sell agreement should define long-term disability in the exact manner as the insurance policy.

Debilitating accidents befall even young healthy people. However morbid it may

- Preserve control among existing owners

- Avoid disruption in managing the closely held business

- Establish market for an otherwise illiquid asset

- Establish a predetermined method for determining a fair price and terms for the buyout

- Reduce financial risk for decedent's family

seem to plan for such unpleasant possibilities, addressing the issue of disability is sound business practice. In addition, buy-sell agreements can be used to accomplish many other strategic tasks as part of an overall exit plan (as discussed in Chapter 17, "The Critical Role of the Attorney").

### 7. Contingency/Emergency Action Plans

The balance of power, particularly in a closely held business, is often very fragile. The loss of the company leader can leave a void that results in power struggles, employee turnover, managerial mistakes, lost customers, and lost profits. Even a vital and profitable company can unravel quickly when its leader is unexpectedly removed from the mix.

The loss of a mentor and business leader may be especially damaging to the crucial management succession grooming process. Not only are the company's profits threatened, but the plan for the long-term development of the successor may become derailed. Successors who are not ready to lead may be thrust prematurely into leadership positions, drastically reducing their chance of success. Other employees may sense trouble and begin to seek employment elsewhere. Important customers and suppliers may react in the same way.

To minimize the chance of this type of panic or power struggle, emergency plans should be developed to account for the sudden absence of leadership. Responsible individuals (such as corporate officers and board members) should be made aware of and empowered to implement these plans should such the occasion arise. Further, these plans should be reviewed periodically and updated as appropriate.

### Case Study: Sample Contingency Plan

Dear Merriam, Jamie, and Bobby:

Our family business has been a joy for me to build and run. I'm proud that it has provided so well for our family for the last thirty years. That said, the business was my passion. I don't expect it to be yours. You have your own dreams to pursue and your own lives to live. As a result, I have created the following plan in the event I die or become disabled. I hope this will make the process of dealing with our family business easier.

**Management:**

Day-to-day executive management should be turned over to John W. Smith, the company's CFO. He should assemble an advisory team made up of Roger Wiley in Operations and Bill Cohen in Sales.

**Compensation:**

John, Roger, and Bill are covered under the stay bonus plan I put in place last year.  Under this plan, they continue to receive their regular salaries, but also will receive a bonus equal to 100% of their base salaries if they stay with our company during the transition period and maintain the company's financial performance.  Jane [my secretary] has the file on the stay bonus plan.  Ken Fecund [my attorney] drafted the plan and can answer any questions.

**Disposition of the Business:**

I believe the company should be sold upon my death or disability. Although John, Roger, and Bill are great managers, I'm not sure they have the drive or the vision needed to continue to make this company a success. I have had preliminary conversations with Richard Jackim, an investment banker in Chicago, about selling the company.  In 1999, he thought the business might be worth approximately $10 million. I have a great deal of confidence in Richard and his team. Please engage them to sell the company for you. He will handle everything, make the process easy for you, and do a great job. His contact information is on the contact sheet attached.

**Advisors:**

Please ask Ken Fecund and Marybeth Kilgore [my CPAs] to work closely with Richard to handle the details.  Their contact information also is on the contact sheet attached.

**Possible Buyers:**

I also listed the names and addresses of people who have contacted me recently and expressed an interest in buying the company when I was ready to sell.  I haven't shared these names with Richard.  Please give him these names when you meet with him. There also are a few people I would ask you not to sell the business to. These are people I've run across during my career, and, for a variety of reasons, I would hate to see them take over.  I've listed them on the contact sheet as well. Please don't sell to them unless there are no other alternatives.

**My Goals:**

My primary goal in having you sell the company is to provide a financial legacy enabling you to live comfortably, pursue your dreams, and have rich and rewarding lives.  I wish I could be a part of those lives, but if I can't be there physically, at least I will have some comfort knowing that I played a part in making it possible.

In addition to my primary goal:

(1) I would love the company to stay in town where it has provided good jobs to our friends and neighbors for the last 30 years.

(2) I would love the company's name to stay the same, as a memorial to me.

(3) I would love it if John, Roger, and Bill could continue to be employed by the company to help continue its success. They have been good and loyal employees.

If you can accomplish my primary goal and any of my secondary goals at the same time, that would be great, but please do not compromise my legacy to each of you in order to accomplish any of these secondary goals.

**Thank You:**

Each of you have been a treasure to me and together you have been the light of my life. I am very proud and honored to be your husband and father. Thank you very much. Remember, enjoy what you do and success will find you.

I love you all so very much.

Roger Dayton (signature)

**Contact Information:**

Attorney -

CPA -

Financial Advisor -

Investment Banker -

Insurance Advisor -

# Summary

If you do nothing else with your clients, at the very least, help them to understand the fundamental importance of a contingency plan. The very worst legacy they can leave their family and loved ones are the headaches that come with trying to wrestle with these issues without the owner's help and guidance. The process of discussing and developing a contingency plan often leads to a mandate to develop a full exit plan as well.

In the next chapter we explore the importance of assembling a multidisciplinary team to help you design and implement your clients' exit plans.

# Chapter 10

# Assembling a Multidisciplinary Team

As you probably noticed, one of the principal themes of this book is that developing a successful exit plan is like assembling a complicated puzzle. Each part must fit with the others in order for the final image to take shape. Given the detailed knowledge of estate planning, business law, mergers and acquisitions, tax law, insurance products, financial planning, and wealth management required during the exit planning process, you are probably not surprised to learn that you must develop a multidisciplinary team to adequately represent your client.

During the course of our careers as investment bankers, we have not come across a single professional with all the knowledge or skills necessary to design a successful exit plan on his or her own. In fact, we have not found a single law firm, accounting firm, or financial planning firm that has all the necessary resources in-house.

I make it a part of my practice to identify top professionals in their fields and to build working relationships with them so I know who to turn to when I help clients assemble their exit planning team.

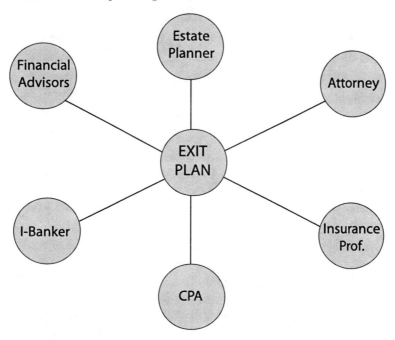

Figure 10-1: Exit Planning Disciplines

In this chapter, first, we review why the multidisciplinary approach makes sense. Next, we look at why it is important to have one advisor act as the "lead" or the "quarterback" for the advisory team. Finally, we explore the roles of the lead advisor as well as each of the key players on the team.

## The Multidisciplinary Approach

Exit Planning is a multidisciplinary process presenting business owners with a comprehensive and strategic approach to the orderly transition of the management and ownership of their companies.

An effective exit plan focuses on all of the important business, personal, financial, tax, estate planning, and wealth-management issues involved in exiting a privately owned business. The planning issues facing closely-held business owners are much more complex than those of individuals of similar net worth who do not own their own businesses. Closely-held business owners must not only account for the preservation of family wealth—through estate, gift tax, retirement, insurance, and investment planning—they also need to deal with a host of additional issues directly related to the enduring success of business operations, such as:

- Addressing compensation planning for successors and key executives (to ensure they stay in the event of transfer)
- Building a long-term business strategy
- Understanding the fair market value of closely held stock
- Developing a formalized "grooming" program for successors
- Evaluating corporate finance and entity structure options
- Designing and implementing shareholder agreements
- Utilizing tax effective ownership-transfer techniques

Despite all of the sound business reasons to do exit planning (many of which were covered in Chapter 1), the fact remains that most privately owned businesses never actually develop an exit plan. Our research shows that the reluctance to plan is attributable to the perceived difficulty of the task (for example, too many business and personal issues to consider, and requiring expertise from too many separate disciplines).

To increase the probability of success, a responsible exit planning program requires enlisting the assistance of many individuals with different areas of expertise, such as income tax specialists, attorneys, management consultants, appraisers, insurance professionals, employee benefit specialists, estate planners, and financial planners. And although well intentioned, these advisors may offer conflicting advice that will confuse and frustrate owners. Add to the mix the constant pressures of day-to-day business management and the reluctance to deal with relational issues, many owners never manage to "find the right time" to develop their succession plans.

## The Need for Exit Planning Advisors

Because exit planning is typically a once-in-a-lifetime event, the process is not something most business owners know anything about. As a result, using an exit planning advisor makes sense. A seasoned exit planning advisor helps to anticipate and identify potential problems otherwise overlooked.

The use of an impartial exit -planning specialist also adds an important degree of professionalism and legitimacy to the process. In many cases, this provides critical leverage because exit planning is often fraught with emotional issues.

Because the emotional component takes a toll on the interpersonal relationships of the stakeholders, one role of the exit planning advisor is that of a facilitator, especially during the critical goal-setting process. A facilitator helps collect candid information from stakeholders, builds a shared understanding of differing viewpoints, manages emotional turmoil, arrives at equitable compromises, and helps build a shared vision for the future. It is often too difficult for an "insider" to effectively accomplish this important and systematic process.

An exit planning advisor must have the following capabilities.

Expertise in:
- Retirement planning
- Business valuation
- Compensation planning
- Corporate finance
- Corporate structuring
- Estate and gift tax planning
- Income tax planning
- Life and disability insurance planning
- Stock transfer techniques

General business skills:
- Goal articulation and business strategy development
- Management development
- Managing interpersonal relationships, particularly family dynamics
- Corporate governance

Other desired perquisites of a good exit planning advisor:
- Substantial experience
- Integrity

- Empathy
- Creativity
- Communication skills

Do not worry if you do not posses all of these capabilities. I hate to admit it, but even this humble author cannot claim to have all of these capabilities. In reality, no single professional possesses the technical skill, consultative experience, and business acumen required to develop a sound exit plan. In fact, most professional firms, including accountants, lawyers, financial advisors, and investment banks, do not have all this experience in-house.

| | CPA | Financial Advisor/ Insurance Professional | Legal Advisor | Investment Banker |
|---|---|---|---|---|
| Identify Owner's Personal Objectives | ✓ | ✓ | ✓ | ✓ |
| Evaluate Business/ Determine Current Value | ✓ | | | ✓ |
| Develop Personal Financial Plan and Retirement Needs Analysis | | ✓ | | |
| Develop Exit Strategy and Plan | ✓ | | ✓ | ✓ |
| Improve Business Performance | | | | ✓ |
| Review Estate Plan | | ✓ | ✓ | |
| Develop Capital Gains and Estate Tax Minimization Plans | ✓ | | ✓ | ✓ |
| Review Insurance Needs | | ✓ | ✓ | |
| Develop Investment Plan for Sale Proceeds | | ✓ | | |
| Execute Exit Strategy | | | ✓ | ✓ |
| Assist Owner with Post-Exit Issues | ✓ | ✓ | ✓ | ✓ |

Figure 10-2: The Multidisciplinary Team

As a result, a coordinated team of specialists representing multiple disciplines should be on call. The role of each advisor is summarized in Figure 10-2., above.

# The Role of Each Advisor

### The Lead Advisor

Although each specialist in the succession-planning team has a different role to play, the lead advisor plays the role of quarterback or coach. The lead advisor could be the financial advisor, attorney, CPA, insurance professional, or investment banker with whom the owner and stakeholders work throughout the exit planning process. In addition to the specialist role, the lead advisor must have a "big-picture" understanding of the owner's personal situation and the succession-planning process so he can show the owner how the pieces fit together.

Although the lead advisor will not possess all the specialized expertise outlined above, that person must have a working understanding of each aspect of an exit plan. One of the lead advisr's primary roles is to help the owner assemble a team of "specialists" when, and as, specific needs arise.

Virtually any member of the exit planning team can play the role of the lead advisor. But often, unless a team member specializes in exit planning, the member finds that the lead role requires more time than he or she has available. In addition, some advisors find they do not have a wide network of other professionals to call on for additional specialist services. As a result, occasionally, an advisor with a strong client relationship may delegate the lead role to another advisor with more hands-on exit planning experience.

In that event, the optimal situation is to find a single professional firm with experience in exit planning and a group of qualified professionals who do nothing else. That group will act as the facilitator, gather the information needed by each of the other professional advisors, coordinate the exit planning process, and prepare the exit planning team's recommendations for delivery to the client. When an outside firm coordinates the advisory team, the team is much more likely to develop an effective, synchronized plan at a reasonable cost in time and fees.

Regardless of who plays the role of lead advisor, this person or group takes responsibility for the net results or the "client deliverable" of the exit planning team. This client deliverable should be a comprehensive, integrated report that contains all the recommendations and planning tools of the exit planning team. This report, then, becomes the "road map" the client uses to figure out what needs to be done, by whom, and when.

Communication between the owner, advisory team, and the professional advisors is critical. The lead advisor must interact effectively with the business owners and stakeholders by communicating concepts clearly, and by understanding the information provided in return. Too often, advisors unilaterally recommend solutions to accomplish tax savings or estate planning steps based on what they feel is best for the business owners. They don't spend sufficient time trying to understand the larger picture and how these steps impact the other goals and expectations of the stakeholders. In a collaborative process, all advisors must be consulted and a team consensus reached. If the team cannot reach a consensus, the differing options need to be summarized and presented to the client for a decision.

Be thorough! The consultants you ask to help construct and implement a client's exit plan should have the best possible credentials—credentials that are in proportion to the magnitude of the task. Remember that the exit planning process is a watershed event in your client's life. Advice given to your clients at this critical junction will affect them for generations. Take the time to assemble the right team!

### Investment Banker

In the exit planning context, the investment banker prepares a detailed business valuation for the company, provides suggestions on ways to increase the salability or value of the company, provides the exit planning team with a real-world assessment of the owner's exit options, and provides an assessment of overall market conditions. During the implementation phase, the investment banker also handles the sale of the company to a family member, key employee, or third party.

Selecting an investment banker is difficult. It is important to realize that not every investment banking firm understands the exit planning process. The truth is most investment bankers do very little true exit planning. They are interested in doing deals as quickly as possible so they can move on to the next deal. This is called "transaction velocity." They are hired to sell the company, not to ensure that the owner accomplishes personal objectives in the process.

An investment banking firm that specializes in exit planning is more interested in a consultative approach designed to help the client address the personal and business issues involved in exiting the company first. This type of investment banker is comfortable working with clients on a long-term basis and selling the company when the owner decides the time and conditions are right.

See Chapter 20 for a more complete discussion of the role of an investment banker in the exit planning process and how that banker helps maximize the value of your client's company.

## Attorney

In the exit planning context, an attorney is typically charged with handling the owner's estate planning work, doing legal due diligence or a pre-transaction audit, and then handling the legal issues involved in the actual sale of the company. If the attorney is part of a firm that has a tax group, his or her firm also may be asked to provide advice regarding ways to minimize ordinary income and capital gains taxes related to the sale.

Given the wide range of legal issues involved in exiting a private company, and the estate and tax ramifications of such a move, no single attorney will be able to handle all of the legal issues. It is therefore best to work with a law firm with estate planning attorneys, business attorneys, tax attorneys, and M&A attorneys in-house. See Chapter 17 for a more detailed discussion of the critical role attorneys play in the exit planning process.

## Financial Planner

In the exit planning context, a financial advisor or financial planner is a professional who helps a business owner develop a comprehensive personal financial and wealth management plan. Unfortunately, the financial planner is an often overlooked but very important member of the exit planning team. The results of the personal financial plan become one of the foundation blocks for the rest of the exit plan. See Chapter 15 for a more thorough discussion of how important sound financial planning is to any exit strategy.

## Insurance Professional

Unfortunately, business owners too often view life insurance as something only slightly better than a poke in the eye and, at best, a necessary evil. This misguided attitude often results in a poorly designed and implemented exit plan. In reality, insurance is a very powerful tool that can help the business owner and the rest of the exit planning team accomplish the owner's personal and business objectives. Therefore, an insurance professional should be included on every exit planning team. Chapter 19 discusses some of the unique applications of insurance in helping business owners achieve their exit objectives.

## The CPA

A talented Certified Public Accountant is an essential member of every exit planning team. At a minimum, the CPA is responsible for preparing the company's financial statements, preparing the company's tax returns, and designing an overall strategy to minimize the taxes paid at the time of sale. In addition, the CPA must be familiar with the legal, financial planning, estate planning, and investment banking issues, and participate in those discussions as well. We strongly recommend working with a certified public accountant who has experience working with business owners on business transactions.

There is a vast difference between a CPA and an accountant. A CPA has passed a very difficult examination and is certified by the state. The CPA designation establishes a certain degree of professionalism and training of the person holding the certification.   Obtaining the CPA designation demonstrates commitment and achievement.  On the other hand, an accountant is a person who practices accounting but has not passed the CPA exam.  A practicing CPA is required by law to keep abreast of the changes in the accounting profession by taking Continuing Professional Education.  Chapter 18 shows how important a CPA's involvement is when it comes to maximizing the value of a client's company.

## Summary

As this chapter demonstrates, exit planning is not a one-person project.  The most successful plans are the result of the combined efforts of the best professionals you can assemble.  In addition to the benefits to the client from this approach, assembling a multidisciplinary team for each exit planning engagement creates a dynamic and synergistic environment for these professionals to work together.

# Chapter 11

# Business Valuation

A comprehensive business valuation is one of the cornerstones of the exit planning process. Without a good idea of what a business is worth, it is impossible to make informed exit planning decisions. In this chapter we explore why business valuation is so important. We also discuss what creates value in a business. Next, we look at the three principal valuation techniques that should be used when valuing a private company. Finally, we examine the adjustments required to ensure the valuation reflects market reality.

Without a business valuation, a business owner is not able to plan for retirement, do comprehensive tax planning, formulate a good estate plan, or understand the full extent of the exit options. A business valuation impacts virtually every component of the exit planning process, including:

- **Financial Planning.** How much will the sale of the business provide for retirement?

- **Choice of Exit Options.** Does the company have intrinsic value that would be attractive to a third party or does it make sense to consider other exit options?

- **Estate tax.** How much estate tax exposure is attributable to the business? What minority and marketability discounts are applicable?

- **Gift tax.** What is the tax cost and benefit of gifting shares in the business?

- **Life insurance.** Is life insurance adequate, given the value of the business?

- **Shareholder agreements**. What value should be included in a shareholder agreement for transfers and buyouts? Will a valuation formula work? Should the agreement call for a formal independent valuation?

- **Value enhancement opportunities.** What factors are driving the value of the business down and is there anything that can be done about them?

- **Corporate finance.** How much loan collateral might be available? How much is the company stock worth in a sale?

As a result, a business owner and his team of advisors cannot begin to formulate an exit plan without a baseline business valuation.

**Case Study:  Missed Opportunity**

Rob was ready to exit his business.  He was 57 years old and always had planned to retire when he reached 55.  The year Rob turned 55, the economy began to soften and his company's revenues and earnings dropped significantly.  He was sure that if he sold his company then, it would be worth little more than its asset value.  As a result, he continued to work in the business well past the point at which he found it to be either fulfilling or energizing.

In doing so, Rob committed two common mistakes: First, he postponed planning his exit based on his gut feeling about the value of his business.  Second, he continued to work in his business after his enthusiasm had waned.

Because Rob failed to get a proper business valuation, he did not realize his business could have been sold for significantly more than just asset value. In addition, because he no longer had the same enthusiasm for his business, it never really bounced back the way it had in the past. As a result, Rob ended up investing six more years trying to "turn his business around." At the age of 63, Rob was diagnosed with prostate cancer and was forced to sell the business.  The business ultimately sold for slightly less than what he would have received six years earlier.

How can you help your clients avoid Rob's situation?  You should:

* Understand there are different types of valuations, performed by different types of valuation advisors, for different reasons
* Appreciate that different appraisers charge vastly different amounts for valuations
* Ask what type of valuation is needed and who should perform it; the answers depend on the purpose of the valuation.

If your clients are ready to exit their businesses now (meaning within a year or two), it's a good idea to get more than just a ballpark idea of value.  You should have a thorough valuation that includes a marketability component—can the company be sold today at its appraised value?  Only an experienced investment banker or business broker who has knowledge of current market conditions can give you an accurate answer to that question.

On the other hand, if your clients are three to five years away from exiting their businesses, you may not need a full-blown valuation.  Instead, a "ballpark estimate" of what the business is worth is usually enough for planning purposes. We recommend owners, with this time frame, obtain an annual ballpark valuation of their businesses to keep track of how well they are doing at building value in their businesses and to stay abreast of the market value of their biggest asset.

Valuing a privately-owned business relies on well documented, studied standards and methodologies. However, in reality, business valuation is as much art as it is science. For some assets, such as cars or real estate, there is an active and efficient secondary market and an abundance of information on comparable sales to help determine fair value. With private businesses, the situation is much different. Although there is an active market for these companies, the market is not liquid. This means that transactions take a great deal of time and effort to conclude. In addition, when private businesses do change hands, information about the terms of these transactions usually is guarded carefully. As a result, there are usually very few publicly available comparable sales for an analyst to use when valuing a private business. For this reason, the valuations of private businesses can be more complex and subjective than those of many other kinds of assets.

Business owners often ask, "How much is my business worth?" It may sound glib, but a business owner also should be asking, "What am I likely to receive in cash at closing today, if I decide I want to exit the business now?" The difference between these two questions and the answers they produce is subtle, but important. One addresses the theoretical value of a company, the other the practical, real-world value and its impact on the business owner.

Financial planners, estate planners, insurance professionals, lawyers, CPAs, and other professionals who work with business owners often discuss valuation issues. Because the business typically represents the majority of an owner's net worth, a proper valuation is a critical element in the financial plan, exit plan, and estate plan.

## Definition of Value

What is often not obvious to professional advisors, is that there is no one "right answer" when valuing a business. Depending on the purpose of the valuation, there is a range of right answers for the valuation question. For example, owners seeking a valuation as a part of a transfer of the business to employees via an employee stock ownership plan would receive a fair market valuation.

As the following diagram illustrates, each exit option a business owner considers has its own corresponding valuation options. As a result, the choice of an exit option has a huge impact on the fundamental value of the underlying business.

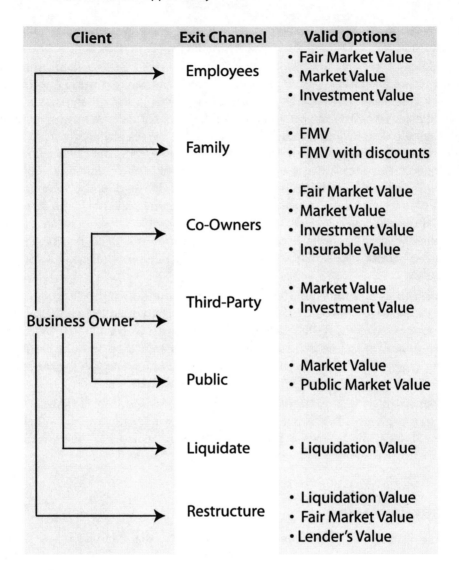

| Client | Exit Channel | Valid Options |
|---|---|---|
| | Employees | • Fair Market Value<br>• Market Value<br>• Investment Value |
| | Family | • FMV<br>• FMV with discounts |
| | Co-Owners | • Fair Market Value<br>• Market Value<br>• Investment Value<br>• Insurable Value |
| Business Owner | Third-Party | • Market Value<br>• Investment Value |
| | Public | • Market Value<br>• Public Market Value |
| | Liquidate | • Liquidation Value |
| | Restructure | • Liquidation Value<br>• Fair Market Value<br>• Lender's Value |

Figure 11-1:  Exit Options and Value Channels

The preceding diagram demonstrates there are three basic definitions of value: fair market value, investment value, and liquidation value.

**Fair Market Value**

Fair market value is defined as the hypothetical price a willing buyer and willing seller, with mutual knowledge of all relevant facts and not acting under any compulsion, would agree upon for the company. When no recent *bona fide* offers from unrelated parties exist, the appraiser is left to speculate on what a hypothetical buyer would pay. The IRS adopts this basic premise for valuations.

Market value is slightly different than fair market value. Market value is the *actual* price a willing buyer and seller actually agree to as payment for the company. Fair market value is an *estimate* of the market value of a company. Market value is the actual value and only is determined by having actual buyers and sellers meet and agree to terms.

**Investment Value**

The investment value of the company represents its value to a specific investor, such as a successor in a family business or a competitor looking for a company to buy. The valuation is based on a specific individual's investment requirements and expectations. For example, a strategic buyer may be a competing corporation that already has enough administrative infrastructure capacity for both companies, thus overhead costs in the acquired company could be eliminated. Combining the two companies may result in greater profit than the sum of the profit generated as two separate, competing entities.

**Liquidation Value**

Liquidation value is based on the assumption the business is worth more dead than alive. This means the company is no longer viable and the owner is selling the company's assets piecemeal rather than as a whole. Liquidation value is affected by the expected timing of the liquidation. The amount of time to sell assets may be immediate (forced liquidation) which would diminish value, or there may be adequate time to sell the assets (orderly liquidation) to several potential buyers which would result in a higher sales price.

**Purpose and Its Impact on Value**

As discussed above, the purpose of a business valuation has significant impact on the results the valuation analysis is likely to produce.

If an owner wants a valuation to set a "fair price" for a buy-sell agreement with other shareholders, the definition of value used should be investment valuation or the value the business has to a particular investor.

As discussed more fully below, the purpose behind a business valuation determines the process by which the business is valued, and hence, dictates the results. The wide range of reasons for a business valuation leads to a correspondingly large range of possible "right values" for a business.

Let us examine the exit options available to business owners and the impact each has on the value of the company and the structure and terms of a likely transaction.

There are valuation authorities who advocate or require specific valuation approaches depending on the purpose of the valuation. For example, the IRS is the governing valuation authority when it comes to gift and estate taxes.

**Case Study: What's It Really Worth?**

Several years ago we represented Richard Narva who owned a heat treating company. Richard wanted to transfer his company, Narva Metal Finishing Co., to his two sons. In analyzing Richard's options, we showed him the following. Table 1 illustrates Richard's exit options, along with Narva Metal Finishing Co.'s corresponding values. Once again, it is important to emphasize that values shown for each exit option are derived using the valuation approaches prescribed by the relevant authorities.

| Exit Channel | Exit Option | Valuation Authority | Value Standard | Resulting Value |
|---|---|---|---|---|
| Family | Gifting/GRAT | IRS | Fair Market Value with Discounts | $6,500,000 |
| Co-owners | Buy-Sell Agreement | Co-owners | Negotiated value or Fair Market Value | $9,000,000 |
| Third-Party Buyer | Controlled Auction | Buyer, Seller and their Advisors | Investment Value or Market Value | $10,250,000 |

**Table 11-1: Values Based on Different Exit Channels**

So the question is, with this information which exit option should Richard choose?

There is no right or wrong answer. This is Richard's choice. He can choose to transfer his company to his sons for roughly $6.5 million, he can exercise the buy-sell agreement and receive $9 million, or he can sell it to a third-party buyer for approximately $10 million. Each choice results in a different value.

In the exit planning context, one business valuation does not fit all purposes. It is important to view business valuation as a multi-step process involving several different iterations. Let us look at how this works.

1. Examine the owner's goals and objectives to identify one or more appropriate exit option.

2.  Consider the likely structure of the owner's exit option.

3.  Prepare a valuation appropriate for that exit option and terms.

4.  Incorporate these valuation results into the owner's financial and estate plan to ensure this exit option and the proceeds likely produced, are consistent with the owner's objectives in these other exit planning arenas.

5.  If the owner's objectives are not consistent, reconsider the owner's exit options, prepare a new valuation, and repeat the process until the business owner and all advisors are comfortable that the exit option and the resulting value meet the owner's personal goals and objectives.

As a result, the first step is to understand all exit options available to the business owner (see Chapter 12). Making a preliminary determination of what exit options are suitable for the client requires experience and usually involves consulting with the client's CPAs, attorneys, or investment bankers.

Ultimately, understanding the breadth and impact of their exit options leads business owners to action because most owners think they have relatively few options from which to choose. Far from being limited, there is a wide spectrum of exit options available to business owners. The final choice of exit option leads to a business value. Thus, if an owner is considering several different exit options, he also is considering several different values for the business.

## Valuation Approaches

When everyone understands the purpose(s) behind the valuation and the appropriate valuation standard(s) to apply, the investment banker can begin the valuation analysis. Before we begin a discussion of traditional business valuation methods and principles, it is important to realize that business valuation is as much an art as it is a science. Even the most highly trained valuation professionals will admit that valuing a business cannot generate exact results. Business valuation is an "educated guess" at best. The valuation process involves comparing several different approaches and selecting the best method, or combining methods based on the analyst's knowledge and experience.

Valuation and finance professionals have developed four, basic valuation methodologies that are the core of modern business valuation theory and practice. These four valuation methods are:

1.  Asset-based valuation

2.  Industry rules of thumb

3.  Comparable transactions analysis

4.  Discounted cash flow

**Asset-Based Valuation**

The asset-based valuation method is based on the premise that the value of a business is best determined by adding the value of all the company's assets and subtracting the liabilities, leaving the net value of its assets. An asset-based valuation is further segmented into five approaches:

1.  Book value
2.  Replacement cost
3.  Appraised value
4.  Liquidation value
5.  Market value

Asset-based valuation methods ignore the importance of company earnings and cash flow. For this reason, this valuation approach generally is not used to determine the market value of a company—especially in the context of an acquisition.

The following table demonstrates a valuation using the fair market value of the assets approach.

Table 11-2: Fair Market Value of Assets

| Asset | Book Value | Adjustment | FMV | Comment |
|-------|-----------|-----------|-----|---------|
| Cash | $400,000 | ($200,000) | $200,000 | Cash that is not needed for working capital is not typically included in a transaction. |
| Accounts Receivable | $1,400,000 | $0 | $1,400,000 | No adjustment needed; all are assumed to be collectable. |
| Equipment | $1,600,000 | $90,000 | $1,690,000 | Several new pieces of equipment have been expensed rather than capitalized to reduce income taxes. |
| Land & Buildings | $2,200,000 | $550,000 | $2,750,000 | The real estate has appreciated in value. |

| Asset | Book Value | Adjustment | FMV | Comment |
|---|---|---|---|---|
| Shareholder Note | $600,000 | ($600,000) | $0 | Shareholder notes are usually just a way for an owner to take money out of the business tax free. |
| Prepaid Expenses & Other Assets | $125,000 | 0 | $125,000 | These are good assets. |
| Total | $6,325,000 | ($160,000) | $6,165,000 | This is the company's adjusted asset value. |

## Industry Rules of Thumb

Industry rules of thumb often provide a useful "back of the envelope" indication of value. Rules of thumb usually are based on industry benchmarks or historical transaction multiples. Although a rule of thumb can give a quick answer to a difficult question, rules of thumb are very limited in that they do not take into account business-specific information that can significantly affect the value of a business.

For example, one rule of thumb for trucking companies is that they sell for the fair market value of their assets plus a premium equal to one times last year's adjusted earnings before interest, taxes, depreciation, and amortization ("EBITDA"). So, for example, a trucking company with $10 million in revenues, $2.3 million in assets, and $500,000 in adjusted EBITDA would be valued as follows:

$2,300,000 plus $500,000 or a total of $2,800,000

Another rule of thumb is that trucking companies tend to sell for 4–5 times EBITDA. This would result in the following value:

$500,000 x 4.5 = $2,250,000

Because the second rule of thumb produced a result less than the fair market value of the company's assets, it should raise a red flag. This rule of thumb should either be disregarded or further investigation should be done to understand why the company's EBITDA is so low.

## Comparable Transactions Analysis

Comparable transactions analysis involves obtaining data regarding other similar, recently sold companies and applying this data to the subject company in order to estimate its value. Comparable transactions should involve companies in the same or similar line of business as the company being valued.

The challenge in using this method is finding comparable transaction data. The IRS recommends using publicly traded companies as the benchmark against which to perform this analysis. The IRS adopts this position because data is readily available on publicly traded companies. The downside of this approach is that very few private companies are sufficiently similar to public companies in terms of size, management depth, financial strength, and other key value drivers to make the comparison viable. So many subjective adjustments are necessary that the data begins to lose its objective integrity.

The alternative is to use data on private transactions involving similar companies. Although this is preferable in concept, it too has some serious drawbacks. First, private transactions are just that—private. As a result, obtaining access to this data in the first place is difficult. Second, private transactions are often a reflection of the values and personalities of the principals involved. As a result, it is difficult to determine whether the transaction was an arm's length deal or if other issues were involved. Finally, the quality of the data is often subject to question. Because there are no standards regarding the reporting of this information, it is unclear whether a transaction summary on a private deal accurately represents the actual transaction.

Despite these weaknesses, the comparable transaction method is one of the best indications of fair market value for a privately-held company. When using this approach, the valuation professional divides purchase price for the comparable company by some performance metric, such as revenues, EBITDA, or assets, to determine a valuation multiple that can be applied to the subject company. The resulting multiples are then applied to the target company's revenues, EBITDA, or assets to obtain a company valuation.

In the following example, we show the comparable transaction method using the revenues and market value of similar companies to develop a revenue multiple for the company being valued.

Table 11-3: Comparable Company Data

| Company | Revenues (Mil.) | Multiple | Value (Mil.) |
|---|---|---|---|
| Comp #1 | $500 | 60% | $300 |
| Comp #2 | $1,750 | 40% | $700 |
| Comp #3 | $950 | 58% | $551 |
| Comp #4 | $2,250 | 68% | $1,530 |
| Average Revenue Multiple | | 56.5% | |
| Subject Company | $22 | 56.5% | $12.4 |

Note: In the above analysis, for simplicity's sake we have assumed that the marketability discount and the control premium cancel each other out and no additional adjustments need to be made.

Depending upon the relative similarity or difference of the target company's characteristics to the group of comparable transactions, analysts may need to adjust the multiple before it is applied to the target company's metrics.

Although comparable transactions analysis can be an important valuation methodology, its usefulness depends on the relevance, quality, and timeliness of historical transactions data. In addition, due to the fact that the overwhelming majority of acquisitions involve privately-held companies, there is often limited financial data available about these transactions.

### Discounted Cash Flow

As a methodology, discounted cash flow (DCF) often is considered the preferred method to value businesses. This approach is preferred over the other approaches because its results are based on the projected, future operating results of the company, rather than historical operating results. This is particularly important, if there is good reason to expect future cash flows will be different from historical results, as is the case when the company is growing rapidly, is in decline, or has recently changed its business model.

Another factor in favor of the discounted cash flow method is that it does not rely on comparisons with other companies that may or may not be similar. The only inputs required in this valuation method are estimates of a company's future cash flows and the expected rate of return a buyer would reasonably expect on those cash flows.

That said, the discounted cash flow method also presents some challenges for valuation analysts. The DCF method relies on the following inputs.

**Projecting Future Cash Flows.** The first step in a discounted cash flow analysis is to project future operating cash flows over a holding period, generally four to five years. These projections are generally done before accounting for debt and taxes to obtain an accurate indication of future free cash flow, without making any assumptions about the company's leverage. The future free cash flow is the cash left over after operating the business, and investing in necessary property, plant, and equipment, but before servicing debt or paying out any cash to owners.

The value of this future cash flow stream is a function of:

- How certain or risky these future cash flows are
- The current returns that could be earned on alternative investments
- The expected growth or decline of the cash stream over time.

**Discount Rate.** The second step in discounted cash flow analysis is to develop a discount rate. The discount rate is best thought of as the rate of return expected by an owner of the company to compensate him or her for the risk associated with the investment. For example, a risky Internet start-up with no track record and no assets commands a higher discount rate than a company with a long history of growth, profitability, and more obvious future prospects.

Discount rates are calculated based on five inputs:

1. The risk free rate (this is the expected return on long-term government bonds—currently about 4 percent)

2. The equity risk premium (this is the expected rate of return on publicly traded common stocks over and above the risk free rate—currently about 8 percent)

3. The size premium (this is the additional rate of return investors expect on smaller, riskier stocks)

4. The private company premium (this is the additional return investors require to compensate them for the lack of liquidity in private companies)

5. The specific risk premium (this is the additional rate of return expected for the risks specific to this particular company)

The final discount rate is the sum of all of the above. This represents the rate of return that a hypothetical investor could get by investing in a similar investment. This "built-up" discount rate is applied to the projected, future cash flows to determine their present value.

**Terminal Value.** The next step involves calculating a terminal or residual value. The assumption underlying this step is that a company is a going concern and its value is a function of its ability to generate cash flow, not just during the four- or five-year projection period, but well into the future. A terminal value calculation combines assumptions used to derive future projections and the discount rate to obtain a current value for a company's long-term future cash flows. A terminal value is calculated by projecting the cash flow in the period beyond the last forecast period. This projected future cash flow is then capitalized based on the company's discount rate. Finally, this capitalized amount is discounted back to the present using the discount rate.

The following table presents a basic, net present value analysis for a typical privately owned, middle- market company.

Table 11-4  Net Present Value Analysis

| Calculation of Discount Rate | | Notes: all as of 1/31/20XX | |
|---|---|---|---|
| Risk Free Rate | 5.7% | 20-Year Treasury Yield | |
| Equity Premium | 7.8% | S&P 500 | |
| Size Premium | 5.0% | 10th Decile NYSE Premium | |
| Private Premium | 3.0% | Private Company Premium | |
| Co. Specific Premium | 3.0% | Customer Concentration | |
| After Tax Discount Rate | 24.5% | | |
| Pre-Tax Adjustment | 9.1% | | |
| Pre-Tax Discount Rate | 33.6% | | |
| Assumed Sustainable Growth Rate: | | 2% | |
| | | P.V. Using | |
| Forecast | Projected | 33.6% | Discounted |
| Period | EBITDA | Disc. Rate | Cash Flow |
| 2005 | 1,900,000 | | |
| 2006 | 1,938,000 | 74.86% | 1,450,793 |
| 2007 | 1,976,760 | 56.04% | 1,107,790 |
| 2008 | 2,016,295 | 41.95% | 845,881 |
| 2009 | 2,056,621 | 31.41% | 645,894 |
| Discounted Cash Flows | | | 4,050,359 |
| **Terminal Value Calculation** | | | |
| Cash Flow in Final Forecast Period | | 2,056,621 | |
| Sustainable Growth Rate following Forecast Period | | 2.0% | |
| Cash Flow for Terminal Value | | 2,097,754 | |
| Times Terminal Value Capitalization Factor | | 2.97 | |
| Terminal Value | | 6,120,895 | |
| Terminal Value | | 6,120,895 | |
| Discount Rate | | 33.6 | |
| Number of Years to Discount | | 4 | |
| Present Value of Terminal Value | | 1,927,036 | |
| Terminal Value | | | 1,927,036 |
| **VALUE (discounted cash flows + terminal value)** | | | 5,977,395 |

Note: Because the cash flows being discounted are pre-tax, it is important to use a pre-tax discount rate. The discount rate using the build-up method demonstrated, above, results in an after-tax rate. As a result, an additional 9.1 percent was added to this rate to convert it to a pre-tax discount rate.

### Capitalized Earnings Method

The capitalized earnings method is another earnings-based approach. As in the DCF method, it does not value the assets of the company. Instead, value is determined by applying an earnings multiple to the historic adjusted earnings of the company. The multiple is based on the buyer's required rate of return and the company's growth potential. Although relatively easy to use, the capitalization of earnings method has a basic flaw, namely, it is based on a company's historic financial performance and does not take into account a company's future prospects. As a result, this method is appropriate only when the company's past is a good reflection of its long-term future growth prospects.

## Valuation Adjustments

Privately owned businesses are often valued by comparing them to alternative investments such as publicly traded stocks or bonds. Valuation analysts therefore use certain discounts or premiums to recognize the inherent differences between owning public and private stock. These discounts or premiums are calculated separately, and applied as a percentage increase or decrease in the appraised value.

It is important to note that some estate and gift tax strategies rely heavily on the use of these discount factors. The overaggressive use of discounts in such a strategy may result in IRS valuation challenges. The recent popularity of the family limited partnership transferring ownership in a family business as an estate and gift tax strategy (which relies heavily on valuation discounts for much of its appeal), has resulted in the IRS's questioning overly aggressive discounts. When using valuation discounts in a succession plan, the best defense against an IRS challenge is to have a formal discount study prepared by a credible valuation specialist.

Each of these specific premiums and discounts is discussed in more detail below.

### Control Premiums and Minority Discounts

One key difference between buying a private company and buying shares in a publicly traded company is the element of control. When most investors buy publicly traded stock, they are buying a small portion of the total number of shares in that public company. As a result, in most cases, these investors are purchasing a minority interest in a public company. On the other hand, in most private transactions, the buyer obtains the majority of the private company's shares and is receiving a controlling interest in that company.

A controlling interest in a company allows the owner to:

- Hire or fire managers
- Establish and change company policy
- Acquire or sell corporate assets
- Approve or reject merger plans
- Determine salaries of employees
- Control dividend payments
- Liquidate the business.

A minority shareholder does not wield any of this power. The absence of this control makes ownership less attractive to a potential buyer. Analysts account for this by applying a premium when a buyer is acquiring a controlling interest in a public company. Likewise, analysts apply a discount when valuing a minority interest in a private company.

Each of the valuation methodologies discussed above assumes a controlling interest is being valued. As a result, the only adjustment needed is a minority interest discount if the interest being valued does not have control.

## Lack of Marketability Discounts

Liquidity is important to every investor. The ability to sell an investment quickly, easily, and inexpensively is how investors define liquidity. The presence of a ready market of willing buyers, therefore, enhances the value of an investment. In the public markets, buyers are able to quickly determine the market value of securities, and buy or sell them within minutes with only a modest transaction fee.

On the other hand, there is no ready market for the stock of a private business. Buying or selling private securities involves a long, time-consuming, and relatively expensive process. This lack of marketability makes an investment in a private company less attractive than a similar investment in a publicly traded company. Analysts account for this by applying a marketability discount to shares of private companies, which can range from 10 to 30 percent or more of the fair market value.

Each of the valuation methodologies in this chapter takes a lack of marketability discount into account.

## Restricted Stock

Some private companies have provisions in their articles of incorporation or in a buy-sell agreement to restrict stock so that it only can be sold back to the company or other owners. To some, this makes the ownership of the stock less desirable. Sometimes, however, the stock restriction may increase the value of the investment because the restriction (that is, the requirement that the company must buy out the owner) creates a ready buyer for the stock. Although stock restriction discounts cannot be used for reducing value for estate tax purposes, they may have a powerful effect on valuations for other purposes, such as divorce proceedings or third-party sales transactions.

## Summary

Any advisor who works with private business owners needs to have a basic understanding of business valuation principals and the workings of the private capital markets in order to help clients successfully evaluate their various options.

Advisors should understand how:

1.  A business owner's exit options or intentions relate to value
2.  Different valuation methods work
3.  The valuation results affect other areas of the exit planning process

For advisors to be effective, they must be able to help clients identify their financial goals, develop strategies to promote the realization of those goals, and ultimately execute tactics to achieve the goals.

As this chapter demonstrates, a baseline business valuation is essential before any exit planning decisions can be made.  In addition, given the importance of the business valuation in the exit planning process, we recommend that this step be handled by a professional with real-world experience valuing and the subsequent sale of private companies.  To get the best possible indication of market value, it is important to work with a professional who has real-world intuition about how the market would perceive the company and what the degree of demand would be.

Consequently, while business valuation firms and CPAs can do valuations, we recommend that clients use an investment bank to value their businesses when preparing an exit plan.  Why?  Because in the end, a business is only worth what a buyer will pay for it.  Investment bankers and business brokers have in-depth knowledge of what active buyers like and dislike about particular businesses. This enables business brokers and investment bankers to bring a real-world perspective to the valuation process.

# Chapter 12

# Understanding Exit Options

Exiting a business means different things to different people. Depending on the client's personal goals and situation, exit strategies can vary by structure and degree. On one end of the spectrum, a client may merely wish to free up time, energy, and resources to explore other interests. At the other end of the spectrum, a client may want to realize his or her investment and walk away from the business without looking back.

This section addresses the eight basic exit options available to owners of private middle-market businesses. Each one presents a different way for the owner to take some or all of his or her investment off the table and realize varying degrees of personal freedom.

Choosing the best exit strategy involves a careful assessment of the business owner's personal and business goals as well as the objectives of each of the other stakeholders. The choice of the best exit strategy also may depend on the personal and financial circumstances of the owner and other stakeholders.

If you understand the pros and cons of each of the basic exit options available to business owners, you are better able to help your clients decide which one will help them leave their business on their terms.

Figure 12-1 illustrates the different exit channels and corresponding options available to business owners.

## 1. Transfer Ownership to Family Members

According to studies, 50 percent of typical business owners want to transfer their business to their children. In reality, less than a third actually does so. Because this option has a low success rate, a business owner also must develop a contingency plan that involves conveying the business to another type of buyer.

**Advantages:**

- It can fulfill a personal goal of keeping the business and family together.
- It could provide financial well-being to younger family members unable to earn comparable income from outside employment.
- It could allow the client to stay actively involved in the business with his or her children.

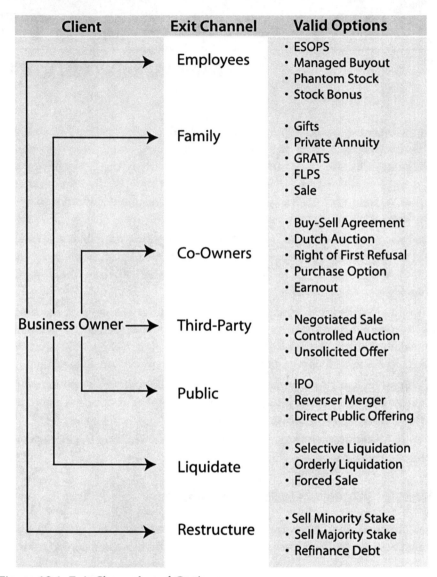

| Client | Exit Channel | Valid Options |
|---|---|---|
| | Employees | • ESOPS<br>• Managed Buyout<br>• Phantom Stock<br>• Stock Bonus |
| | Family | • Gifts<br>• Private Annuity<br>• GRATS<br>• FLPS<br>• Sale |
| | Co-Owners | • Buy-Sell Agreement<br>• Dutch Auction<br>• Right of First Refusal<br>• Purchase Option<br>• Earnout |
| Business Owner | Third-Party | • Negotiated Sale<br>• Controlled Auction<br>• Unsolicited Offer |
| | Public | • IPO<br>• Reverser Merger<br>• Direct Public Offering |
| | Liquidate | • Selective Liquidation<br>• Orderly Liquidation<br>• Forced Sale |
| | Restructure | • Sell Minority Stake<br>• Sell Majority Stake<br>• Refinance Debt |

Figure 12-1  Exit Channels and Options

■  It could afford the owner the luxury of determining how much he needs or wants for the business, rather than be told how much he will get.

**Disadvantages:**

■  This option also holds great potential to create or increase family discord and feelings of unequal treatment among siblings.

- The normal objective of treating all children equally is difficult to achieve because one child will probably run or own the business at the perceived expense of the others.

- Family members cannot usually afford to pay cash at closing. As a result, the selling family member has to accept payment over time.

- Financial security is normally diminished rather than enhanced. Many businesses suffer when they are transferred to a family member who either cannot or will not run it properly.

- In addition, family dynamics may diminish the owner's control over the business and its operations significantly, increasing rather than diminishing the owner's level of personal stress and anxiety.

## 2.  Sell to Other Shareholders

Not all business owners have this option, but, if your client has other shareholders in the business, there could be a ready market for his or her shares. In a well-prepared company, shareholders would have a buy-sell agreement governing what happens when one or more shareholders want to exit. The benefits and pitfalls of selling to other shareholders are linked closely to the quality or existence of such an agreement.

**Advantages:**

- The business stays in the "extended family."
- A fellow shareholder knows the business and does not have to be convinced of the prospects and value thereof.
- The owner is dealing with a buyer who is willing to purchase stock, rather than insisting on an asset transaction.
- A well-prepared shareholders' agreement can facilitate the transfer process.
- The departing shareholder can arrange an automatic "purchase" of his or her shares by the company or by other shareholders in the event of death. The purchase price can be funded then with key man life insurance.

**Disadvantages:**

- If a company is sold to other shareholders pursuant to a poorly prepared shareholders' agreement, its terms may force the departing shareholder to accept a price that is not reflective of the company's fair market value.
- The departing owner may be locked into selling his shares only to fellow shareholders, creating a limited market, and thereby, depressing the company's value.

- Selling to other shareholders does not typically result in the maximum value for the company.
- If the purchase price for the departing owner's share is not funded with life insurance, the terms of the shareholder agreement or buy-sell agreement may require an extended payout, creating financial risk for the departing owner's family.

## 3. Sell to Management ("MBO" or "LBO")

With this exit option, the business owner can sell all or part of the business to the company's management team (or part of the team). The transaction is called a Management Buyout (MBO) or management-led Leveraged Buyout (LBO). In this situation, the management team uses the assets of the business to finance a significant portion of the purchase price. Management, on its own or in conjunction with outside investors, contributes equity to make up the difference between the debt raised and the final purchase price. Management's expertise in running the company is important to both the lenders and the outside equity investors, and management becomes an integral part of the ongoing operation.

**Advantages:**
- The business stays in the "extended family."
- The management team knows the business and can do a good job of selling its merits to a lender or equity investor.
- There is less risk in this situation because the management team is not disrupted and can continue to perform, as it always has.
- The partnership with an equity investor can provide additional growth capital not otherwise available to the company.

**Disadvantages:**
- Normally, a lender requires members of the management team to contribute 30 percent or more of the purchase price in equity. Depending on its members' circumstances, the management team may not be able to do this without outside help.
- The deal may require the participation of an equity investor. This could cause cultural or management style conflicts.
- If the company's assets are insufficient to fully leverage the transaction and management cannot make up the difference, the owner may be asked to take a note to finance the gap. This effectively means some of the client's equity investment stays in the business until management can earn enough profit to pay off the note.

## 4. Sell to an Employee Stock Ownership Plan ("ESOP")

If the business owner wants to sell the business to the company's employees rather than just the management team, an Employee Stock Ownership Plan (ESOP) may provide an attractive means of cashing in a part of the owner's interest in the business. In an ESOP, the company uses borrowed funds to acquire shares from the owner and contributes the shares to a trust. The trust is funded by a bank and the repayment of the loan is a function of the distributions the company is capable of making to the trust. The company's ability to make these distributions is what is used to determine the borrowing capacity of the trust, and hence, the cash available to purchase owner's shares. Each participating employee has an account in the ESOP trust. Employees become vested owners of the shares when they leave the company at which time the company must offer to buy the shares back from the employee.

### Advantages:

- The business stays in the "extended family."
- The shares for the ESOP are bought with pre-tax dollars.
- The taxable gain on the shares sold to an ESOP may be deferred in certain circumstances.
- An ESOP is an employee benefit.
- Owning shares in a company may make employees think and act like owners and may increase productivity.

### Disadvantages:

- ESOPs are complicated and expensive to set up and maintain.
- An ESOP may not be suitable for an "S" Corporation.
- If shares are being sold to employees, the company needs an exemption from securities registration.
- The company is compelled to offer to buy back shares from employees when they leave.
- An ESOP generally is suitable only for a gradual exit over time.

## 5. Sell to a Third Party

A sale of a business to a third party can take many forms. The buyer may be a competitor, customer, or supplier in the same industry. These buyers are called strategic buyers. On the other hand, the final buyer may be a financial group like a private equity group, hedge fund, or institutional investor.

Buyer characteristics are an important factor in any deal. A business owner should consider carefully how different buyer characteristics fit the owner's personal and business goals and objectives. For instance, a financial buyer might be the best fit for an owner who would like to liquidate his investment in the business while staying involved in a management capacity. A strategic buyer also may offer an owner a "partnership" type solution with a simultaneous realization of at least a part of an owner's investment. A strategic buyer may be the solution for an owner who has a specific business goal that he cannot realize on his own. For a well prepared business, a sale to a third party may the best way to cash out.

## Advantages:

- The fundamental advantage of a third-party sale is that most sellers receive a majority of the purchase price in cash at closing.
- This exit strategy also typically results in the highest valuations for a business because the natural market forces are allowed to work.
- The price obtained from a third party is more likely to be equal to the fair market value of the company, if not more.
- A third-party sale is the only exit option that offers a seller the potential of access to buyers with a strategic or synergistic motive, leading to a sale at a premium to fair market value.
- A sale to a third party may be the best option for a business that is too valuable to be purchased by someone in the "extended family."
- The large variety of available buyers makes it possible for an owner to find a buyer that will allow him or her to satisfy exit needs relating to soft issues, such as time and involvement, as well as money issues.

## Disadvantages:

- An owner who desires to stay on after a sale to a third party may suddenly find himself in the role of an employee rather than owner. This is often difficult.
- Many third party buyers require the seller to finance a portion of the purchase price with a seller note or earn-out structure. If little or no exit planning was done and the company is not properly prepared for sale, this exposes the seller to risk.
- This process typically takes 9–12 months to execute.
- The process of marketing for a third-party buyer could result in loss of customers and employees, if confidentiality is not well managed. However, using a good investment bank should provide peace of mind.

# 6. Refinance or Recapitalize the Business

Refinancing or recapitalizing a business may be a feasible exit strategy. Recapitalizing a business means finding new ways to fund the company's balance sheet. This could involve using debt to allow the business owner to take some cash out of the business. The company could leverage its assets to arrange for a debt facility to provide partial liquidity to an owner. In effect, what the owner has done is bring a lender in to act as a partner in the business.

The same type of arrangement is possible with equity investors. In some cases, a business owner may be willing to sell a minority or majority interest in his company to another party while keeping some personal interest, himself. Both situations may be applicable when the owner wants to stay around or continue to be involved in the company, but wants to take some chips off the table.

**Advantages:**

- The owner maintains an equity interest in the company and can participate in its future growth.

- The owner is able to take some money off the table and diversify his or her risk.

- The owner can remain involved actively in the management and growth of the company.

**Disadvantages:**

- If debt is used to create liquidity for the owner, the increased leverage may make the company's future performance more risky.

- If debt is used, the lender may require a personal guarantee from the owner which does not accomplish the owner's objective to diversify his risk.

- If equity is used to create liquidity, the business owner now has partners who may be minority investors or have a controlling interest in the company. Either way, accounting to investors may not be compatible with the owner's personal style and past practices.

# 7. Go Public

Going public or conducting an Initial Public Offering (IPO) is often viewed as the ultimate exit strategy for a business owner. There is no doubt going public is very exciting and has been a successful exit strategy for many entrepreneurs. However, going public, for all its strengths, has a number of important weaknesses many business owners are not aware of. In addition, going public is not a realistic option for the vast majority of private companies.

**Advantages**

- Going public provides additional capital to help fund a company's growth. Almost all companies primarily go public because they need money. The typical (firm-commitment) IPO raises $20 to $40 million, but offerings of $100 million are not unusual either.

- Going public creates liquidity for the business owner, his key managers, and other employees.

- Going public tends to give a company a higher profile than private firms have. This is important in industries in which success requires customers or clients to make long-term commitments. Many big companies prefer to work with public companies because their public stature creates a sense of security.

- Going public and being able to offer employees liquid shares may improve a company's ability to attract top-notch management.

- Valuation multiples for public companies are generally, significantly higher than the multiples paid for similar private companies.

**Disadvantages**

- Going public is not an available exit option for most owners of private companies. This option is typically available only to high growth companies with significant revenues and earnings.

- Going public means diluting ownership. If a company is sitting on a gold mine, this means this future gold will be shared with new stockholders. However, if the price is right, it may be worth it. After the typical IPO, about 40 percent of the company remains with insiders, but inside ownership can vary anywhere from 1 to 88 percent.

- A public company is, by definition, no longer private, and consequently gives up a great deal of privacy. After a company goes public, it must regularly file reports with the SEC and whatever exchange the company is listed on. The company also must comply with state securities laws ("blue sky"), NASD, and exchange guidelines. All this disclosure can be disconcerting for a company that traditionally valued its privacy. This disclosure also may reveal important information to competitors.

- Going public typically means a loss of control for the business owner. In fact, investors can buy a sufficient stake in the company in the public market to take control and fire the founder.

- An IPO is a costly undertaking. A typical firm spends about 15 to 25 percent of the money raised on direct expenses. It is even more costly if you consider indirect or opportunity costs like management time and disruption of business.

■    Going public does not provide existing shareholders with immediate liquidity. Business owners who select an IPO face various restrictions that do not permit them to cash out for 18 months or longer following the IPO.

## 8. Liquidate the Business

If there is no one to buy your business, the client may have to shut it down. In liquidation, the owners sell their assets, collect outstanding accounts receivable, pay their bills, and keep what's left, if anything, for themselves.

Liquidation typically makes sense only if a business lacks sufficient income-producing capacity (apart from the owner's direct efforts) to support the investment required in the company's assets. For example, if the business can produce only $75,000 in profits each year and the assets themselves are worth $1 million, it would make the most sense to sell the assets at liquidation value. The value of the assets is higher than the value of the cash flow. As a result, no one would pay more for the business than the value of the assets.

**Advantages:**

■    The process is fairly simple and fast.

■    The entire company does not have to be liquidated. The owner may decide to liquidate only a portion of the company and keep the more profitable parts.

**Disadvantages:**

■    Liquidation usually results in the lowest possible value for a business because it reflects the fair market value of the assets with no consideration for client or customer lists, employee knowledge, name or reputation, or any of the other intangible assets associated with a going concern.

■    The cost of liquidating a company is almost as high as the cost of selling a going concern, so the perception it is the least expensive option is often incorrect.

■    Employees and key managers lose their jobs.

## Summary

One of the overall themes of this book is how interconnected all of the components of the exit planning process are. This is one of the primary reasons the process seems so daunting to business owners.

As this chapter points out, a good exit plan should present a business owner with an objective analysis of all exit options. However, to be effective, it must help the business owner understand the pros and cons of each option as it relates to the personal goals and objectives of the business owner as well as the other stakeholders. It also should reflect the information revealed by the owner's financial plan, business valuation, estate plan, and tax plan.

By incorporating this information into a pros and cons discussion of each exit option, the owner and stakeholders are empowered to make informed decisions that help ensure their goals are met in the process.

# Chapter 13

# Maximizing Value

For most business owners, a personal goal is to maximize the amount of money they put in their pocket when they exit their business. As one of our colleagues once said, "Every business owner should strive to make a mountain out of a molehill."

To accomplish this, effectively, a business owner needs to do three things. First, he/she must maximize the fundamental or underlying value of the business itself. Second, he/she must use a sales process that maximizes what the market is willing to pay for the business. Third, he/she must pay as little as possible in capital gains taxes when the company's ownership is sold or transferred. Doing any one of these things has some impact on the ultimate value the owner receives, but doing all three simultaneously is like hitting a home run.

In this chapter we explore the first of these considerations—maximizing the fundamental value of the underlying business. To accomplish this, business owners need to do three things: first, understand the value factors/value drivers that create value in a business; second, create measurement tools to monitor a company's progress while working on identified value drivers; and, three, create a formal process for revisiting value enhancement goals as they are met or change.

## Value Factor Analysis

As you know, when you sell a house a fresh coat of paint, new carpeting, and a few other quick improvements can improve the value of your home dramatically. The same is true with the client's business. The trick is figuring out which things need to be "fixed" or "spruced up" in order to maximize the value of the business.

Professional buyers look at a number of key aspects of every business to determine its value. To increase business value, the business owner must target these same elements. These elements—characteristics that both reduce risk and improve return—are referred to as value drivers.

Value drivers come in two varieties: generic (common to all industries) and industry specific. Some of the generic value drivers are as follows:

- A stable and motivated management team
- Operating systems that improve sustainability of cash flows
- Operating profit margins at least as good as the industry average
- A solid, diversified customer base
- Facility appearance consistent with asking price
- A realistic growth strategy
- Effective financial controls
- Good and improving cash flow

Each industry also has specific or unique value drivers. For example, if your client owns a distribution company, a potential purchaser looks at the strength of the manufacturers the company represents, the number of inventory turns per year, and the level of technical expertise the company's salespeople possess.

How do you help your clients implement value drivers in your business?

First, learn more about value drivers by reading about them here, and in other materials.

Second, talk to the other exit planning team members and perhaps a business consultant with expertise in the industry.

Third, encourage your client to stand above the fray at least one-half day per month. Help your client look at his or her business through the eyes of people interested in buying it. What do they see that would cause them to pay top dollar for your business? What would cause them to pay less for the business? When answering these questions, your client should look both at what the business is doing and what it is not. Viewing the business in this way is what we mean by working *on* a business, not just in it.

As we discussed in Chapter 11, business buyers consider a number of factors when they value a company. Peter Christman and I developed a proprietary process that examines 54 different factors sophisticated buyers consider when determining how much to pay for a business.

We ask the business owner to complete a detailed, 60 page questionnaire that collects data on a wide range of topics including the company's history, its current operations, its markets, products, or services, its facilities and assets, its personnel and management, and its financial performance. After we have reviewed that information, we schedule a 4–6 hour interview with the client to probe for additional information a questionnaire cannot capture.

This is a time-consuming process. Fortunately, much of this same information is required for developing a detailed base line valuation of the company. It also is useful when developing an Offering Package for the company, should the client decide a sale to a third-party buyer is his best exit strategy. Spending the time to collect this information is an important part of the process. If the right information is collected, it also can be shared with other professionals to help them with their jobs so there is no duplication of effort or additional burden on the client.

After we have all of the information we need about the business, we prepare a detailed analysis of the company and provide the client with a score card grading the company on each of the 54 value factors.

Each factor is rated as either a positive, neutral, or negative. A positive means this particular attribute of the company is a strength and adds value. A neutral means this particular attribute does not influence the company's market value, one way or the other. A negative (or what we call an Opportunity for Improvement) is an area in which the company performs poorly and detracts from market value. The following is a partial list of the 54 value factors we look at when analyzing a company.

Table 13-1: Value Factors (partial list)

| | | | |
|---|---|---|---|
| • | Attitude of Owner | • | Market Position |
| • | Family/Partner Consensus | • | Corporate Structure |
| • | Barriers to Entry | • | Lawsuits |
| • | Historical Performance | • | Taxes |
| • | Products/Services | • | Environmental |
| • | Management Team | • | OSHA |
| • | Sales and Marketing Literature | • | Intellectual Property |
| • | Customer Base | • | Track Record |
| • | Product/Service Quality | • | Operating Margins |
| • | Employees | • | Shareholder's Equity |
| • | Fixed Assets | • | Economy |

For example, one of the factors we rate is the depth of the client's management team. If the business owner acts primarily as a CEO, and has recruited and trained a management team that is able to run the business without the owner's day-to-day involvement, this is a positive and enhances the value of the business.

If the business owner has a management team that is well trained and competent at operations, but still requires daily guidance, this would be considered a neutral. The business owner is still very much involved in operations, but he has developed a management team that could continue the operation if someone else stepped in to set the vision and provide the appropriate guidance. This is common for most well-run private companies. As a result, it doesn't increase or decrease the company's market value.

On the other hand, if the business owner is the spirit and energy behind the company, and is involved in managing key client relationships as well as directing operations on a daily basis, this is a negative. Buyers would be concerned that the business is too dependent on the owner and would not be able to predict with confidence how the business would perform without the owner at the helm. As a result, this detracts from the value of the business.

This is just an example of one of the 54 value factors we look at. For each value factor, we describe our observations about the company, describe how it would impact the value of the company, and why. This process helps business owners see their businesses through the eyes of an objective, third party. It also becomes the basis upon which we develop our Value Enhancement Recommendations.

After we have identified a number of Opportunities for Improvement for a client, the next challenge is to help the owner focus on which recommendations will help the owner accomplish his or her goals most effectively. In the real world, achieving goals often means making some trade-offs. Any goals your client sets will require some investment of time, effort, and money, and may necessitate sacrificing other goals.

One way to figure out whether a goal is worth pursuing is to do a cost-benefit analysis. This doesn't have to be complicated. Simply draw a line down the middle of a piece of paper to create two columns. On the left, list the benefits of achieving a given goal. On the right, list what it will cost you to get there. This simple analysis can give a business owner a better idea of whether a given goal is worth investigating further.

## Action Plans

The difference between a dream and a plan is that the first simply expresses a desire to achieve something, whereas the second expresses a method for accomplishing the first.

If you really want to help clients achieve their dreams, you need to develop a plan to show them how to get from here to there. A good plan prioritizes what needs to be done. It also should contain benchmarks against which to measure progress, and tools to monitor how well everyone is doing.

In our practice, when we present our Value Enhancement Recommendations, we provide the business owner with a matrix showing each Value Enhancement Recommendation. Next we rank each recommendation based on how much relative value that recommendation is likely to deliver and how meaningful it is to the business owner, given his or her objectives. This process enables a business owner to identify quickly which recommendations will have the biggest impact on value depending on the owner's priorities.

For example, assume we identified that a company should have its financial statements audited rather than simply compiled. This is a relatively small investment considering the significant value that it can add during a transaction, both in terms of increasing the salability of the company and ensuring that financial problems are not uncovered during the deal. Although audited financials will not result in a buyer's paying a significant premium for a company, having audited financials statements makes the company more salable. In this case we would rank the value contribution as a low.

In addition to discussing the value impact this recommendation could have, we also point out whether addressing this issue helps accomplish the owner's overall goals and objectives. In this case, let's assume that the owner wants to exit within 12 months. Audited financial statements help a business sell more quickly and attract better buyers. In addition, audited financial statements can add value even within that short time frame. Three years or more of audited financial statements is preferred, but one year is better than nothing. Depending on how important the audit actually was, the accountant could prepare audited statements on a historical basis as well. Possessing such statements would get a high score on the Appropriateness Scale.

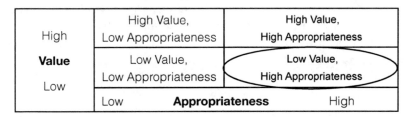

Figure 13-1 – Low Value, High Appropriateness

Contrast this with a recommendation that the owner should develop and implement a lean manufacturing process on the plant floor. This would certainly reduce costs and add value to the company, but the process would require an investment of around $500,000, be disruptive to existing operations, and take about a year to implement fully. The business owner's goals included spending increasingly less time at the company and exiting the business within two years. As a result, this recommendation would get a high ranking on the Value Scale, but a low ranking on the Appropriateness Scale.

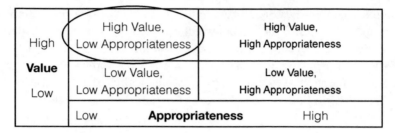

Figure 13-2 – High Value, Low Appropriateness

So, the goal is to identify those value enhancement opportunities that score high on both the Value and Appropriateness scales. Those recommendations have the biggest impact on both the value of the company and the ability of the owner to achieve his or her goals.

## Establishing Measurement Tools

An important part of any plan is establishing a way to tell when you have reached important points in the process. These mile markers can be composed of any number of measurement tools or benchmarks. Overall sales revenue is a common measurement. Many companies recognize the first year they topped $1, $5, and $10 million in sales. Revenue is an obvious, important, and easily grasped benchmark. You also can look at sales growth rates and overall sales volume as valuable benchmarks.

Sales, however, is not the only benchmark. You also can look at benchmarks for critical variables such as number of stores, number of customers, and transaction volume. Many industries have benchmarks unique to that industry. For instance, air carriers think in terms of percentage of seats filled and revenue generated per mile flown; e-commerce businesses measure unique web page views and time spent on each page. Your client's business may be concerned with different benchmarks, such as new business from previous customers or utilization factors per piece of capital equipment.

Not all benchmarks need to be financial. You can set benchmarks related to customer satisfaction, error rates, employee turnover, or virtually any other aspect of your client's business. The only characteristics all benchmarks share are that they should be significant, relevant, and measurable.

One of the biggest differences between small and large companies is the amount of effort each devotes to performance measurement. Big firms are famous for measuring all kinds of performance data. They generate reports describing what is happening in a company on almost a daily basis. These "dashboard" reports are handy for companies with thousands of employees spread all over the country because they help management stay in touch with what is going on.

However, if a business owner runs a middle-market business and he or she has been personally involved in hiring all employees and works with them on a daily basis, a lot of measurement and reports may seem like a waste of time. The truth is, owners of middle-market companies tend to be hands-on managers. They manage directly from the shop floor.   That said, entrepreneurs' ability to make decisions is hampered often by a lack of adequate information about their own companies. Although their intuitive knowledge of their companies and "seat of the pants" management may produce results superior to many Fortune companies, the truth is that entrepreneurs usually could do a better job of gathering data about their companies.

Entrepreneurs often lack enough data to be able to answer the following questions.   What is my most profitable product? What are the common characteristics of my best customers? Which types of promotions have the highest payback? What is my market share?

Business owners find implementing a value enhancement program much easier if they create measurement tools to tell them how they are doing along the way.   These measurement tools do not need to be overly complex. Part of the process involves deciding which items are most critical to achieving the desired growth and then finding a way to measure them.

For example, if competitive pricing is the main factor that affects overall enterprise value, the Opportunities for Improvement may include the suggestion that the business owner assign one employee to make a weekly or daily call to several distributors carrying the company's products along with those of the competition.   This simple step can provide a wealth of real-time market data.

It is important to recognize that measurement for measurement's sake delivers no value.   A business owner should not spend valuable resources collecting data that won't be used.

## Revisiting Goals

The value of a goal lies in the way it provides a relatively, steady unblinking light toward which to steer when the business owner is caught in the fog of everyday business life.   However, that does not mean a goal should be as immovable as a lighthouse. As an exit planning advisor, you should periodically (at least annually) encourage your clients to take a fresh look at their goals to see whether they need to be changed, or perhaps, eliminated. Changes in your clients' personal situations, such as a health issue, a change in business performance, the birth of a grandchild, and so on, may cause some old goals to become irrelevant and new goals to emerge. Of course, the best reason to scrap a goal is because it has been accomplished.

Psychologists at Harvard University found there was only one common denominator among successful people. This single common trait crossed cultural, ethnic, racial, economic, and educational boundaries. The one thing all successful people did was to create a set of *written* goals for themselves and then pursue those goals. The study showed that only 1 out of 100,000 people routinely set written goals for themselves and then measure their progress toward those goals. The study also found the success of these people was not a function of accomplishing all of their goals; instead, it was simply due to the process of working toward a clearly defined set of goals.

Last, but not least, it is important to remember that goals are just goals. Goals are not preordained events that occur whether or not you work toward them. In other words, just having a goal of reaching $10 million in sales does not mean your client will achieve it. At the same time, reaching or exceeding a goal should not be considered the only measure of success. Reaching $9 million in sales is surely a lot better than not accomplishing anything at all. The process of working toward a strategic set of goals will produce tremendous results for your clients over and above the net results realized from accomplishing or not accomplishing any single goal.

## Summary

In this chapter we learned that to help clients maximize the proceeds a client receives upon exit, the client must do three things. First, the client must maximize the fundamental or underlying value of the business itself. Second, the client must use a sales process that maximizes what the market is willing to pay for the business. Third, the client must pay as little as possible in capital gains taxes when the company's ownership is sold or transferred. Doing any one of these things has some impact on the ultimate value the owner receives, but doing all three simultaneously is like hitting a home run.

This chapter focused on maximizing the underlying value of the business itself. To that end, we learned that the business owner needs objective, specific, and pragmatic advice on how to reduce the risk level a buyer perceives when looking at the company. To ensure that this advice is appropriate, each action step should be analyzed on the basis of how well it helps the business owner accomplish his or her personal goals. Finally, to maximize its value, the plan's progress must be measurable and the plan periodically revised as the owner's goals change or evolve.

# Chapter 14

# Key Employess—The  Key to Value

In the previous chapter we discussed how to help business owners increase the value of their companies.  As their professional advisors, it is our role to point out that although entrepreneurs and business owners are attracted to building additional value, it is at least equally important that they protect the value they have already built.

When it comes to protecting the value of a company, business owners often forget that the biggest asset of most companies does not show up on the company's balance sheet; it walks out the door every night.  This asset is the company's employees.

In this chapter we discuss how to protect this important asset and explore how to keep and retain key employees during an ownership transition.  This chapter explores two basic techniques to keep key employees: employment agreements and special compensation for key employees.

One of the greatest fears of buyers is that a company's key employees will walk out the door as a result of a change in the management and ownership of the company.  Key employees often walk, if they feel they have been overlooked or unfairly treated during the exit process, or if they are not comfortable with the new owners or managers.

If the key employees are members of the executive, sales, or operational management teams, the value of the company could be dramatically affected by their departure. For this reason and others, finding a way to keep these key employees is a critical element in an exit plan whether it involves selling to a third-party buyer or a transition to a younger generation family member.

At the same time, a prudent business owner always needs to think about damage control.  If keeping these key employees is not possible, the owner must be able to minimize whatever potential damage they can do to the company if they go to work for the competition in order to protect the value of his company.

## Keeping Valuable Employees

The first step in retaining key employees is to determine who is key or essential to the business and who is not.  In developing a business exit plan, the business owner and his or her advisors should consider what impact the loss each employee would have on:

■ Sales and profits

■ Potential exposure of trade secrets and loss of employees to competitors

■ Plans for expansion

■ Operations

■ Morale/loyalty of other employees

■ Mentoring of successor managers

■ Customer relations

Key employees should be identified and considered in the exit planning process. As discussed earlier in this book, key employees are really stakeholders in the business. Their goals and expectations should be understood by the owners and accounted for in the overall plan. Often, creative compensation plans, such as those discussed later in this chapter, can assist in retaining key employees for the long term.

**Types of Compensation.** There are two overriding issues to be considered when developing a compensation strategy for key employees:

(1) The proper and equitable benefit to the appropriate employees.

(2) The most tax-effective manner allowable by law for both the business and the employee.

Fortunately, there are many compensation strategies that address both concerns. The following chart shows several different types of compensation strategies and tax implications for each.

| Employee Compensation | Employee Taxable Income | Employer Tax Deduction |
|---|---|---|
| Salaries & Bonuses | Yes | Current |
| Nonqualified Deferred | Deferred | Deferred |
| Qualified Deferred | Deferred | Current |
| Qualified Fringe Benefits | No | Current |
| Dividends | Yes | No |
| Stock Bonuses | Yes | Current |

**Figure 14-1: General Tax Implications of Common Types of Compensation**

# Salaries and Bonuses

Although cash is king, cash is the least effective type of compensation from a tax standpoint. Although cash, salary, and bonuses result in income tax deductions for the employer, additional payroll taxes generally apply, and employees are subject to ordinary income tax rates on the earnings. Despite its tax implications, cash compensation is here to stay. The reality is that many employees need a large portion of their compensation in cash to support their families and lifestyles. This is especially the case with relatively young executives who have not had time to accumulate significant amounts of liquid disposable wealth.

It is universal advice from financial planners: employees who have achieved a comfortable lifestyle should participate to the maximum extent allowed in an employer-deferred compensation plan.

## Qualified Deferred Compensation

The Internal Revenue Code provides tax-favored treatment for certain types of employer-sponsored, deferred compensation arrangements designed primarily to provide employees with retirement income. These arrangements include qualified defined contribution and defined benefit pension plans such as qualified annuities, tax-sheltered annuities, savings incentive match plans for employees (known as "SIMPLE" plans), and simplified employee pensions ("SEPS"). For simplicity, these plans are referred to collectively as "qualified employer plans."

A qualified deferred, compensation plan needs to be one or more of the IRS-approved retirement plans or benefit plans mentioned above. A qualified retirement plan is intended to provide cash to the employee during retirement years, whereas a benefits plan provides non-cash benefits to employees such as medical, disability, or death benefits.

A qualified retirement plan may be either a defined contribution plan or a defined benefit plan. The difference between these two types of retirement plans is simple. With a defined contribution plan, annual contributions by the employee and employer accumulate in an investment account and the balance in the account is available for the employee to draw upon during retirement. In this case, the employee bears the investment risk.

In a defined benefit plan, the employer promises to provide a defined level of benefit to the employee at retirement. An actuary calculates the annual amount the employer must contribute into the retirement account each year in order to accumulate sufficient funds to meet the commitment. In this case, the employer bears the investment risk.

As illustrated in Figure 14-1, contributions to a qualified deferred, compensation plan are generally tax deductible for the employer and result in deferred income (until withdrawal) for the employee. This results in a significant tax advantage for both the employer and employee. It is important to note that qualified retirement plans are subject to a set of IRS rules that limit the amount of annual contributions to the plan, require equal participation for all rank and file employees, define an acceptable vesting schedule, and require annual reporting to the plan participants and the IRS.

## Non-Qualified Deferred Compensation

Non-qualified deferred compensation can be a powerful retirement planning tool, particularly for owners of closely-held corporations. Non-qualified deferred compensation plans offer flexibility, something qualified plans lack.

With non-qualified deferred compensation plans, the employer can discriminate freely. The employer can pick and choose among employees, including him- or herself, and benefit only a select few. The employer can treat those chosen differently from everyone else. The benefit promised need not follow any of the rules associated with qualified plans. The vesting schedule can be whatever the employer would like it to be. By using life insurance products, the tax deferral features of qualified plans can be simulated. Properly drafted, non-qualified and deferred compensation plans do not result in taxable income to the employee until payments are made.

To obtain this flexibility, both the employer and employee must give something up. The employer loses the up-front tax deduction for the contribution to the plan. However, the employer will get a deduction when benefits are paid. The employee loses the security provided under ERISA. However, very often the employee in question is the business owner, which mitigates this concern. Also, techniques are available to provide the non-owner employee with a measure of security.

A non-qualified deferred compensation plan is a written contract between the corporate employer and the employee. The contract covers employment and compensation provided in the future. The non-qualified deferred compensation agreement gives the employee the employer's unsecured promise to pay some future benefit in exchange for services today. The promised, future benefit may be in one of three general forms. Some non-qualified deferred compensation plans resemble defined benefit plans in that they promise to pay the employee a fixed dollar amount or fixed percentage of salary for a period of time after retirement. Another type of non-qualified deferred compensation resembles a defined contribution plan in which a fixed amount goes into the employee's "account" each year. The employee is then entitled to the balance of the account at retirement. The final type of non-qualified deferred compensation plan provides a death benefit to the employee's designated beneficiary.

Nonqualified plans can be either funded or unfunded: funded plans actually hold cash in an account for the employee; unfunded plans are merely a contractual promise to pay the benefit at a future date, subject to the terms of the agreement. Funded plans usually are preferred by employees.

If the plan is funded, care must be taken to avoid the IRS Doctrines of Constructive Receipt and Economic Benefit, which disallow deferral of income tax to the employee if the employee does not have a "substantial risk of forfeiture" in the account. In other words, an employee cannot simply instruct an employer to invest a portion of salary in trust and defer income tax.

This requirement can be met in many ways, including placing a requirement in the plan that the employee must stay with the company for a defined period of time before the benefits vest, or by using IRS's prescribed vehicles such as a Rabbi Trust.

The flexibility of non-qualified deferred compensation plans makes them very useful to companies facing succession issues. They also are useful in attracting, retaining, and motivating key employees. Non-qualified plans can be used by employers to help successor-generation employees accumulate capital to buy the owner's stock. They can provide a tax-deferred source of retirement income for employee-owners and may be used to save estate and gift taxes.

## Qualified Fringe Benefits

Qualified fringe benefits afford the best of both worlds: a current deduction for the employer and no income tax for the employee. Therefore, qualified fringe benefits provide a benefit for both the business owner and employee.

The fringe benefits outlined below are examples of what generally may be deducted from the taxable income of the employer and excluded from taxable income by the employee:

- Work-related fringe benefits (for example, use of the company car for business purposes)
- Payment for group health insurance
- Qualified transportation fringe benefits (for example, bus passes, or employer-paid parking)
- Reimbursement of qualified moving expenses
- Qualified employee discounts
- Qualified dependent care services
- Free services (for example, stand-by flights by airlines to their off-duty employees)
- Minor workplace fringe benefits (for example, free use of copier, cell phone, or computer for personal purposes)
- Payment for group life insurance coverage up to $50,000
- Payment for accident or health plans
- Payment of certain educational expenses

However, the tax rules covering qualified fringe benefits are complicated, and you should consult with a qualified benefits or compensation advisor to help navigate these waters. Generally speaking, fringe-benefit plans are not allowed to favor certain employees over others, but some benefits may be extended to retired employees, disabled, former employees, or the widows/widowers of deceased employees.

## Dividends

Dividends are a portion of a company's net income paid to stockholders as a return on their investment. Dividends are declared or suspended at the discretion of the company's board of directors.

Due to the corporate "double tax," paying corporate dividends is the least desirable way for business owners to compensate key employees if the company is a "C-Corp." Regular "C" corporations are separate legal entities that must pay income tax on their earnings; this is the first level of tax. When the corporation distributes cash dividends to its shareholders, it triggers a second level of income tax, which is paid by the individual shareholders who receive the dividends; this is the second level of tax.

The corporation receives no deduction for these dividends. Given this fact, the key employees receiving dividends from a regular "C" corporation may actually receive only about 25 cents on every dollar of the company's net profits, after income taxes. Because of this, many business owners prefer to pay key employees higher salaries so the company at least receives a tax deduction for the salary paid.

Aware of this tendency on the part of business owners, the IRS challenges excessive salaries paid to key employee who also are shareholders, alleging these payments are really in lieu of corporate dividends.

## Stock Bonuses

Some employers may provide stock bonuses in lieu of cash compensation to key employees, but this effectively grants equity ownership to the key employee. As a result, this decision has long-term consequences and needs to be thought through, carefully. There may be many other ways to motivate a key employee to stay without having to give up equity.

That said, stock bonus programs may be an effective way to gradually transfer ownership from one generation of owner-managers to the next. From a tax standpoint, a stock bonus is just like cash compensation: the current value of the stock bonus is subject to ordinary income tax for the employee and generates a current income tax deduction for the company. Therefore, some family businesses employ stock bonus programs to transfer ownership between family members because there is no tax cost to the family group as a whole. Plus, a *bona fide* stock transfer—from one generation to the next—through the use of a stock bonus, will not produce any estate or gift tax.

It is important to note that the IRS may challenge a large stock bonus from one generation to the next as a disguised gift, and may assess gift taxes, accordingly. As a result, care should be taken to ensure the value of the stock and amount of compensation also are reasonable.

Although a stock bonus generates cash flow for the company (through the associated tax deductions), it may cause cash flow problems for recipients. The recipients of the stock bonus receive illiquid stock in the transaction, but not any cash to pay the associated tax. The result is much like winning an expensive car in a contest and then having to sell it in order to pay the taxes. Of course, there are ways to solve these problems, but they can be complicated and expensive to implement.

## More Sophisticated Compensation Techniques

It would be impossible to cover all the possible compensation techniques in this book. If this is an area of interest, or there are unique problems that need to be solved, adding a compensation specialist to the exit planning team may be appropriate. The following are just a few examples of some of the more sophisticated compensation techniques we have used in our exit planning practice:

### Restricted Stock

As discussed above, some employers may provide stock bonuses instead of cash compensation to key employees. Stock bonus programs also can be an effective way to gradually transfer ownership from one generation of owner-managers to the next. A variation on this approach involves giving a "restricted" stock bonus to key employees as part of an ownership exit plan. Restricted stock requires the executive or stockholder to return the shares to the company upon some triggering event, such as termination of employment, over a specified number of years. If properly structured, a restricted stock bonus will satisfy the IRS Doctrine of Constructive Receipt which requires a substantial risk of forfeiture in order to defer income taxes to the employee. Thus, a properly structured restricted stock bonus allows for transfer of ownership to employees without triggering any current taxable income for the recipient or employee.

When the stock restriction lapses, the employee is then deemed to have fully "received" his or her stock and is subject to ordinary income tax on the value of the shares as of the date the restriction is lifted. The corporation is afforded a corresponding tax deduction at that time.

**Phantom Stock**

Phantom stock programs are one solution we regularly recommend to our clients. A phantom stock program allows employees to participate in company success and growth, just as owners do, but without actually receiving any ownership interest. Each year, amounts are credited to the key employee's account based on the agreed-upon formula. At some specified date, when a triggering event occurs (which can be defined by a number of years, termination of employment, death, retirement, or sale of business), the company buys back the phantom stock and pays the employee cash based upon an agreed-upon formula in the plan.

Phantom stock plans are not subject to the qualified plan rules regarding participation, contribution limits, vesting, or annual IRS reporting. Phantom stock plans can be either funded or unfunded. Sometimes life insurance policies are put in place with unfunded plans to help fund the payoff in the case of the death or disability of the employee.

Phantom stock plans can be a powerful way to retain and motivate key employees without actually transferring ownership. This is often an important consideration, especially in the case of a family-owned business where there are key, non-family executives who want the benefits of ownership, but the family owners do not wish to transfer ownership outside the family.

If properly presented and administered, participants in a phantom stock plan act and feel like owners. They receive periodic statements that reconcile the number of stock units posted to their accounts and disclose the current value of the units, just as if they owned actual stock. They see they are sharing in the appreciation in the value of the company and receive tax-deferred treatment on the contributions and appreciation in the plan.

In addition, phantom stock ownership has advantages over common stock ownership. For example, the phantom owners do not share in the risk of loss the common owners bear. If the company profits fall off, the phantom owners risk only the loss of their phantom stock balances. Only the actual owners of the business would be expected to contribute personal assets or guarantee bank loans to get through hard times. Also, many phantom stock plans are set up so that account balances are not reduced in years when the company loses value. These factors can make a phantom stock plan very appealing to employees, sometimes even more appealing than an actual employee stock ownership plan.

**Incentive-Based Compensation**

The CEOs of the largest and most successful publicly-owned companies earn the majority of their compensation through incentive-based bonuses and stock options. Incentive-based compensation planning can play a major role in attracting and retaining the best managers in private businesses as well.

It is difficult for key employees to argue with an incentive-based system. We recommend getting the input and participation of key managers when designing an incentive-based compensation program.    If the managers participate in the design process, they will take ownership of the plan going forward. This reduces the chance of anyone claiming the program is unfair or biased when it is implemented.   Some examples of different incentive plans include:

■ **Group Incentives**:   Monthly/annual bonuses based on achievement of a group or department's performance goals during that period. An example could be a bonus to a Sales Manager for his group meeting its monthly, quarterly, and annual sales targets.

■ **Team-Based Rewards**:   Payment of rewards or bonuses based on the performance of a certain team within a group. An example might be a bonus for the team responsible for the launch of a new product.

■ **Profit Sharing**:   Awards based on overall financial performance of the company.   The size of the award is generally uniform across eligible employees.   Although this type of plan sounds attractive at first blush, it often fails to motivate for specific results. The overall financial performance of the company is so far removed from the individual control of any one employee that it can be hard for employees to understand exactly what they need to do to achieve the goal.

■ **Gain Sharing**:   Rewards are given to employees who demonstrate gains in productivity using predetermined formulas.   The same program can be used with team or group performance.

■ **Goal Sharing**:   Rewards employees for achieving specific, usually non-financial goals such as successful completion of an internal project or process.

■ **Competency Pay**:   Rewarding employees who demonstrate superior performance on the job. An example would be rewarding a shift manager who has been able to increase production while at the same time reducing accidents or absenteeism during his or her shift.   Competency pay should not be confused with seniority pay, which is not performance based.

We recommend that incentive compensation arrangements not simply be added on top of an existing base.   To make the programs truly meaningful and effective, incentive compensation plans should involve the trade-off of substantially higher compensation in exchange for some portion of the employee's guaranteed base salary.   This "at-risk" portion doesn't have to be huge, but it does need to be significant enough so the employees receive the psychological message that they have some "skin in the game."

## Employment Agreements—Damage Control

In the event that a key employee does leave the company during the exit planning process or sale of a company, it is important for the business owner to be able to control the situation. Controlling this type of situation means several things. First, it means having a basic understanding of what potential disruption to business the departure of the key employee could cause.

Second, it means the company's trade secrets, including its client or customer lists and trade practices, are protected. This means making sure each key employee's employment contract includes a nondisclosure clause, a non-compete provision, and a non-solicitation clause.

A non-disclosure clause prevents a former employee from revealing a company's trade secrets. Trade secrets are broadly defined in common law, but it is important that each non-disclosure provision spell out exactly what is included under the terms of this specific agreement to ensure each company's unique secrets are protected. That said, it should be noted that even the best drafted non-disclosure agreements are notoriously hard to enforce. To make an injunction secure restricting disclosure, you must prove that imminent and irreparable harm will be done to the company, if the former employee continues in a course of action. If you can establish this "prima facie" case, the company may be able to secure an injunction barring the former employee from further action. On the other hand, if the actions have already occurred, the company must prove economic damage in order to enforce the nondisclosure agreement. If that is not possible—and often it is not—trying to enforce this clause may not make sense.

---

**Typical Defined Terms in Employment Nondisclosure and Non-compete Agreements**

**Confidential Information.** "Confidential Information" as used in this Agreement shall mean any and all confidential and proprietary information of Employer, including without limitation, techniques, concepts, drawings, models, inventions, intellectual property, proprietary processes and procedures, forms, marketing materials, databases, software programs, software source documents, and formulae related to the current, future, and proposed products and services of Employer, its suppliers and customers, and shall include Employer's market research, financial information, purchasing information, customer lists, business forecasts, sales and marketing plans, and information. For purposes of this Agreement, Confidential Information shall not include: (i) information in the public domain or generally known by competitors in the industry; (ii) information that enters the public domain through no fault of the Employee; (iii) information received by Employee from a third party having a bona fide right to disclose such information without being bound by a confidentiality obligation; and (iv) information independently developed, created, or produced by Employee whether before, during, or after the term hereof.

---

**Nondisclosure and Nonuse Obligations.** Employee will use the Confidential Information solely to perform client projects for Employer. Employee agrees to treat all Confidential Information with the same degree of care as it accords to its own Confidential Information, and Employee represents that it exercises reasonable care to protect its own Confidential Information. Employee agrees that it shall disclose Confidential Information only to people who need to know such information and certifies that people will have previously agreed, either as a condition of employment or in order to obtain the Confidential Information, to be bound by terms and conditions of a confidentiality agreement approved by Employer. Employee agrees to assist Employer in remedying any unauthorized use or disclosure of the Confidential Information.

A non-compete clause prohibits a key employee from accepting employment from a competitor. To be enforceable, this clause needs to be carefully drafted so it is not too broad or overreaching. Most states are "right to work states," which means state courts read non-compete clauses with a bias toward the employee. As a result, they need to be drafted so they restrict the employee only for a specific period, often 6 to 18 months, and within a specific geographic range, i.e., at a 500-mile radius of the former employer. See the following example:

**Typical Defined Terms in Employment Nondisclosure and Non-compete Agreements (continued)**

**Non-compete.** For a period of 1 year after termination of employment for whatever reason, Employee shall not, either directly or indirectly, either alone or as a director, proprietor, partner, employee, consultant, agent, independent contractor, or otherwise, accept any employment with a competitor of Industrial or engage in any business which is competitive with Industrial's business, within 100 miles of Industrial's principal place of business without the prior written consent of Industrial.

A non-solicitation clause prohibits a key employee from soliciting the company's clients, customers, or prospects. It also may apply to soliciting the company's other employees for purposes of leaving the company. These clauses are much easier to enforce than a non-compete clause because state courts generally recognize the investment a company's clients, customers, prospects, and other employees represent as part of the intellectual property of the company. As a result, courts believe protecting these assets is important. At the same time, they have concluded that restricting a former employee's ability to solicit this business does not interfere with an employee's ability to work in his or her chosen profession or to earn a living. See the following clause for an example:

---

**Typical Defined Terms in Employment Nondisclosure and Non-compete Agreements (continued)**

---

**Non-solicitation.** Member agrees for a period of 24 months following termination of this Agreement by either party, for any reason whatsoever, Member shall not solicit (1) Investment Bank's clients, seller leads, or prospects for whom Member performed services or to whom Member made a presentation for the purpose of providing investment banking services similar to those provided by Investment Bank; and (2) Investment Bank's employees or independent contractors for the purpose of hiring them or inducing them to leave their employment or relationship with Investment Bank.

---

Despite the difficulty that comes with enforcing provisions like these, it is important to have these clauses in every employment agreement with key employees. The presence of these clauses accomplishes two things. First, from the perspective of your key employees, these clauses have what is called an "in terrorem" effect. The legal term "in terrorem" means providing "a warning or deterrent." That means these provisions put your key employees on notice that there are legal consequences if they engage in any of the prohibited activities. The general effect is that employees are more likely to abide by the spirit of the agreement than they are to violate it.

Second, from a potential purchaser's perspective, it demonstrates that the business owner has taken all reasonable and prudent precautions to protect against the potential damage a former key employee could cause the company. It also provides the buyer with the necessary tools should he/she need to take legal action in the future to protect the company against 1) a breach of confidentiality; 2) the key employee's joining up with a competitor; or 3) a former employee's trying to steal clients, customer, prospects, or employees.

## Summary

In this chapter we have shown you several ways to develop compensation programs to help a business owner proactively protect a large part of the value of the company he or she has built. These compensation plans can be as simple or complex as the owner wants them to be. The important point is that by involving key employees in the exit planning process as stakeholders, and addressing these compensation issues early, the business owner and the key employees can help each other achieve their personal goals and objectives.

# Chapter 15

# The Strategic Importance of Financial Planning

Business owners face special challenges when it comes to managing family wealth. Due to the demands of time and energy required to stay on top of business operations, many business owners find little time to personally manage their investments. Because the demands of managing a company are so great, business owners typically have little interest in educating themselves about or reviewing and monitoring their investment performance. As a result, business owners often make "seat-of-the-pants" investment decisions, delegate these decisions to others, or put off making any investment decisions entirely.

As a result, the owner's investment performance or portfolio may not be optimal. In addition, the investment strategy being used is often not in line with the owner's goals. Investment diversity also presents a special challenge for closely-held business owners. Growing a business requires capital. During periods of growth, many business owners answer part of the need for capital by constantly reinvesting profits back into the company. As a result, even for many very successful business owners, the accumulation of a diversified investment portfolio is often not an option. Investment planning thereby ends up being relatively low on the owner's priority list.

Exit planning, however, changes everything. Often the transfer of ownership calls for purchase of a founder's stock through an outright sale or an alternative estate planning mechanism. The result may be that the owner, who for years has concentrated on managing and growing the business, must suddenly change focus and worry about managing a large amount of liquid wealth. Although some individuals approach the management of their personal wealth as their retirement "vocation," others are better served through professional investment advice. In such situations, if you are a financial advisor you can play an invaluable role.

To understand this point, consider the following case study.

### Case Study: How Much is Enough?

**Situation:** Mack and Sarah jointly owned a successful trucking company. They had been married for forty years and in business together for 39 of those 40 years. They were considering selling their company. They received an unsolicited offer for their company, for which they would receive $35 million. Based on the terms of the deal they would receive $7 million in cash at closing and $28 million in the stock of a large, publicly traded trucking company.

On the personal side, Mack and Sarah wanted to leave money to their church and their children when they died. In the meantime, they figured they would spend the investment income from the $7 million and approximately 2 percent of their nest egg each year. Mack and Sarah felt this was very conservative and were very comfortable with their prospects. Was their optimism warranted?

Before accepting the offer they came to us to ask our advice. Our first move was to introduce Mack and Sarah to a financial advisor. He prepared a sophisticated financial planning model that showed the couple that, given the proposed structure and their personal goals, they had a 1 in 4 chance of running out of money during their lifetime. The financial planner used a planning model that looked at more than 10,000 possible combinations of market ups and downs and found that 25 percent of these combinations resulted in the couple's being unable to accomplish their personal financial goals—even after selling their company for $35 million! Mack and Sarah were shocked. They were not prepared to roll the dice with those kinds of odds.

The new information the financial advisors provided helped us negotiate a better deal with the buyer. Although the total value of the transaction transpired, we were able to shift more of the consideration from restricted stock to cash. With this structure, the financial advisor told Mack and Sarah that they would be able to build an investment portfolio that gave them a 95 percent chance of meeting all their personal, family, and philanthropic goals.

As part of the post-closing wealth management plan, the financial advisor recommended that Mack and Sarah make some adjustments to the couple's portfolio by investing the proceeds in a balanced portfolio of bonds and equities. He also recommended that they gradually sell off the stock they received at closing so that within three years the couple would no longer have any significant concentration in that asset. This new investment approach reduced the probability of the couple's running out of money from 1 in 4 to less than 1 in 100. Mack and Sarah could live with this risk.

Whatever your client's plans, formalizing retirement goals—and the application of a timetable for achieving those goals—proves an invaluable exercise. But help your clients be realistic in their goal setting. A future retiree without a clear picture of potential requirements increases the chances of falling short of vital retirement needs. Some individuals arrive at retirement with cash flow levels that are far less than their pre-retirement annual expenses, while others may actually plan to increase their spending after retirement. The important thing is to understand—*and* try to quantify—those desires in detail.

Clearly, there is tremendous benefit for the client in this situation, but think of the benefits to the financial advisor. By identifying a significant problem of which the clients were not aware and helping them address it proactively, the financial advisor saved the day! That financial advisor quickly joined the circle of the client's most trusted advisors. It is hard to imagine a client shopping for another financial advisor to help him or her manage this new liquid wealth going forward.

Developing a strategic, personal, financial plan needs to be an integral part of any comprehensive, exit planning process. Exit planning allows financial advisors to probe for and receive information about a business owner's:

- Overall investment goals and objectives
- Personal risk tolerance
- Level of knowledge relating to investing
- Current investment strategy
- Current investment portfolio

To offer the best counsel in relation to succession or exit planning issues, financial advisors need to work closely with other advisors to understand these important issues related to the owner's exit:

- The tax ramifications
- The practical and financial ramifications
- Short-term and long-term individual liquidity needs
- Possible future business concerns, such as financing or capital obligations
- The founder's retirement plans
- The founder's estate plan
- The founder's insurance needs
- The founder's income tax situation

## The Importance of a Financial Plan

It is beyond my expertise to explain how to develop a comprehensive and well-designed financial plan for a high-net-worth client. This is why I advocate the use of a multi-disciplinary team in the exit planning process. However, my experience as an investment banker has demonstrated repeatedly how important and how often overlooked personal financial planning is when an owner is thinking about selling his or her business.

Unfortunately, most business owners make decisions to sell based on assumptions and guesses about what they need to retire; they simply hope and pray they will net enough from the sale of the business to accomplish their goals.

For these business owners, selling a business and receiving a check for $10 million dollars feels like winning the lottery. But $10 million does not go as far as it used to.

Most business owners assume a nest egg of $10 million (choose whatever number you like) is more than enough to support their retirement lifestyle and leave a comfortable legacy for their families. But this important assumption needs to be carefully evaluated. There are inherent risks in certain types of investment strategies or asset combinations that often go unnoticed and cause this assumption to be terribly wrong. Unfortunately, during our professional careers we have had the misfortune to work with a number of clients who made this assumption.

In the high-stakes process of exiting a business, many business owners forget to check their assumptions, and therefore, do not ensure their long-term financial needs are being addressed. Exit planning is not just about business issues. The process also must account for the personal welfare and financial security of the company's owners and their families.

As one of the financial advisors I work with says, "There are only 4 things a successful owner can do with his money following an exit from a business. He can spend it, give it to the people he cares about, give it to charity, or give it to the government."

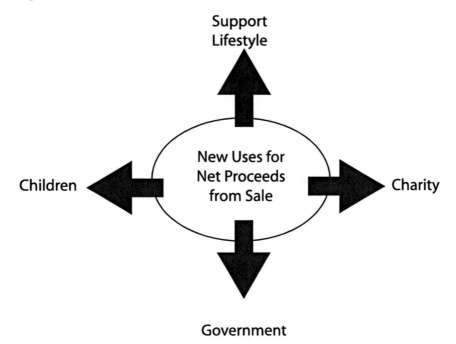

Figure 15-1: Use for Sale Proceeds

In addition to dealing with business issues, it is crucial that owners employ a quantitative framework to create a personal financial plan—including asset allocation, spending, plans for family gifting, and charitable giving—so that a business owner can rest assured he will not lose control over his retirement nest egg or the legacy he wants to leave to his heirs.  During this process, careful consideration must be given to non-business issues such as:

- Defining retirement goals
- Spending and cash flow needs
- Post sale investment strategy to balance risk and reward
- Estate and gift tax strategies
- Life insurance planning

## Professional Wealth Management

Money does in fact change everything.  Financial challenges increase exponentially as you add more zeros to your net worth.  Individuals with significant assets have a genuine need for professional wealth managers.  But what exactly is wealth management?  Wealth management means taking care of the needs of affluent clients, their families, and their businesses as part of a long-term, consultative relationship. At its best, it functions as a full-service model offering clients advice on investment management, estate planning, retirement, tax, asset protection, cash flow, and debt management.

One of the desires clients express to us is not to be tied down by their new liquid wealth.  They realize picking individual securities can be challenging and that it is not easy to create and maintain a truly, diversified portfolio.  Instead of doing it themselves, former business owners typically want their money to be professionally managed.  Once they approve of an investment approach, they do not want to have to approve their financial advisor's individual investment recommendations.  As a result, we find managed accounts are an attractive option for former business owners.

In a managed account program, the client's money is managed by third-party, professional money managers.  Managed accounts are typically attractive to individuals with at least $500,000 to invest.

In most sound, managed account programs, the investor has the option to select from dozens of experienced and professional money managers to personally manage the investor's portfolio.  These managers are often some of the best and most, respected specialists in their field.  They typically manage money for the super affluent or large institutional investors such as universities and pension funds.

Providing the client with a variety of professional money managers allows the client to choose from a wide array of investment styles and specialties ranging from managers who specialize in investing in small, midsize, or large company stocks, to real estate investment trusts (REITs), international securities, and tax-exempt bonds.

Managed accounts provide the client with a high degree of personal freedom former business owners want. After the professional managers are chosen, they make the day-to-day investment decisions for the client's portfolio, following formal investment philosophies and risk profiles.

Because most former business owners are not knowledgeable about investments, they look to their personal financial advisor to help them understand investment basics and risk tolerance, and to help choose a combination of managers to meet their investment goals.

Another feature high-net-worth business owners find attractive about managed accounts is the ability to keep track of portfolio performance through consolidated reports showing the individual performance of each manager, the current asset allocation, the portfolio's current value, and its short- and long-term performance. Such reports deliver the convenience and "simplicity" these folks seek.

High-net-worth former business owners are, like the rest of us, sensitive to paying professional fees. As a result, they appreciate that managed accounts give them access to a wide range of services and features for one inclusive fee. Most of the larger financial services firms providing managed accounts include the following services in the annual management fee:

- An investment strategy review to understand the client's current and future financial needs, goals, and risk tolerance
- The ability to work with their personal financial advisor to craft an investment policy regarding investment styles and diversification strategies
- Tracking the purchase and ownership of the securities that make up the client's portfolio so the client has a cost basis for his or her positions

Other successful financial planning and wealth management firms adopt a slightly, different approach to building and preserving wealth for their clients. These firms advocate a comprehensive approach in which they provide many of the same services as a wrap account, but provide these services in-house under one roof, rather than using outside managers. For lack of a better term, let's call this type of firm a discretionary wealth manager.

One of the attractive features of the discretionary wealth management approach is that the client and his financial advisor are able to develop a truly, customizable investment philosophy based on the unique needs and tax profile of the client. Advocates of this approach say that wrap accounts are not truly customizable. Instead, clients may choose between many different third party managers, but once the manager is selected, the client is basically locked into the portfolio the manager runs for all of that manager's clients, much like when a client buys a mutual fund.

In a discretionary wealth management account, the client and his financial advisor have access to several different, money managers who specialize in different investment styles, like in a wrap account program.   The difference, however, is that in a discretionary account, the client and his money managers develop an investment philosophy unique to that client.   Once the philosophy is agreed to, the money manager customizes the client's portfolio as long as the manager stays within this investment philosophy.   This means each money manager effectively invests and manages each client's portfolio separately to ensure the client's unique needs, situation, and personal preferences are taken into account.

Another feature that makes this approach different is that the client and financial advisor have direct access to each manager.   As a result, the client's portfolio is managed and re-balanced on a regular basis taking into account the client's changing needs, tax situation, and the performance of individual securities across the client's entire portfolio regardless of manager or investment style.

Advocates of this approach believe that actively managing significant wealth using a comprehensive and holistic approach generates better returns for the client.   In addition, because the money managers used are in-house and not third-party contractors, the financial advisor provides these services without an additional layer of fees making the relationship more cost effective from a client's perspective.

Until recently, this investment approach has only been available to ultra-high-net-worth clients, but increasingly firms are offering these services to clients with $1 million in investable funds.

Both wrap accounts and discretionary wealth management are attractive options for business owners who are about to realize a significant liquidity event. As a trusted advisor to business owners, it is our job to introduce clients to these options as early in the exit planning process as possible.

## Summary

No exit plan is complete without a detailed and thorough financial plan in place. A good financial plan addresses the key question, "how much do I need to net from a sale in order to accomplish my goals?" Without that key information, the best exit plan in the world runs the risk of not meeting the owner's personal goals and objectives.   As a result, each financial plan must define the business owner's retirement goals, spending and cash flow needs, and post closing investment strategy.   It must create a forum in which the financial advisor and financial family can work most productively to accomplish the business owner's goals.

Chapter **16**

# Estate Planning

For business owners, estate planning is much more than a contemplation of what do with the client's estate after he or she dies. Estate planning in an exit planning framework is closely related to the two primary goals at the forefront of each business owner's mind: minimizing taxes and making sure that owners accomplish their personal goals during their lifetime as well as at death.

Because the wealth of closely-held business owners is typically tied up in illiquid assets, the imposition of the estate tax may force heirs to sell the respective businesses in order to pay the taxes. Without proper estate planning, your client's business may need to be liquidated in order for your client's heirs to pay estate taxes.

Therefore, it is essential for all business owners to work with a financial advisor to determine the value of the owner's current estate and for assistance in projecting its future value. The first step is to determine the extent of estate tax exposure in order to prepare the way for further exit planning. Building an estate plan entails more than setting up wills, trusts, and health-care directives. When developing an effective estate and gift tax plan, business owners also must consider other elements of exit planning, such as developing and motivating future managers, transferring ownership, retaining key employees, dealing fairly with family members and other stakeholders, contingency planning, and retirement cash flow and investment portfolio strategies.

Well-planned family and charitable trusts can reduce capital gains taxes, ordinary income taxes, and estate taxes. Trusts also can help ensure income for spending needs, provide for financial security for future generations, fund charities, and help to accomplish the business owner's personal goals.

## Lifetime Gifting

Gifting can be a very simple and powerful way to transfer wealth from one individual to another without incurring transfer tax—especially when the gifting program is followed over a period of years. Furthermore, after a gift is made, the asset is removed from the donor's taxable estate so any future appreciation on the gift also is removed from the donor's taxable estate. The trade-off in making a gift is that the recipient of the gift gets the same tax "basis" in the property received as the donor prior to the gift. If the same property were bequeathed at death, the recipient would receive a free "step-up" in basis in the property.

The IRS allows any individual to gift up to $11,000 of value to another individual each year without paying any transfer tax and without eating into the lifetime credit against estate and gift taxes everyone is allowed under the law. (Note: Although the current figure was raised from $10,000 in 2002, future increases to account for inflation can be expected.) Married couples can gift $22,000 per year per recipient. In order to qualify as a *bona fide* gift, the donor must give up all rights of ownership and control. Any strings attached will nullify the gift.

In addition, an individual can pay another person's educational or health-care costs without the payments constituting a gift as long as the payment is made directly to the school or health-care provider. This can dramatically increase the amount of money one person can give another without triggering any gift tax issues.

## The Importance of Using Trusts

Trusts are used for a variety of purposes; indeed, the flexibility of trusts is perhaps the major reason they are so widely used in estate planning. Trusts can be created and funded during a lifetime (*inter vivos* trusts) or they can be created by the terms of the will (*testamentary* trusts). The terms of a trust may allow it to be changed or even revoked by the grantor, or the terms of the trust may be fixed or irrevocable at the date of creation.

Several of the primary purposes for using trusts in estate and financial planning include:

**Managing Assets.** The responsibility of making investment decisions and maintaining adequate records can be transferred to either a corporate or an individual trustee.

**Protecting Assets.** In certain situations, a properly drafted trust can protect the assets in a trust from creditors of a beneficiary. In addition, the assets may be protected from a spouse in the event of the divorce of the beneficiary.

**Providing Privacy.** The assets, terms, and conditions of a trust are generally not subject to public inspection.

**Avoiding Probate.** The assets held in a trust created and funded during the grantor's lifetime are controlled by the terms of the trust, not by the terms of probate. In some states, avoiding probate can save time and reduce administrative expenses.

**Providing for Multiple Beneficiaries.** A trust can be created for the benefit of multiple beneficiaries and can allow the trustee to use discretion in making distributions.

**Providing for Special Needs.** A beneficiary may have a special need relating to education, health, and so on. A trust can be used to address those special needs.

**Tax Planning.** A trust can be used to help take full advantage of the combined marital deduction and the unified credit while assuring all necessary assets are available to meet the needs of the surviving spouse. For example, your client could leave his or her assets to a spouse, except the amount equivalent to the estate tax exemption amount. This amount would go into a "by-pass" trust for the benefit of the spouse and family. Although the spouse would be able to benefit from the entire estate, the trust assets would not be included in the estate of the surviving spouse on his or her subsequent death.

The business owner may implement a trust arrangement during his or her lifetime or under the terms of the owner's will. In addition, the client can establish a trust during his or her life to begin operation upon the client's death. In the latter case, property passing under the terms of the client's will could be directed to "pour over" into an already existing trust. A trust established during the client's lifetime (*inter vivos*) can be used with respect to estate planning for certain types of assets. For example, insurance proceeds and employee benefit plans, if made payable to the trust, would be collected by the trustee immediately following the client's death without the potential delay and administrative difficulty that may be associated with a trust established under the client's will (*testamentary*). In some states, this approach has the added benefit of avoiding the continuing, probate court jurisdiction sometimes imposed on trusts established under wills.

In fact, it may be beneficial to place title to certain assets in an *inter vivos* trust, as well as to designate the business owner as trustee during his or her lifetime to avoid the probate process. Such arrangements are often referred to as a self-declaration trust, or *living trust,* and can be effective in minimizing probate time and avoiding publicity and expenses without incurring any unnecessary trustee fees.

In creating a trust, particular attention should be paid to the choice of a trustee—the individual or institution—that will be responsible for the management, investment, and distribution of funds. The level of competence of an individual selected to serve in such a fiduciary capacity will vary, depending on such factors as business judgment and experience. Perhaps more important is the fact that an institutional trustee's existence is "perpetual" whereas an appointed individual may die or become incapacitated, thereby negating the personal continuity of trust administration.

If you want to name an individual as trustee, you should consider naming a corporate trustee as a backup, if the individual is subsequently unable or unwilling to serve. (Note: One of the advantages of a trust is its flexibility to adapt to changing circumstances. Although a trust is generally irrevocable following the death of the individual who created it, a provision can be included that gives the beneficiary the ability to replace the trustee. This authority can be granted to any individual, but typically is reserved for an adult beneficiary, such as the surviving spouse.)

A corporate trustee can provide management and record-keeping expertise for almost any type of asset and is trained in the responsibilities of serving as a fiduciary. In addition, the corporate trustee's existence is generally enduring and can be counted on to be there long into the future to respond to the needs of the beneficiaries. There *are* fees associated with the selection and use of a corporate trustee. The cost of professional expertise should be weighed in each situation. You may want to consider naming both a professional and other relevant individual as co-trustees. In this way, you can obtain professional management expertise coupled with the individual's knowledge of the family (as applicable) and awareness of the needs of the individual beneficiaries.

The two clients, Mack and Sarah, who were the subject of the case study in the previous chapter, were prime candidates for a "living" estate plan. After carefully laying out their goals, they opted to maintain their current lifestyle and make annual gifts to charity and their children, totaling approximately, $750,000 per year. In addition, they wanted to leave a legacy of $10 million to their children. Finally, they wanted to always maintain a nest egg of $10 million as a "safety net."

The couple's financial advisor was able to work with the clients' other advisors to set up the following "living" estate plan for them:

- A Charitable Remainder Trust (CRT) to hold the main portfolio and provide a regular income stream to the couple. This also provided the clients with a method to efficiently diversify their assets, protect their principal, secure significant tax breaks, and ensure a final distribution to a number of favored charities.
- A Grantor Retained Annuity Trust (GRAT) that allowed for a substantial transfer of wealth while minimizing estate and gift taxes. In a GRAT, the grantor or investor contributes assets to the trust, and in exchange, receives a stream of fixed payments each year from the trust. The payments are typically based on an IRS-approved interest rate and the life expectancy of the grantor. Whatever is left in the trust when the grantor dies is passed on to the beneficiaries, tax free.

Let's look at these two estate planning tools in more detail. Used separately or combined, they are very effective tools in the context of exit planning.

## Charitable Remainder Trusts (CRTS)

Most business owners hold highly appreciated stock in their businesses which they are reluctant to sell because of the significant, capital gains taxes they would owe. At the same time, the business owner may be looking for ways to increase his/her income or diversify his/her portfolio. Usually, this means selling those highly appreciated assets, paying the high taxes, and reinvesting the net proceeds. Fortunately, the Charitable Remainder Trust provides an option.

The Charitable Remainder Trust, also known as a CRT, was created by the tax reform act of 1969. It is an irrevocable trust designed to convert a business owner's or investor's highly appreciated assets into a lifetime income stream without generating estate and capital gains taxes.

CRT's have become popular in recent years because they not only represent a valuable, tax-advantaged investment, but also enable clients to provide a gift to one or more charities that have special meaning to them. A CRT can:

- Eliminate immediate capital gains taxes on the sale of appreciated assets such as stocks, bonds, real estate, or just about any other asset.
- Reduce estate taxes (which can be up to 55 percent) so the client's heirs do not have to pay as much at the time of the client's death.
- Reduce current income taxes with a sizable, income tax deduction.
- Increase the client's spendable income throughout the rest of his or her life.
- Create a significant charitable gift.
- Avoid probate and maximize the assets the client's family receives after the client's death.

When a client establishes a CRT, the business owner or another beneficiary, such as his or her spouse or another family member, receives a fixed income stream from the trust for life, or for up to 20 years, whichever is longer.

When the trust ends, the remaining assets pass to the qualified charity or charities of the business owner's choice.

## Grantor-Retained Annuity Trust

A grantor-retained annuity trust (GRAT) allows a business owner to give away trust assets to designated beneficiaries but keep an income stream from the gifted assets for a period of years. If the assets increase in value during the term of the trust, this appreciation passes to the designated beneficiaries at a dramatically reduced estate and gift tax cost.

A GRAT is an irrevocable trust to which a business owner contributes the stock of his company. The business owner or client then retains the right to receive a fixed annuity payment from the trust for a specified period of years (typically from two to seven years), based on several factors including the market value of the asset contributed to the trust, the length of the annuity, and an IRS-approved interest rate.

At the end of the trust term, any remaining trust property is distributed to the GRAT's beneficiaries as the grantor originally specified in the trust agreement. Generally, this distribution is made either outright or in the form of a further trust for the benefit of the grantor's children or other family members.

One of the attractive features of GRATs is the manner in which they are treated for federal gift tax purposes. When a GRAT is established, it is subject to federal gift tax. However, tax is not assessed on the full value of the property gifted to the GRAT. Using IRS-approved formulas and assumptions, the donor calculates the amount expected to remain in the trust at the end of the trust term (after the donor has received all the annuity payments to which he or she is entitled). Only this actuarially, computed remainder is subjected to gift tax. In most cases, the GRAT is structured so the actuarial value of the annuity payments is approximately equal to the value of all the property initially contributed to the trust. In such a GRAT, the projected trust remainder is nearly zero. When a GRAT is structured this way, it is referred to as a "zeroed-out" GRAT, and little or no gift tax is due.

It is important to note that if the donor dies during the term of the GRAT, the GRAT will be subject to estate taxes, which results in the forfeiture of any potential tax savings generated using this technique. As a result, this option is not a good choice for business owners in poor health. However, assuming a happier scenario in which the business owner survives the GRAT term and the property in the trust appreciates at a rate greater than that reflected in the IRS assumptions (which, in recent years, often have been in the 6 to 8 percent range), the excess appreciation passes to the beneficiaries or remainder-men, free of both gift and estate taxes.

As a result, a GRAT often is used by business owners who are considering selling their business in the next three to five years. By using this technique, they can contribute their stock to a GRAT at a depressed value and pass it to their children, free of gift and estate taxes. The children can later sell the business. When they sell, the business will have a higher cost basis than that of their mother or father, and the children will pay substantially lower capital gains taxes.

A GRAT offers these donors an opportunity to allow children or other beneficiaries to receive a financial legacy from the business owner while substantially reducing the total taxes due. At the same time, it allows the business owner to receive a generous annuity stream during the term of the GRAT.

In the case of Mack and Sarah , the GRAT was set up before the transaction closed, and it served as a powerful, tax minimization tool. By using a GRAT, the couple's exit planning team valued the shares contributed to the GRAT using a significant discount. This meant, for tax purposes, the clients' privately held shares could be valued at less than their potential future market value. This was due to the fact that at the time the trust was established, the shares represented a minority interest and lacked liquidity and marketability. The couple's advisors calculated IRS would allow a 30 percent discount from the fair market value for these attributes.

Roughly 50 percent of Mack and Sarah's shares in their company were contributed to this GRAT. When the company was sold, the buyer actually purchased shares from Mack, Sarah, and the GRAT. The GRAT was set up to last 4 years and would generate payments in each of those 4 years. In a second step, the proceeds Mack and Sarah received were used to fund the CRT. This allowed them to recognize a significant charitable deduction that was used to offset some of the capital gains that they realized.

In addition to the CRT and GRAT discussed above, there are other estate planning strategies that every professional involved in exit planning should know about.

## Generation-Skipping Tax

The estate tax is imposed on each generation at death. For example, before 1986, if a parent left his estate to his child and the child subsequently left the same estate to his child, the estate would be subject to the estate tax twice—at the time of the parent's death and again at the time of the child's death. As a result, many individuals figured out they could "skip" at least one generation of estate tax by transferring wealth directly to their grandchildren. By leaving the estate directly to a grandchild, the estate would be subject to tax only once.

Of course, the IRS was not going to stand for this. As a result, in 1986, Congress enacted the generation-skipping transfer tax that taxes direct generational "skips" (described above) at the highest marginal estate tax rate. Under this legislation, each individual may transfer up to the generation-skipping exemption amount during his or her lifetime to individuals two or more generations removed without incurring the generation-skipping tax. Any amount over the exemption amount is subject to the generation-skipping tax.

The existence of the generation-skipping tax (even with the exemption) presents potential challenges that must be accounted for. Some common trouble spots include:

1. Leaving property outright to a grandchild or great grandchild while the lineal ancestor is still living

2. Leaving some property in trust to a child and the remainder—which is not included in the child's estate—to a grandchild

3. Leaving property in trust, with the trustee paying out amounts to a grandchild while the child is still living

Although a detailed discussion of the generation-skipping tax is beyond the scope of this book, there are techniques that address these complications. In addition, there are planning vehicles such as dynasty trusts can be used to help preserve family wealth far into the future. A dynasty trust is a special trust that holds family assets for perpetuity. The trust allows family members to use those assets and pay income to family members from those assets over many subsequent generations. However, because the assets are perpetually held in trust and never inherited, no estate tax will be levied. Over a period of generations, the value of the trust assets will grow at a rate far in excess of the value of the assets, had they been subjected to transfer taxes from one generation to the next.

**Qualified Terminable Interest Property (QTIP).** Generally, property transferred from one spouse to another upon death is not subject to estate tax because of the "marital deduction." An unlimited deduction is allowed for a surviving spouse when property is transferred from the first to die, but is subject to the estate tax when the surviving spouse dies. There are qualifications that must be met in order to get the marital deduction. One of the more significant qualifications is that taxpayers get the unlimited marital deduction only for property that passes to the surviving spouse without a "terminable interest." A terminable interest occurs when the property passes to the surviving spouse with an ownership interest that terminates during the surviving spouse's lifetime.

However, there is an exception to the terminable interest rule. This exception is known as Qualified Terminable Interest Property (QTIP). QTIP property must meet the following requirements:

4. The property, say a house, must pass from the decedent.
5. The surviving spouse must have a qualifying income interest for his or her entire lifetime, payable at least annually. In the case of a house, it might be the ability to live there rent free for life.
6. No person may have the power to appoint any part of the property to anyone other than the surviving spouse during his or her lifetime. In the case of a house, no one could sell or otherwise force the surviving spouse to move out.

So when a QTIP election is made for an asset, the surviving spouse gets the income for his or her remaining lifetime, the surviving spouse includes the asset in his or her estate upon death, and a separate designate inherits the asset upon the death of the surviving spouse. If properly structured, there is no estate tax due on QTIP property when the first spouse dies, even though the surviving spouse may have inherited a terminable interest.

QTIPs often are used in cases where there is a second marriage and the family wants to preserve assets for the children from the initial marriage while providing income for the second surviving spouse, and avoiding the payment of estate tax when the first of the couple dies. This strategy is typically sound. However, if the second spouse is very young (so young as to be the same age as the children from the initial marriage), this strategy may not be advisable.

Remember that QTIP property must provide the income interest in the QTIP asset for the spouse's full lifetime before the transfer to the ultimate recipients. In this case, the younger, second spouse may live as long as or longer than the children from the initial marriage. And the children from the initial marriage will not get their inheritance until the younger spouse dies. In this case, the children from the initial marriage may never actually receive any inheritance at all.

QTIPs also are useful in situations where the surviving spouse may not be able to manage or control spending, or lacks financial acumen. In anticipation of those circumstances, the first to die can provide for the comfort and continued income of the surviving spouse while simultaneously protecting the *corpus* of the individual's estate (that is, dictating the ultimate inheritor[s] of the assets). No taxes are incurred upon the first spouse's death. QTIP trusts also are used by business owners to transfer ownership to the next generation while saving estate taxes.

Here is a brief scenario to illustrate the technique. The founder of a business makes lifetime gifts of minority interests in the business to his children. Let us assume they received 20 percent of the company's shares (10 percent for each child). The taxable value of these minority interests is discounted because of the lack of control and marketability. The owner retains 80 percent ownership and sets up his will to bequeath half of his ownership (40 percent) to his spouse and the other half (40 percent) to a QTIP trust. The children are the ultimate beneficiaries of the shares held in the QTIP trust and will inherit the remaining shares upon the death of the surviving spouse.

Because of the unlimited marital deduction, no estate tax is due when the owner dies. When the surviving spouse dies, the stock in the QTIP trust (40 percent) plus the stock bequeathed outright (another 40 percent), or a total of 80 percent pass to the children. Minority ownership discounts may be applied separately to the surviving spouse's 40 percent interest and the 40 percent QTIP interest, even though the combined ownership interest being passed to the children does not represent a minority interest (80 percent). The logic for separating the two 40 percent blocks for purposes of discounting the value is that the shares in the QTIP trust are not under the control of the surviving spouse; that is, the surviving spouse could not sell the QTIP shares. Therefore, the blocks of shares are considered to be two entirely, separate ownership interests—each entitled to a minority discount.

**Charitable Deduction for Estate Tax.** As with the marital deduction, individuals may transfer assets to qualified charitable organizations without incurring estate or gift taxes. This estate and gift tax exemption for charitable giving specifically exists in the tax code. Furthermore, qualified charitable gifts are deductible (subject to certain limitations) on the donor's individual income tax return. There are numerous, tax-friendly techniques for charitable gift giving using split interest gifts (such as charitable lead trusts, charitable remainder trusts, charitable remainder unitrusts, and pooled-income funds), which when properly structured, result in full benefits received by the charity and tax savings to the donor and trust beneficiaries.

Several relatively, common estate-tax planning techniques have been covered above. There are many more elaborate and powerful techniques to consider as well. Yet, it is important to remember there are many different disciplines on the exit planning platform that must interact in order to save estate and income taxes, preserve family wealth, protect shareholders and employees, encourage business success, and promote family harmony.

## Summary

Estate planning and exit planning are often confused as being one and the same. This is unfortunate. As this chapter demonstrates, estate planning is a very valuable subset of an overall exit plan, but estate planning, by itself, only addresses one small part of the entire exit planning process. When estate planning is done as part of the overall exit planning process, both the estate plan and the exit plan are more effective.

# Chapter 17

# The Critical Role of the Attorney

As covered in Chapter 10, "Assembling a Multidisciplinary Team," a good attorney is one of the critical members of the Exit Planning Advisory Team. Unfortunately, most business owners who are thinking of selling their businesses consult with their attorneys only after they have a signed offer on the table. That does not give the attorney enough time to help the owner address all the estate planning, business structuring, due diligence tax issues, asset protection, and personal liability issues involved in exiting a company. When attorneys raise these issues with clients in the middle of a transaction, clients often accuse them of being "deal killers" rather than "deal makers." This is unfair. These attorneys are just trying to represent and protect their clients.

The best way to ensure that attorneys are deal makers rather than deal killers is to involve them early in the process so they have time to adequately discuss and address all the estate planning, tax, personal liability, asset protection, due diligence, and transactional issues in a constructive manner.

The purpose of this chapter is to outline a few issues the legal advisor of the exit planning team needs to address. We hope this chapter gives readers a sense of the importance and wide scope of these issues.

## Shareholder or Buy-Sell Agreements

The formulation of a good exit plan would not be complete without careful consideration of either existing shareholder agreements or buy-sell agreements, or the need for new ones. A shareholder agreement, or buy-sell agreement, is a contract between shareholders or other stakeholders (family members or key employees) that outlines a procedure for buying an ownership interest in a closely-held business upon the occurrence of a specific event (for example, retirement, death, disability, divorce, termination of employment). A well-designed, buy-sell agreement can help ensure there is a predetermined buyer for the business owner's interest and that his interest in the company does not end up being sold to someone other than the predetermined buyer. A good buy-sell agreement helps business owners address the following concerns:

### What happens to the business if the owner dies?

If the estate lacks liquidity, the owner's heirs may have to sell the owner's interest in the company to pay estate taxes and administration costs. The shareholder agreement may provide a blueprint for the mechanics of the buyout from the decedent's estate which can help minimize the confusion that often results from the departure of a shareholder.

### What happens if the business owner's partner dies?

What happens to the partner's interest in the company? Will the deceased partner leave it to someone in his immediate family? Will that person want to receive a salary or actively participate in the business? Or, perhaps the deceased partner's heirs will choose to sell the interest to someone else, even a competitor, in order to pay estate taxes or get fast cash.

### What happens to the business if the owner becomes permanently disabled?

How will the business keep key employees? Should the family sell to a third party, to another shareholder, or to a key employee? What would the disabled partner have wanted?

### Will there be a market for the owner's interest in the business?

Some owners are worried there may not be a third party who is willing to buy an interest in the business. How will the owner eventually receive value for his or her shares?

### What is the value of the owner's interest?

What is a fair buy-out price? This is a key issue to resolve, and having a previously agreed to formula, results in great peace of mind. Sometimes, the buy-sell agreement refers to a valuation formula upon which the shareholders previously agreed. The formula may be a multiple of the company book value, cash flows, or both. Some agreements require an appraisal by a qualified professional to determine the fair price of the stock. Other agreements allow the selling shareholder to first offer shares on the open market to third-party investors or strategic purchasers, while allowing the remaining shareholders the right to match the third-party offer before any outside sale can take place.

There is a lot of flexibility in defining the buyout price. The key is to address the valuation issue specifically in the agreement. If the buyout price is not clearly defined and understood by the owners, the result may be a long, painful, and expensive legal dispute over a fair price.

There is one catch. You cannot set the valuation too low. The IRS will not allow the valuation formula in a buy-sell agreement to be used as a mechanism to transfer ownership in a closely-held business from one generation to the next at discounted prices, in order to avoid or reduce estate and gift taxes. The IRS wants to ensure the value is comparable to similar value that would be used by any reasonable person in an arm's-length transaction.

It also is important to note that the value agreed to in a buy-sell agreement may not necessarily be used to determine the value of a business interest for estate tax purposes, even though it may be enforceable between the buyer and seller. Therefore, keep in mind that the estate tax valuation may be different from the actual price paid for the interest.

## How will the agreement be funded?

There are two common alternatives to provide the liquidity to implement the buy-sell agreement provisions: (1) establish a sinking fund or (2) purchase insurance.

Usually, funding a buy-sell agreement using insurance is the most practical alternative. Sinking funds can take years to fully fund in an amount equal to the buyout price. As a result, if the owner suddenly dies before the sinking fund is fully funded, there is not enough cash to fund the buyout.

Furthermore, retaining large amounts of cash in a regular "C" corporation for buyout purposes may cause the IRS to tax these accumulated earnings. C corporations are allowed to retain only "reasonable" amounts of cash within the business. If a C corporation has a large sinking fund, the IRS may assert that the corporation is not distributing enough dividends to its shareholders in order to delay the individual ordinary income tax that would be due from the shareholders receiving dividend payments. When this is the case, IRS assesses a special penalty tax on the excess cash retained in the business.

For these reasons, life and disability insurance policies are often purchased on each shareholder in order to provide cash for the buyout. When the shareholder dies or becomes disabled, the policy benefit is used to buy the stock from the selling shareholder or the estate.

Generally speaking, the insurance premium payments are not deductible and the insurance proceeds are not taxable. However, insurance proceeds received by a "C" corporation are potentially subject to the alternative minimum tax and may result in additional corporate income tax. When funding a buyout resulting from a triggering event, other than death or disability, the required cash must come from a shareholder's personal assets, company cash reserves, or loan proceeds. Some buyout agreements allow for the negotiation of a seller-financed, installment note in exchange for withdrawing the owner's shares. There are many options, so the best advice we can give is to get an insurance professional involved on the exit planning team.

## Types of Buy-Sell Agreements

The most common types of buy-sell agreements are the following:

   7.  Cross-purchase

8. Redemption

9. Hybrid cross-purchase/redemption

**Cross-Purchase Agreement.** In a cross-purchase agreement, the remaining stakeholders purchase the shares from the selling shareholder or the shareholder's estate. Accordingly, a cross-purchase agreement may require the shareholder maintain liquidity in amounts sufficient to buy out the other shareholders at any time.

An advantage of a cross-purchase agreement is the surviving owners receive a "step up" in tax basis to the extent of the purchase price paid for the stock. When the acquiring shareholders eventually sell their shares, the capital gain will be less. However, if the acquiring shareholder plans to retain the stock until death, this advantage may not be realized because the heirs who inherit the stock will get the "inheritance step-up" in basis.

A disadvantage of a cross-purchase agreement is complexity and risk. A cross-purchase agreement is only as good as the ability of the parties to satisfy its terms. The selling shareholder must trust that the applicable partners will be able to pay cash for the shares. If they have not adequately reserved cash or kept up with the insurance premiums, the seller may not be able to cash out according to the terms of the agreement. The greater the number of owners in a closely-held business, the more difficult a cross-purchase agreement is to administer. Although it may be possible to use a partnership to hold and maintain the cross-purchase buyout insurance, many businesses with more than a handful of owners find a cross-purchase agreement to be overly risky and cumbersome.

**Redemption Agreement.** With a redemption agreement, the company, not the individual stakeholders, buys the stock of the company from the selling shareholder. In this case, it is the company that must have the needed liquidity. An advantage of the redemption approach is control, liquidity, and administrative ease. With a redemption agreement, the shareholders do not have to depend on each other individually to maintain cash reserves or insurance policies on each other's lives. The company has this responsibility. It is much easier for the board of directors to monitor and control adequate buy-out cash reserves and/or insurance on the company's records, than it is for them to monitor the financial records of each individual shareholder. Remember that with a cross-purchase agreement, the ability to sell shares for a stated price is only as good as the personal, financial condition of the other shareholders. For some owners, the risk that the partners will not be able to come up with the needed cash on a buyout date makes a redemption agreement preferable.

A disadvantage of the redemption approach is that when the company redeems the selling owner's stock, the other stakeholders do not receive any "step up" in the tax basis of their stock, because the company, not the shareholders, bought the shares. Thus, the repurchased stock is simply retained in the corporation as treasury stock and each individual shareholder's stock basis remains unchanged although the ownership percentages increase proportionately.

**Hybrid Cross-Purchase/Redemption Agreement.** The hybrid approach to a buy-sell agreement provides the greatest flexibility. This approach is set up so the shareholders may choose to cross-purchase or execute a corporate redemption, whichever makes the most sense at the time. It can be referred to as a "wait-and-see" approach. A hybrid agreement generally allows the corporation to have the first option to purchase any or all of a shareholder's shares upon a triggering event. If the corporation elects not to redeem the shares, the existing shareholders have a secondary option to purchase any or all remaining stock.

Regardless of the business owner's final objectives, having a well-defined buy-sell agreement in place just makes common sense. But, buy-sell agreements are complicated and clients need the input of a seasoned attorney to help them draft an agreement that works.

# Pre-transaction Due Diligence

Pre-transaction due diligence is another area that business owners overlook. However, anyone who has been involved in helping business owners exit their companies knows there is no such thing as being too prepared.

What is pre-transaction due diligence? *Webster's Dictionary* defines "due diligence" as:

1. An investigation or audit of a potential investment. Due diligence serves to confirm all material facts in regards to a transfer of ownership.
2. The care a reasonable person should take before entering into an agreement or transaction with another party.
3. A review of all financial records plus anything else deemed material to a transfer of ownership.
4. A way of preventing unnecessary harm to either party, or the entity involved, in a transaction.

Pre-transaction due diligence is the proactive preparation of a business for a transfer of ownership and a crucial step in maximizing the value of the company prior to exit. The goal of a pre-transaction due diligence review is to identify and fix any perceived problems or issues so they do not detract from the value of the company or affect the success of a future transaction.

Pre-transaction due diligence involves doing the same kind of investigation of the company that a buyer, banker, or investor would do just prior to closing. It involves two types of analysis: a financial audit and a legal audit.

The financial audit involves a third-party review of the quality and depth of the financial information that will be presented to a potential buyer, banker, or investor. The business owner must ensure that every line item on the balance sheet and income statement for the company and the backup information used to generate the statements is absolutely correct.

In addition to a pre-transaction financial due diligence, business owners need to conduct a top-to-bottom, legal due diligence to ensure that, among other things:

- All corporate housekeeping records have been kept correctly
- All employment practices are current
- There are no hidden or unknown liabilities
- There are no environmental issues
- All licenses, filings, and permits are up-to-date
- All legal contracts, including leases, are valid, binding, and up-to-date
- The company has good title to its tangible and intangible assets
- The company has adequately protected its intellectual property, including any technology, trademarks, or patents

Both the attorney and CPA should work together during the pre-transaction due diligence process to assemble a "due diligence chest." This filing cabinet should contain copies of all records and documents a buyer, banker, or investor will request when such persons come in to perform their due diligence. Having copies of these important documents in one easy-to-access location will greatly reduce the disruption that a buyer's, banker's, or investor's due diligence has on your client's business. It also demonstrates to buyers how well organized and efficient your client is. This reflects well on the business owner and can positively influence a buyer's perception of the client's company.

The point is for you to find potential problems and issues before the buyer, banker, or investor does. When a buyer identifies a problem during due diligence, it can have a huge impact on the value of a company, if not derail a situation completely. There is nothing worse for a business owner than having to admit there is an unknown skeleton in the closet, especially if the skeleton is spotted by the buyer. Even if the ultimate effect on the company's operations is minimal, the problem or issue can result in a loss of confidence on the part of the buyer, banker, or investor. It causes them to be suspicious of any additional information provided by the business owner. It also provides negative fodder for negotiations.

The same issues are just as important if the business owner is considering a generational transfer or a transfer to an existing management team. In both cases, the owner wants to hand over a business to the new owners in clean condition without any last-minute surprises. Last-minute surprises can undermine an otherwise positive experience for everyone.

The cost of doing a pre-transaction due diligence can vary widely depending on how well organized a company is and what kinds of problems are identified. That said, it may be one of the best investments a business owner can make, if the process identifies and fixes a problem that could have derailed a transaction. The net result of this process is the peace of mind that comes from knowing there will be no last-minute surprises for the client to impact the value of the company.

Consequently, we strongly recommend business owners begin the pre-transaction due diligence on their company as soon as they can. The pre-transaction due diligence can be conducted simultaneously with the investment banking process. But, retaining a good attorney and giving him or her sufficient time to do due diligence in advance reduces the likelihood that any surprises surface during the buyer's due diligence, and helps ensure the owner gets the price and terms he wants.

## Transaction Structure

A third, but no less crucial, role for the attorney involves helping the business owner and his other advisors determine the best structure for a transaction. This decision needs to be made early in the exit planning process because it affects the owner's tax strategy, estate plan, business valuation, and financial plan.

Transaction structure includes determining what will be sold. Will it be the business and the real estate or just the business? Will it be the company's assets or the company's stock? Will the owner provide any type of seller financing? All these decisions have far-reaching implications.

For example, deciding whether to sell a company's stock or assets can have significant tax and personal liability implications for the owner. Current tax law provides that when a C corporation sells assets, it must recognize a gain to the extent the sales price exceeds its basis in the assets sold. If a C corporation subsequently makes distributions to shareholders, there is a second tax. This two-tiered tax structure significantly increases the total tax cost of an asset sale by the corporation.

Generally speaking, the seller of a C corporation prefers to sell stock because the owner is taxed only once, at the personal level. In addition, a stock sale is simpler, mechanically, because it involves only a single asset. For employees, a sale of stock results in the continuation of employee benefit plans unless the plan is specifically terminated and plan assets are distributed to the participants.

Another reason most sellers dislike structuring a transaction as an asset sale is that sellers have to pay the Depreciation Recapture or Built-in Gains Tax.

A C corporation that later makes an S election is subject to a corporate-level tax if it sells appreciated assets during the first 10 years following its change to an S corporation (Internal Revenue Code 1373). The code defines the term "built-in gain" as the excess of the total value of the C corporation's assets on the day it became an S corporation over the tax basis of all such assets on that day (i.e., the gain).

The built-in, gain provision applies only to recognized gain. This corporate-level tax may be avoided by deferring the recognition of gain beyond the 10-year period. Deferral may be achieved, for example, by holding the property under a lease arrangement rather than transferring ownership.

You should note that the selling taxpayer must report depreciation recapture as income in the year of sale, regardless of the cash received in the transaction. So, for example, structuring a transaction as an installment sale will not defer the taxes due. As a result, if an installment sale is not carefully negotiated, the seller may have to pay more in taxes than he or she receives from an installment sale in the first year.

Although business sellers generally prefer stock sales, business buyers almost always prefer to purchase a company's assets. There are several reasons for this. First, the buyer can specifically identify assets it wants to acquire, and those assets receive a step-up in basis to reflect their fair market value. From a buyer's perspective, this is good because it increases the amount the buyer can depreciate, which in turn reduces the income on which the company must pay tax. Second, the buyer will not assume any contingent or unasserted liabilities of the selling corporation. This lowers the buyer's risk profile and increases the value of the company in the eyes of the buyer. Third, for tax reporting, the Internal Revenue Code permits buyers to use installment reporting for both asset sales and stock sales that do not involve publicly traded property.

As discussed above, buyers prefer asset purchases because they can avoid assuming any contingent liabilities that may come with the corporation. Which of a company's liabilities a buyer assumes is usually one of the most hotly negotiated aspects of a deal.

In a stock transaction, a buyer acquires all the assets and liabilities a company has, including any liabilities that exist but have not yet been asserted. These could involve unasserted tax liabilities, warranty claims, workers compensation claims, and other items. If the parties agree to a stock sale, negotiations usually include the seller providing the buyer with either partial or full indemnification against these liabilities. However, buyers realize enforcing an indemnification or the financial participation of the seller after the transaction is closed can be very difficult.

One potentially significant liability that may never disappear involves environmental issues. Generally speaking, any entity ever connected to a piece of real property, whether as an owner, a lessor, or a lessee, may be responsible for clean-up costs. It is virtually impossible to estimate the amount of this liability with any real accuracy. As a result, an environmental study performed by a reputable firm is absolutely imperative for both the seller and the buyer before entering into any sort of real estate contract for sale, acquisition, or lease.

Obtaining good legal advice early on to address these and many other issues is vitally important in the exit planning process.

## Summary

As previously mentioned, the discussion in this chapter is by no means a complete or exhaustive discussion of all legal issues involved in helping a business owner prepare an exit plan and successfully exit a business. We hope by discussing a few issues we impressed upon the reader the need to involve a legal advisor in the exit planning process as early as possible. More often than not, business owners do not talk with their attorneys about their exit plans until after a purchase offer has been signed. At that point, it is often too late for the attorney to truly add value. The message here is to involve a competent attorney in the exit planning process and make that person part of the "deal making" team.

# Chapter 18

# The CPA's Role in Maximizing Proceeds

In Chapter 10, "Assembling a Multidisciplinary Team," we discussed the importance of recruiting a good CPA to be part of the exit planning team. The following outlines a few of the ways in which a CPA can add tremendous value in the exit planning process and maximize value and proceeds.

## The Importance of Accurate Financial Statements

We learned in the Chapter 11, "Business Valuation," that a company's value is based usually on both objective and subjective factors. All these factors are intended to help a buyer or investor determine how risky the company is. It is important to understand that value is inversely related to risk. The less risky a company appears, the more a buyer will be willing to pay for it. The more risky, the less valuable a company will be.

One of the measures buyers use to gauge risk is to examine a company's historical financial performance. The financial reporting fiascos at Enron and WorldCom underscore the importance of preparing financial statements that are complete and accurate. Financial statements that stand up to close scrutiny are not important just for large, publicly traded companies. Even a private company, whose owner may not be planning to retire for several years, should have a financial reporting system that provides accurate management data and produces financial statements that can be trusted by future buyers. In order to do this, it is important to maintain complete records that give an accurate picture of the company's financial performance.

The more confidence a business owner can instill in a buyer or investor regarding a company's historical financial performance, the lower the buyer's perception of risk. This is an important step in maximizing the value of a company prior to the owner's exit.

As a result, it follows logically that having a company's financial statements prepared by an outside certified public accountant (CPA) gives the company's financial statements more credibility, and in turn, enhances the company's value.

There are three types of financial statements that a CPA can prepare:

**Compiled financial statements** are prepared by an outside certified public accountant and are based solely on the information a business owner provides.

These are frequently used in small businesses because they are the least expensive and easiest option. Although compiled financial statements are independently prepared, they do not offer the business owner or a buyer any assurance a company's financial statements are accurate or that they conform to "generally accepted accounting principals" (GAAP). For larger businesses with an experienced, in-house accounting staff, compiled financial statements may not offer much value over internal financials. In an exit planning context, compiled financial statements have little value over and above a company's internal financial statements.

**Reviewed financial statements** are subject to higher professional standards of review. The CPA makes inquiries into such matters as accounting principles, methods, and record-keeping practices. Reviewed financial statements provide a limited degree of assurance that a company's financial statements conform to GAAP because none of the information is verified with third parties. Reviewed statements often contain footnotes explaining the accounting treatment of certain items as well. Reviewed financial statements offer the user a greater degree of confidence in the accuracy of the data, and hence, have some value in the exit plan context.

**Audited financial statements** are prepared in accordance with generally accepted auditing principles (GAAP) and provide assurance to the public that the audit has been conducted in a professional manner. The CPA confirms certain information in the client's records with third parties, for example, accounts receivable. At the end of the audit process, the CPA, exercising professional judgment and drawing upon his or her knowledge of the business, reaches a conclusion about the financial statements. This is the "opinion" expressed in the auditor's report. Audited financial statements provide the greatest degree of assurance to the reader, but also are the most costly due to the extensive amount of work performed and the fact that the auditor is taking on risk in certifying them.

So what kind of financial statement is right? That really depends on who needs to see the company's financials. Buyers, investors, and banks or other third parties may require reviewed or audited financial statements. As a result, owners who intend to exit within the next three to five years should seriously consider the value of audited statements because this simple step can reduce risk in the eyes of buyers and increase the value of a company.

## Tax Strategies

In addition to helping maximize the value of the company by preparing a sound financial record, a good CPA can advise business owners on creative means to minimize both ordinary income and capital gains taxes. In many instances, this advice is rendered by a tax specialist rather than the auditor. The capital gains tax, along with the inheritance tax, is often referred to as a "voluntary" tax. Why? Because business owners control whether or not to pay this tax. With careful planning it is possible, and legal, to reduce, defer, or in some cases eliminate these taxes.

Let us look at a few basic ways business owners can do this.

## IRS Allocations Rules

When a business owner sells his or her business, the owner is really selling a collection of assets, some tangible (such as real estate, machinery, inventory) and some intangible (such as goodwill, accounts receivable, a trade name). If the transaction is structured as an asset sale, the purchase price must be allocated among the assets that are being sold. According to IRS rules, the buyer and seller must use the same allocation, so the allocation should be negotiated and included as part of the purchase and sale agreement. Both the buyer and seller are required to report the allocation they used to the IRS.

As you can imagine, the IRS has come up with some rules for making allocations of the purchase price. Generally speaking, the IRS requires each tangible asset be valued at its fair market value (FMV). The total FMV of all assets in each class are added up and subtracted from the total price paid before moving on to the next asset class. Asset classes are prioritized in the following order: (1) cash; (2) CDs, government securities, readily marketable securities, and foreign currency; (3) all other assets except intangible assets (see definition below); and (4) intangible assets such as goodwill.

This means intangible assets such as goodwill are assigned the "residual value," if there is any. However, remember that fair market value is in the mind of the appraiser. There is still some latitude in allocating the purchase price among the various assets provided the allocation is reasonable and the buyer agrees to it. The odds are even better if the allocation is supported by a third-party appraisal.

Given that minimizing taxes is often a big goal for buyer and sellers, allocation of purchase price is often a big issue. To reduce taxes, the seller wants as much money as possible allocated to assets on which the gain is treated as capital gains, rather than to assets on which gain is ordinary income. The reason is that the tax rate on long-term capital gains is limited to 15 percent for sales and exchanges beginning May 6, 2003 through 2010, while the tax rate on ordinary income can be as high as 35 percent. Most small business owners who successfully sell their companies are already in a high tax bracket, so the rate differential is very important.

The buyer, on the other hand, typically wants as much money as possible allocated to assets that are deductible from current income, such as a consulting agreement, or to assets that can be depreciated quickly under IRS rules. This improves the cash flow of the business by reducing its tax bill in the first few years after the purchase.

## Sale of Stock vs. Sale of Assets

As discussed earlier in Chapter 17, "The Critical Role of the Attorney," if your client's business is a corporation, the owner has a choice to either sell the owner's stock in the corporation or have the corporation sell its assets to the buyer, leaving the empty corporate "shell" with your client.

A good CPA is important to help quantify the impact of a stock sale versus an asset sale. Talking in principle about the pros and cons of one approach or another is good up to a point, but when a decision needs to be made, it helps to have real numbers to work with.

For example, one point to consider when thinking about the two options is that the seller's tax bill from an asset sale is usually larger than the savings the buyer receives from such a sale. On the other hand, a stock sale usually results in the lowest total tax paid to the IRS and the most money left in the hands of both parties. Theoretically at least, a client's exit planning advisors should take advantage of a stock sale by adjusting the client's sales price to reflect the future tax burden to the buyer. Also, in a sale of stock the IRS does permit the buyer to elect to have the transaction treated as a purchase of assets (that is, the buyer can get a step-up in basis for the assets), if the buyer pays tax on the difference between each asset's current basis and its fair market value in the year of the transfer. Having an experienced CPA on the team helps assign real world numbers to these concepts and put them in context.

## Delaying the Second Tax

As explained in Chapter 17, "The Critical Role of the Attorney," if the seller owns a C corporation and sells assets, the transaction is normally taxed twice—once when the corporation sells the assets and again when the corporation distributes the proceeds. Because the company effectively has no assets other than cash, the corporation is often liquidated. However, sometimes this second tax at the shareholder level can be deferred, if the corporate "shell" is maintained rather than liquidated. In a family-owned corporation, the shell can become a holding company for family investments. For example, the proceeds of the sale are held by the corporation and invested in publicly traded securities, real estate, or another business. As you can imagine, the IRS generally does not like it when people find ways to avoid or defer paying taxes, so, in addition to the regular corporate income tax, the "shell" may have to pay personal holding company tax to the tune of 15 percent. However, a business owner can generally avoid this result, if the shell corporation pays out all its after-tax income as dividends. Again, a good CPA is usually the best resource with whom to discuss this issue.

### Electing S Corporation Status

With an S corporation, there is usually just one tax to shareholders rather than the two levels of tax in a C corporation. If a client is contemplating the sale of his or her business several years down the road, you may want to consider advising the client to switch to an S corporation now. By doing so, the client can usually eliminate the double taxation on any appreciation after the date of the switch. It is important to get a good CPA involved, if this route is being considered. Keep in mind, the Built-in Gains Tax must be paid on any appreciation in value, over and above the value set at the time of S corporation election. This applies if the company is sold during the first 10 years of S status. As a result, it is important to have an appraisal done at the time of the S-Corp conversion.

**Tax-deferred Reorganization.** One exit strategy available to a business owner is a merger with another company. If a business owner does not want to create immediate liquidity for himself or his family, he or she may decide to merge with another business through a tax-deferred reorganization, and avoid significant current tax effects. There are a number of ways to restructure two separate organizations into one entity. According to the IRS, tax-deferred reorganizations must have continuity of ownership and continuity of the business. This continuity exists, if at least half of the equity in the target company is acquired in exchange for stock of the acquiring company. The down side is this does not result in a liquidity event for the seller, but it may help the owner accomplish other goals. Again, the advice of a good CPA and attorney is important for anyone considering this exit strategy.

## Summary

The role of the CPA in the exit planning process constitutes more than simply answering questions about historic financial statements. A business owner's CPA is an important part of the exit planning team. As covered in this chapter, CPAs are instrumental in preparing and presenting accurate financial statements that present the company in the best possible light, determining the overall tax impact of a transaction or structure, and designing an effective way to minimize, defer, or eliminate the total taxes due at closing. CPAs need to be involved early in the process in order to help business owners take advantage of the tax saving structures available. Unfortunately, as time passes, so do a business owner's tax options.

# Chapter 19

# The Important Role of Insurance

Life insurance is a basic tool to manage the risk of loss, and can effectively provide income replacement for a family or business upon the death of a business owner or key employee. For closely-held business owners, proceeds from life insurance policies may be used to fund the transfer of the business from one generation to the next.

Life insurance proceeds also may be used to pay estate taxes. From an income tax standpoint, assets in a life insurance policy: (1) can enjoy tax-free build-up; (2) provide for tax-free withdrawals in certain circumstances; and (3) in the case of death benefits, are generally not subject to income tax.

## The Insurance Review

A business owner's exit-planning team of consultants should include at least one individual who concentrates exclusively on independent insurance planning. This professional works with the business owner to understand the owner's current insurance. This approach helps business owners avoid common insurance problems such as carrying too much insurance, paying premiums that are too high, or carrying outdated policies. Possible unaddressed insurance issues include:

- Children and grandchildren are born, married, and divorced, requiring insurance restructuring
- Beneficiary designations may not be current; beneficiaries on policies sometimes predecease donors
- Policy ownership may not be structured in the most tax-effective manner
- Ancillary documents may not be properly in place
- Currently owned insurance may be out-of-date, inappropriate, inadequate, or overly expensive

## Life Insurance Basics

For many people insurance is a mystery. Despite all of the different types of insurance coverage available, there are basically two types of insurance: term life and whole life. Other insurance offerings such as second-to-die policies are variations, combinations, or enhancements of these two basic types.

**Term Insurance.** Term insurance provides life insurance coverage for a limited period of time, or term. There are basically two elements to a simple term policy; the cost of the policy, usually stated in terms of the premium payments, and the death benefit. The premiums are payable during the term of the life insurance coverage. If the insured dies during the term, the policy pays the stated death benefit to the beneficiaries named in the policy. If the insured outlives the term of the policy, no death benefit is paid and there is no return of premiums.

There are three types of term insurance: annual renewable term, level term, and decreasing term. With annual renewable term insurance, the cost of the coverage goes up as the insured ages. Level term locks in the cost for a period of 5, 10, 15, or 20 years. At the end of each period, the cost can increase dramatically. The cost remains fixed at the new level until the end of the next period, when it increases again. Over the long run, level term is less expensive than annual renewable term because the insured has locked in a long-term relationship with the insurance carrier. Decreasing term is the opposite of annual renewable term. The annual cost of the insurance stays the same going into the future, but the death benefit is reduced.

The biggest advantage of term insurance is cost. Generally, term insurance is the least expensive way to provide relatively short-term coverage. Term insurance also can be canceled by simply not paying the premium. This is an advantage because sometimes changes in circumstances impact the usefulness of a life insurance policy. Because there is no cash value or return of premium to consider with term insurance, obsolete term policies may be allowed to simply lapse.

However, the biggest disadvantage of term insurance is also cost. Term insurance premiums increase with the age of the insured. Although term coverage provides comparatively, inexpensive coverage over a stated term, the cost to renew the policy after the original term expires may be very expensive. It is possible the insurer may decline to renew the term policy and the insured will be unable to find coverage at any cost.

A variation on basic term insurance is called "permanent term" insurance. These term policies are automatically renewable at the end of the original term. These are especially valuable to an insured who has developed health difficulties that would negatively impact the ability to obtain new insurance. However, insurance companies charge more for this feature and the premiums become much more costly as time passes. Some term policies have a provision allowing the insured to convert the term insurance into some form of whole life insurance. This feature serves as a sort of hedge against the chance medical complications will affect the insured's ability to find additional coverage at the end of the term policy.

**Whole Life.** Whole life insurance evolved as a solution to the difficulties relating to the renewal of term policies described above. Remember that after a term policy expires, the insured may find he or she is unable to find additional coverage at any price due to advanced age and medical conditions. Whole life or permanent insurance was designed to address this problem. With a whole life policy, the insured is guaranteed coverage for life and the premiums are structured in a fixed series of equal payments. As long as the premium payments are made, the insurer cannot cancel the policy. To accomplish this benefit, a portion of each payment is placed in a sort of savings account or sinking fund, which serves to reduce or amortize the financial obligation. Over the years, this sinking fund grows in value and is referred to as the policy's "cash value." The insurance company may use the sinking fund to make up any shortfall between the annual cost of the insurance coverage and the annual premium payment required.

With traditional whole life insurance, the sinking fund earns a guaranteed, conservative rate of return, typically between 4 and 8 percent. Although this amount grows tax-free the performance may be disappointing, if there is high inflation or if better returns are available in other investment vehicles.

Typically, owners of whole life policies can borrow against the cash value of their policies. These loans are very easy to obtain, the repayment terms are flexible, and the cash can be accessed quickly. However, the amount of the loan reduces the face amount of coverage under the policy, and the interest is not deductible for income tax purposes. A whole life policy can be cashed in with the insurance company at any time. After the owner receives the cash, the policy is simply canceled. The cancellation of a whole life insurance policy is typically a taxable event. Losses on the cancellation of a whole life policy are not typically deductible.

**Universal Life.** Universal life is a variation of traditional whole life insurance. The universal life concept came about to address consumer dissatisfaction with the conservative, guaranteed rates of return provided by the traditional whole life sinking fund. In the early and mid-1970s, people figured out they could cancel their whole life policies, buy cheaper term insurance, and invest the premium savings in other investment vehicles that significantly outperformed the guaranteed rates provided in the whole life sinking funds. In doing so, they created an individualized sinking fund paying a much higher return.

To counter this exodus from the traditional whole life insurance product, insurance companies developed universal life. Universal life policies work just as whole life policies do in that the insured's policy cannot be cancelled and a portion of each premium payment is placed in a sinking fund with a guaranteed minimum return. The difference with universal life is, if the sinking fund actually earns more on investments than the guaranteed minimum return, the insured gets the higher return. Because the sinking fund is earning a higher rate of return, the cost of the policy is less.

The downside, of course, is that the sinking fund investments may not perform as predicted.   If the insurance carrier fails to earn the assumed return on the sinking fund, the insured's premiums increase to make up the shortfall. In the worst case, insured individuals may not be able to make the higher premium payments and the policies will be canceled.

**Variable Life.** The third type of permanent insurance is called variable life. It was developed to try to improve on the shortcomings of both whole life and universal life policies. This type of policy allows the insured to invest the sinking fund into mutual funds or money market accounts. As long as the investments perform well, the insured does very well with this arrangement, outpacing the more conservative other whole life policies.   But if the insured invests entirely in a stock fund that experiences significant declines in value, the policy may be canceled for lack of funds. With variable life, there are no guarantees, so this type of policy is the riskiest.

**Term/Whole Life Mix.** A popular strategy is to purchase a mix of term insurance and whole life insurance. In this situation, the term policies provide the greatest death benefit for the least premium in the short run, whereas the whole life policies provide insurance coverage with a steady predictable premium that cannot be canceled in the long run. This mix allows a whole life product to be competitive in price with universal life prices by having dividends on the investment portion buy additional guaranteed insurance, called paid-up additions, as earned. If the investment rate of return is as predicted, the term/whole life mix will be able to sustain a targeted cash value at a lower premium than that of straight whole life.

## Insurance Strategies

Life insurance is almost always a consideration when developing an exit plan, because as new succession strategies are developed, old insurance needs may become obsolete while new insurance needs may arise. The following discussion of various insurance strategies illustrates some of the different roles life insurance plays in exit planning.

**Income Replacement.** The primary reason most people buy life insurance is to replace income streams from the deceased wage earner in the family. This need is sometimes overlooked by business owners in the middle of exit planning. This is because many owners plan to leave the business to their family members and assume the family members will continue to reap the same cash flow from the business after the owner's death. This reasoning does not consider the fact that the family may lose the income stream from the deceased's salary. If no one in the family is competent to take over the owner's duties that salary will need to go to an "outsider" brought in to perform those duties.

**Estate Tax Liquidity.** The second reason most people buy life insurance is to provide liquidity for estate planning purposes.  As discussed in the chapter on estate planning, life insurance is the most widely used financial tool for paying estate taxes upon death. Often, the estates of closely held business owners are made up of illiquid shares in the owner's business. This can cause a liquidity crunch when the estate tax comes due. Insurance on the life of the business owner can provide the liquidity needed to help pay some or all the estate taxes and thereby leave a larger estate for the owner's heirs.

**Key Person Insurance.** The third reason business owners buy life insurance is to protect the value of the business they built.  They realize a portion of the value of their business is based on the active involvement of one or more key people.  Key person insurance provides closely-held businesses with protection in case one of these key people dies. The business generally makes the premium payments and is the beneficiary of the policy. The premium payments are not deductible for income tax purposes but the death benefit is generally excluded from the taxable income of the business. We recommend key person insurance be maintained in appropriate amounts on the lives of all family members who are active in the business, as well as selected key, non-family executives.  The sudden and unexpected loss of a key executive in a closely held business can have a devastating effect on operations, not to mention an emotional impact on everyone in the company. Emotions may affect the swiftness of the response by company management in replacing the lost executive, especially in the case of a family business.

When the company owner dies unexpectedly, the impact is magnified. Loyal customers and suppliers may re-evaluate their relationship with the company. Special relationships and business deals based on personal relationships with the deceased owner may be retracted. Shareholders may become concerned about the security of their investment. Employees may worry about the security of their jobs. Bankers may become concerned about the ability of the company to sustain loan covenants without the leader of the business in place, and may be more cautious in dealing with the company going forward.  All these difficulties will affect business cash flow.

The proceeds from key person insurance can help the company through the transition process. Bank loans can be paid down. A stronger balance sheet (cash reserves and less debt) can help creditors, customers, shareholders, and employees feel more secure about the ability of the company to remain viable. If sales decline temporarily, the company will have excess cash reserves to continue through the rough times. Finally, the insurance proceeds can be used to help recruit and train the deceased executive's successor.

**Funding a Buy-Sell Agreement.** The fourth most common reason for business owners to buy life insurance is to fund a buy-sell agreement.  The death of a closely held business owner is often a triggering event in a company's buy-sell agreement that mandates the purchase of the deceased owner's shares by the company or the other shareholders. Life insurance is a very effective way to fund such a purchase.

Typically, buy-sell agreements are designed as either redemption agreements (the company buys the stock from the deceased shareholder) or cross-purchase agreements (the other shareholders buy the stock from the deceased shareholder). If the buy-sell calls for a redemption, the company should purchase adequate life insurance coverage on the lives of all shareholders. If one of the shareholders dies, the proceeds from the life insurance policy are used by the company to purchase the stock from the deceased shareholder's estate. If the buy-sell agreement calls for a cross-purchase, all shareholders should buy insurance policies on the lives of all other shareholders. In the event of the death of any one shareholder, the surviving shareholders can use the proceeds from the life insurance to buy the stock personally from the deceased shareholder's estate. (Buy-sell agreements are discussed in more detail in Chapter 16.)

**Compensation.** The last reason business owners use life insurance is to attract and retain key employees.  Life insurance can be a valuable benefit used to enhance employee compensation packages. The most common example of such a strategy is to set up a split-dollar insurance plan. In a split-dollar arrangement, the employer and employee split the cost of the life insurance premiums on the key employee's life. Upon the death of the employee, the company receives the cash value of the insurance policy while the employee's beneficiary receives the death benefit over and above the policy's cash value. To put it another way, when the employee dies, the company gets back the premiums contributed under the split-dollar arrangement and the employee's beneficiary gets the rest of the proceeds.

Viewed another way, a split dollar arrangement allows the employer to basically lend money interest free to the employee so he or she can purchase insurance. The overall cost of such an arrangement to the employer is relatively small because the employer eventually gets back the premium dollars contributed under the arrangement.

Life insurance also is commonly used to fund non-qualified deferred compensation plans for key employees. Although non-qualified deferred compensation plans do not have to be structured with life insurance, employees find it reassuring when their plan benefits are reinforced by the existence of a life insurance policy. Typically, the company buys an insurance policy on the life of the employee, naming the company as the beneficiary. If the employee dies before retirement age, the insurance death benefit is used by the company to pay the obligation under the non-qualified deferred compensation to the deceased employee's heirs. If the employee lives to retirement age and cashes out the balance in the non-qualified deferred compensation plan, the company can use the cash value in the policy to help fund the obligation to the employee under the plan.

## Disability Insurance

In addition to life insurance, disability coverage is an important but often overlooked consideration for most business owners.  Exit planning and contingency planning also should examine the possibility that the business owner might suffer a serious disability that impacts the future operations and success of the business.

When it comes to disability planning, business owners have more responsibility than regular employees. If a regular employee who owns disability insurance is injured or becomes ill and is unable to work, the employee's family receives payments from the insurance company to replace the paychecks until the disabled earner returns to work.

It is not as simple for business owners. They need disability insurance to provide income for their families in the event of disabling injury or sickness, just as everyone else does. But business owners also must plan for the survival of the business in the event of diminished capacity. No exit plan is complete without a contingency plan to ensure the survival of the business.  The owner's personal legacy and family's wealth may depend on it.  See Chapter 9, "The Contingency Plan," for additional information on disability insurance.

## Summary

Unfortunately, insurance is one of the much maligned things business owners only want once it is unobtainable.  Many people forget that insurance, properly used, is one of the most effective business planning tools available.  It can facilitate all types of financial and structural arrangements not otherwise available to small- or medium-sized businesses.  Insurance can be used as a cost effective way to fund compensation packages to retain key employees; it can be used to reduce ordinary income taxes, capital gains taxes, and estate taxes; and, it can dramatically increase the after-tax net proceeds available to a business owner's heirs.  As a result, an insurance professional can be a valuable, but often overlooked, member of a business owner's exit planning team.

# Chapter 20

# Investment Bankers, Business Brokers, and Maximizing Value

If your client's exit plan calls for maximizing the proceeds the owner realizes when he/she exits the business, you and your client need to understand how a well run sales process can help achieve that goal.

As discussed in Chapter 13, "Maximizing Value," there are three ways to maximize the net proceeds a business owner receives at closing;

(1) Maximize the fundamental or underlying value of the company

(2) Minimize the amount of taxes paid to Uncle Sam

(3) Maximizes the amount a buyer is willing to pay for the company

Each of these steps can have a significant impact on the net proceeds an owner receives at closing, but to "hit the ball out of the park," you need to do all three simultaneously.

In previous chapters we have discussed how to do steps one and two. In this chapter we explore how using the right business broker or investment banker and sale process can make a dramatic difference in the sales price of a company.

## Understanding the Playing Field

Buyers of middle market companies come in many shapes and sizes. In the following sections we examine the various types of potential buyers.

### The Individual Buyer

In our experience, qualified individual buyers are either typically high-net-worth individuals who have taken either early retirement from an executive position with a Fortune 500 company, or successful entrepreneurs who previously built and sold a business. In both cases, these individuals are looking for their next challenge.

Although these individuals may be financially qualified and have the skill set required to buy and run a middle market company, these buyers are often "shoppers." This means that, generally speaking, they do not know exactly what they want and they look at everything available to see whether something "fits." As a result, these buyers often look at acquisitions they could not possibly afford in the first place. Generally speaking, individual buyers purchase companies with market values of between $100,000 and $5 million. When a company's market value gets higher than $5 million, it requires an exceptional individual buyer to be able to consummate a transaction.

This is not to say that individuals are not good prospective purchasers. However, when dealing with individual buyers it is important that the investment banker collect as much information as possible about the buyer before revealing confidential information or investing too much time with the prospect. A basic information request to an individual buyer should include the buyer's background, financial resources, acquisition criteria, business/banking references, and search history.

### The Strategic or Industry Buyer

Strategic buyers are usually large companies looking to grow by acquiring smaller companies in the same industry or in related industries. Strategic buyers are usually following either a vertical growth strategy or a horizontal growth strategy. These strategies are illustrated in the modified Porter diagram shown in Figure 20-1 below.

A horizontal growth strategy might involve acquiring a competitor in a neighboring territory in order to expand its geographic footprint, increase its customer base, eliminate a competitor, lower transportation costs, and so on.

A vertical growth strategy might involve purchasing a supplier of a key product or component used in the acquirer's manufacturing process. This may make sense because it reduces costs, increases margins, guarantees supplies, and provides control over quality.

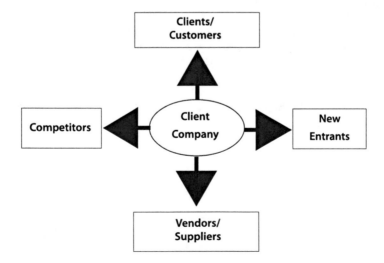

Figure 20-1: Modified Porter Analysis

Each of these strategies provides the acquirer with potential synergies and economies of scale. However, in order for the acquisition to make sense to the acquirer, the target company cannot be too big or too small. One rule of thumb is that the ideal acquirer is 3 to 4 times the size of the target. The acquirer must be large enough to be able to afford, and then, successfully integrate the target into the acquirer's existing operations. In addition, the acquirer wants the target to be large enough that its purchase will have a significant impact on the acquirer's performance. If the target is too small, it will not have the desired impact on the acquirer's financial performance. If it is too large, the deal may be too difficult to finance or successfully manage after the acquisition.

Generally speaking, industry buyers are interested in companies with revenues of at least $10 million. However, as the acquiring company gets larger, the size of the target company needs to get larger too. The challenge to investment bankers is to identify the best possible industry buyers using a blend of potential synergies and size.

## Financial Buyers

Financial buyers or private equity groups are professional buyers that are generally funded by institutional investors such as public and private pension funds, insurance companies, banks, and ultra-high-net-worth individuals. The federal government even funds some private equity groups called Small Business Investment Corporations (SBICs) through the Small Business Administration.

During the last decade there has been an incredible proliferation of professionally run private equity groups. Institutional investors have provided these groups with billions of dollars over the last few years. Each group has a mandate from its investors to put the money to work by investing in good companies that meet a preset acquisition profile. These private equity groups look to provide a return to their investors as an alternative to investments in the public markets. Private equity groups typically look for a 20 to 25 percent rate of return on the money they invest. Because private equity groups typically use bank debt to increase the rate of return on their investments, the price they are willing to pay for a company is usually a function of how much of the transaction can be financed with debt. Typically, these groups want to invest $1 or less in equity for every $2 in debt they can raise.

Generally speaking, a financial buyer is not in a position to pay as much for a company as a strategic buyer because the financial buyer does not stand to benefit from any synergies or economies of scale. However, as the private equity community matures, more and more private equity groups are making strategic add-on acquisitions for their existing portfolio companies. This makes them think like a quasi-strategic buyer. As a result, in many cases, private equity groups are actually paying as much or more than strategic buyers.

Private equity groups are generally segmented by the size of the investments or acquisitions they make. One subset of this community invests in companies with adjusted EBITDA of between $1 and $5 million. Another subset focuses on companies that have adjusted EBITDA of $5 million and up. The challenge to the investment banker is to target the right private equity groups based on size preference, industry preference, and potential synergies within existing portfolio companies.

## Investment Bankers vs. Business Brokers

Investment bankers and business brokers provide similar services but there are some important differences to consider when selecting which to work with. To use a golf analogy, business brokers and investment bankers are like two different golf clubs. One club is not better than the other, but each has its unique purpose. Half of the secret to success in golf is knowing which club to use and when.

So what are some of the difference between an investment banker and a business broker? One difference is the level of education, training, and experience of the individuals and the organizations involved. Most investment bankers have MBAs or other advanced business degrees. Some also may be former attorneys or CPAs. Business brokers do not usually have these qualifications, although increasingly, many do.

Another difference between business brokers and investment bankers is the size of the clients they represent. Business brokers, usually work with and are very good at selling smaller companies. These companies typically have annual revenues of $5 million or less and have earnings before interest and taxes of less than $500,000. Business brokers tend to present their sell-side clients to individual buyers and local entrepreneurs. While many business brokers could represent larger companies, they usually do not have the network of financial and institutional buyers that an investment banker does. Companies that generate less than $1 million in earnings before interest and taxes are generally not of interest to large, sophisticated corporate or institutional buyers. That said, business brokers are much better at selling small companies than investment bankers.

Investment bankers, on the other hand, concentrate on the acquisition or sale of larger companies. Some investment bankers focus on middle market companies, some on lower middle market companies, and others on large companies. Keep in mind that each investment banking firm has its own definition of "middle market." For large or "bulge bracket" investment banks, the middle market is defined as companies with revenues of under $1 billion. Many smaller boutique investment banking firms define middle market companies as meeting at least one of the following characteristics:

- Annual gross revenues of $5 million to $150 million
- Earnings before interest, taxes, depreciation and amortization (EBITDA) of $1,000,000 or more

The lower middle market is where I have spent the last 20 years of my career and where there is the greatest need for exit planning and professional investment banking services. Because investment bankers typically represent larger companies, their clients are of interest to sophisticated corporate and financial buyers. These buyers are usually located in a different state or even a different country than the seller. Many corporate and financial buyers look at hundreds of potential acquisitions each year. To get the attention of these buyers it helps if a client's company is marketed in a professional and well-thought-out manner.

A third difference between business brokers and investment bankers is the approach or process each professional uses to create a market for a client's company.  Business brokers typically use a real estate brokerage model.  They advertise companies for sale in local newspapers and on selected websites that play the same role as the multiple listing service does for residential real estate. As a result, they typically sell companies using a "negotiated sale" approach by dealing with buyers on a first come, first served basis.  They attempt to negotiate the best deal they can for their clients in sequential fashion.  If they are not able to get the buyer and seller together on price and terms, they move on to the next buyer.

Investment bankers, on the other hand, use a controlled auction process that proactively solicits a targeted group of hundreds (sometimes even thousands) of previously identified buyers.  Interested buyers are dealt with simultaneously rather than sequentially.  This often creates a competitive market that drives up the price buyers are willing to pay for a company.  We discuss this process in more detail later in this chapter.

As a result, when deciding whether to work with an investment banker or a business broker, consider the size of the company involved, the complexity of the transaction or exit planning engagement, and the characteristics of the ideal buyer(s).

## Specialist vs. Generalist

When deciding which investment banker to use, business owners often think that working with an industry specialist makes more sense than working with a generalist.  Industry specialists know many of the industry players on a personal basis and may already know your client's business.  This is usually a strong selling tool.

However, industry specialists also come with certain baggage most business owners and their advisors fail to consider.

An industry specialist's success is tied closely to relationships with industry players.  An industry specialist counts on these relationships for future sell-side, buy-side, and consulting engagements.  As a result, it becomes difficult to tell where the industry specialist's loyalties lie.  Can an industry specialist truly be objective about a buyer or the terms of the transaction they are negotiating, if the next day the advisor is working with the same buyer on another project?

One of the strengths of generalists is that they have no particular allegiance with any buyer or industry.  They can be truly objective when representing your client.  A generalist identifies buyers based on market research and networking, not on personal relationships.  A generalist negotiates transactions by creating a competitive market environment, not by working in a closed, old-boy network.

Specialists think in terms of their network of industry contacts. They tend to arrange transactions by calling a group of selected business acquaintances in the hope of negotiating a one-on-one deal.  This can be very powerful, if your client's company is in financial distress and needs to be sold quickly with little or no disclosure to your competitors, vendors, suppliers, or customers.  However, it is important to realize this is not the way to maximize the value of your client's company.

The best way to sell a profitable and thriving company is to create a controlled auction environment which solicits interest from buyers who are not only in the same industry, but related industries as well. A good investment banking process also should contact a broad universe of financial buyers.  In many cases, financial buyers prove to be the best for private, middle market companies.  In fact, due to current market conditions, financial buyers actually have been paying as much if not more than strategic buyers.

If you work with an industry specialist and if the competitive forces of the market place are not allowed to dictate negotiations, you and your clients will never know whether you have maximized the value of your client's company.  A good generalist should be able to present your client with <u>multiple offers</u> from industry buyers as well as financial buyers.  This strategy puts your client in control and enables you to choose the buyer and offer that best to meet your client's objectives.

Industry specialists often approach engagements with an industry template.  One of the goals of specialization is to become efficient at what you do.  To accomplish this, specialists tend to standardize as much as possible and try to fit clients into predefined industry templates or models.  A generalist approaches each engagement with a clean slate and customizes his or her approach for each client.

Let's face it.  Most businesses are unique.  Most companies do not fit into an industry "template."  A good generalist designs each client's marketing program from scratch based on that client's unique business, the client's personal objectives, and thorough market research.  A good generalist "thinks outside the box" about who the best strategic and synergistic buyers might be.

A business owner should be much more concerned about an investment banker's accessibility.  Developing an exit plan for a business owner and then selling the owner's company is a hands-on, time-intensive project requiring a great deal of communication, collaboration, and interaction.  As a result, working with an investment banker who is within a day's drive is often a much smarter move than working with an industry specialist half a continent away.

In addition, the process of selling a privately held business must be closely coordinated with the owner's legal advisors, personal financial planner, estate planner, insurance advisor, and tax planner in order to ensure the sale accomplishes the owner's personal objectives.  The investment banker should be expert at working with your other trusted advisors to ensure everyone is rowing in the same direction in order to accomplish your goals.

After the investment banker is selected and the exit planning process is complete, the owner must decide when to pull the trigger and implement or execute the most appropriate exit option.  At that point, the investment banker begins to prepare a formal offering package for the company.

## The Offering Package

The first step in selling a middle market company is to prepare a professional looking, offering package that presents the company to the marketplace.  Good investment bankers spend considerable time and effort preparing a thorough, well-thought-out, and well-researched offering package composed of a seller profile, a nondisclosure agreement, and a detailed offering memorandum.  The offering memorandum serves several purposes including the following:

- Tells the company's story
- Provides relevant facts buyers want to know, including:
  - Legal structure of company
  - Ownership
  - Key management
  - Organizational chart
  - Customer breakdown
  - Machinery
  - Marketing
  - Historical financial performance
- Potential growth opportunities
- Possible synergies or economies of scale
- Proposed deal structure

The seller profile is the first point of contact with potential buyers. As such, it summarizes the key selling points and describes the company without revealing any identifying information. A nondisclosure agreement is typically prepared in advance and presented to buyers along with the seller profile.

It is important to note that none of the materials in the offering package contain any information about an asking price for the company. The reason for this is explained in the next section.

## Maximizing Value and the Sales Process

When the offering package is complete, the business owner and his or her business broker/investment banker need to decide on the best marketing approach.

However, before discussing the different marketing processes and their pros and cons, it is important to realize that maximizing the value of a business often means it needs to be sold to an outside third party, not to an insider such as a child, key employee, or co-owner. Outside third parties typically have the cash and are able to pay a higher price for a business than insiders.

There are two basic methods investment bankers use to market and sell a private company to a third party:

- A negotiated sale
- A controlled auction

Each approach has its own strengths and weaknesses.

Maximizing the amount of cash your client receives upon the sale of his/her company is the business owner's equivalent of hitting a hole in one. To do this, you and your clients must know which club to use.

Business brokers and investment bankers typically use a negotiated sale approach to sell small companies. In a negotiated sale, the business broker or investment banker markets a company to a broad, untargeted audience often through newspaper ads and Internet postings. An asking price for the company is usually included in the preliminary information buyers receive.

When buyers show an interest, the business broker or investment banker talks with each buyer on a first come, first served basis, and attempts to negotiate the best deal for the client. If negotiations fall apart with one buyer, the business broker or investment banker continues to market the company in order to find the next buyer (assuming there is one). With this approach, the seller loses control over timing, price, and terms, and typically has little leverage in negotiations. This why experienced business brokers and investment bankers say "one buyer is no buyer."

With larger companies, business brokers and investment bankers prefer to use a controlled auction process, in which the broker or investment banker creates a competitive market for a company.  This is done by actively soliciting a large group of targeted qualified buyers simultaneously, and then letting them submit bids to set the price for the company.  At the beginning of this process, the business owner sets a floor or a reserve price at which he has told his broker or investment bankers he will not sell.  It is the broker or investment banker's job to generate enough excitement and interest in the company, stimulating offers above this amount.  As a result, companies in a controlled auction environment are brought to market without an asking price.  To understand how a controlled auction works, it is useful to use a real-world case study.

As the following case study demonstrates, a properly organized and orchestrated investment banking process can dramatically increase the amount of cash an owner receives.

## Case Study: The Controlled Auction Process

Tom, the owner of an industrial tool company, was approached by a national competitor. Preliminary negotiations led to an offer of $7 million for his company. Before he accepted this offer, he called us with the good news. This was more than Tom thought his company was worth and it met his financial goals.  Nonetheless, he wanted to make sure the valuation was right and that he wasn't leaving too much money on the table.  We urged him to allow us to orchestrate a controlled auction for him—a strategy Tom thought would scare off his suitor. The strategy scared the buyer all right—the buyer offered Tom another million dollars just to avoid the auction. Subsequently, Tom hired us and we sold his company (to another buyer) for $10 million. How?

First, Tom was clear about his objectives. He told us exactly what he needed financially, when he wanted to exit, how long he was willing to stay, in what capacity, and which companies he absolutely would not sell to. Using those criteria, we developed a buyer profile and began to identify potential buyers.  In the end, we identified 700 financial or private equity groups and 121 strategic or industry buyers.

Next, we developed an Offering Memorandum that described Tom's company in detail.  We then contact each buyer individually using a combination of letter, e-mail, and telephone calls. We provided each with a confidential profile that described our client in some detail, but did not reveal any information that would allow the buyers to identify the client. Once a buyer showed interest, they were asked to sign confidentiality agreements prior to receiving the Offering Memorandum.

After studying the Offering Memorandum, buyers were asked to submit qualifying bids that spelled out how much they thought the business was worth, the terms they were prepared to offer, and any issues they saw.

Out of the 821 initial buyers contacted, four submitted qualifying bids. Based on these "preliminary offers," Tom decided to meet with three buyers. These buyers were invited to have a lengthy, face-to-face meeting with Tom, and tour Tom's plant.

After these "buyer visits" were completed, two buyers submitted final offers for the company, knowing they were bidding against another buyer. Ultimately, Tom selected the buyer who met the exit objectives he spelled out in his exit plan. The closing was held and Tom left the table with $10 million, or $3 million more than he was originally offered by his "friendly" buyer.

The flow chart in Figure 20-2 illustrates the steps involved in the controlled auction process we use.

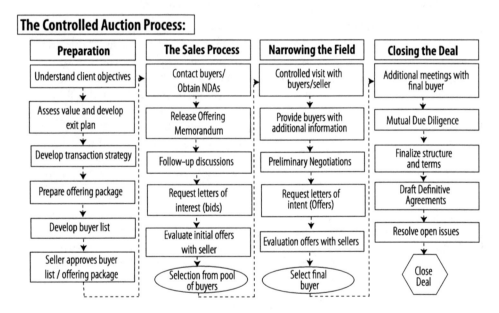

**The Controlled Auction Process:**

| Preparation | The Sales Process | Narrowing the Field | Closing the Deal |
|---|---|---|---|
| Understand client objectives | Contact buyers/ Obtain NDAs | Controlled visit with buyers/seller | Additional meetings with final buyer |
| Assess value and develop exit plan | Release Offering Memorandum | Provide buyers with additional information | Mutual Due Diligence |
| Develop transaction strategy | Follow-up discussions | Preliminary Negotiations | Finalize structure and terms |
| Prepare offering package | Request letters of interest (bids) | Request letters of intent (Offers) | Draft Definitive Agreements |
| Develop buyer list | Evaluate initial offers with seller | Evaluation offers with sellers | Resolve open issues |
| Seller approves buyer list / offering package | Selection from pool of buyers | Select final buyer | Close Deal |

Figure 20-2: The Controlled Auction Process

Keep in mind a controlled auction is not appropriate for all companies. This approach works best when both of the following are true:

1. The size of the company is in the mid-market (at least $5 million in revenues and at least $1,000,000 in adjusted earnings). This ensures that the company is large enough to attract the interest of multiple, sophisticated buyers.

2. The owner's transaction advisors have the skills and resources needed to conduct a successful controlled auction. The auction process is

complicated, time intensive, and time sensitive, so having the right experience and resources is important.

# The Controlled Auction Process in Detail

In the next few pages, we review each step of the controlled auction process presented in Figure 20-2.

## Preparation

**Understand client objectives.**  This step is covered in detail in Chapter 5.

**Assess value and develop exit plan.**  These steps are covered in Chapters 9 and 10.

**Develop transaction structure.**  This step is covered in detail in Chapters 16 and 17.

**Prepare offering package.**  As discussed above, an offering package consists of three key components.  The first is a carefully crafted Client Profile describing the client company without revealing its identity.  The second component is a detailed Offering Memorandum or Business Review.  The third component is the Nondisclosure Agreement (NDA).

**Develop buyer list.**  An investment banking buyer list for use in a controlled auction process should include both financial buyers and strategic buyers. Financial buyers include private equity groups, insurance companies, pension funds, angel investors, small business investment companies or SBICs, and so on.  Strategic buyers include competitors, customers, vendors, and companies in related industries.

Finding the right balance between financial buyers and strategic buyers is important, and is governed by factors including the nature of the client company, the size of its industry, the importance of confidentiality, and the market conditions.  The investment banker takes the lead in preparing the buyer list, but works closely with the business owner to ensure all financial and strategic parties the owner is aware of are included.

**Client approves buyer list/offering package.**  Protecting a client's privacy and confidentiality should be of paramount importance to any investment banker. The client should approve any written material prepared about his or her company.  In addition, the client should approve any buyer list prepared by the investment banker.  Buyers who are not approved by the client are not contacted.  After a buyer signs and returns an NDA, the client should be given one final opportunity to sign off on disclosure to the buyer.

## The Sales Process

**Contact buyers/Obtain NDAs**. All buyers on the buyer list should be contacted simultaneously. After buyers receive the Client Profile, they call or e-mail the investment banker to express preliminary interest in the company and ask additional questions. Before additional questions can be answered, the investment banker should request an NDA from the interested buyer.

**Release Offering Memorandum**. After the buyer has signed an NDA, the investment banker sends the buyer the Offering Memorandum.

**Follow-up discussions**. The investment banker then calls each buyer to ensure he or she received the Offering Memorandum and to answer any preliminary questions the buyer may have.

**Request Indications of Interest (bids)**. After 45 days, buyers are requested to submit a qualifying bid to the investment banker, if the buyer has an interest in continuing the dialogue with the investment banker and meeting with the business owner. Depending on the size and type of company being sold, it is not uncommon to have anywhere between 4 and 25 qualifying bids on the table.

**Evaluate initial offers with seller**. The investment banker then evaluates all the qualifying bids with the seller to help determine which of the interested parties the client should meet with and who should be put on "hold." Screening these buyers is important, because no one wants to waste time or money talking or working with unqualified buyers. Eliminating non-serious contenders also is a good way to protect confidentiality.

## Narrowing the Field

**Controlled visit with buyers/seller.** The investment banker then arranges meetings between the client and the buyers the client has decided to meet. The investment banker works with the owner to prepare for these meetings so the owner and the company are presented in the best possible light. It also is important for the seller to use these meetings to learn more about the buyers and to determine with whom he feels comfortable continuing a dialogue.

**Provide buyers with additional information.** The investment banker then follows up with each buyer after the meeting to provide additional information or to answer any additional questions.

**Preliminary negotiations.** The investment banker fields inquiries from buyers and begins to gently steer buyers toward the pricing and terms the client prefers. At the same time, the investment banker will communicate to the seller any areas of sensitivity or issues raised by buyers so everyone is negotiating with full knowledge of the points that are important to the other party.

**Request letters of intent (Offers).** After the buyers have adequate time to ask questions and review the information provided, the investment banker asks them to submit a final binding offer or letter of intent for the company.

**Evaluate offers with seller.** The investment banker then evaluates each of the offers or letters of intent with the seller to help him decide which offer is the best deal based on personal goals and objectives.

## Closing the Deal

**Additional meetings with final buyer.** After the seller selects the buyer with whom he wants to work, the investment banker arranges additional meetings so the two parties can get to know each other better and develop a personal rapport.

**Mutual Due Diligence.** The investment banker plays an active role in coordinating each party's due diligence on the other party. The investment banker becomes the conduit through which the parties exchange information during the due diligence phase. When site visits are required, the investment banker coordinates those to ensure they do not disrupt the seller's business. Because most middle market transactions involve some component of seller financing, it is important that the seller perform the same due diligence on the buyer as a bank or lender would perform. Although the investment banker typically does not perform the due diligence for the client, he or she plays an active role in determining what information should be requested, facilitating the exchange of information, and making sure that it gets done.

**Finalize structure and terms.** After the mutual due diligence is performed, the investment banker meets with both parties and the legal team to discuss any open issues and to finalize the terms of the letter of intent. These terms are documented usually in a revised or final letter of intent from the buyer.

**Draft Definitive Agreements.** The buyer's attorney then prepares the final purchase and sale agreement and sends it to the seller, his attorney, and the investment banker for review and comments. Additional documents may be prepared, as necessary, depending on whether it is a stock or asset sale and how the assets to be sold are owned.

**Resolve open issues.** After the seller and his attorneys have reviewed the purchase and sale documents, the investment banker works with both sides to negotiate any legal or business issues that popped up during the drafting phase.

**Close Deal.** An estimated 50 percent of letters of intent fall through, resulting in deals that do not close. It is therefore important the investment banker is proactive and keeps the buyer, seller, and their respective advisors on track. It also is important for all parties to anticipate issues and resolve them before they develop into a crisis.

### Investment Banking Fees

Most investment bankers charge two types of fees, a retainer or upfront fee, and a success fee paid upon the successful completion of the engagement.

**Retainer/Upfront Fee.** At the start of an engagement, an investment bank will require a retainer or up-front free from the client. Retainers are structured either as a monthly fee or a fixed fee paid at the beginning of the engagement.  The size and structure of the retainer is linked usually to the amount of initial work the investment banker must put into a project.  Some investment bankers credit the retainer against the success fee at closing; others do not.  This is typically a subject for negotiation.

**Commission/Success Fee**.  In addition to a retainer or up-front fee, most investment banks charge a commission or success fee.  This is where the vast majority of a good investment banker's income should come from.  A success fee is usually a percentage of the total transaction, much like the commission earned by a real estate broker.  However, unlike a real estate commission, most investment bankers work on what is called a Modified Lehman Formula.  Every investment bank has modified the original Lehman Formula slightly; but the basic concept is that the commission percentage gets smaller as the transaction gets larger. For example, one variation of the Lehman Formula looks like this:

**Modified Lehman Formula**

| |
|---|
| 6% of the first five million (10% x $1 - $5,000,000), plus |
| 4% of the next five million (8% x $5,000,001 - $10,000,000), plus |
| 1% on anything over $10 million (1% x balance over $10,000,001) |

Table 20-3  Modified Lehman Formula

For example, using this formula, the success fee on a $4 million deal would be $300,000 or 6 percent of the total transaction.  However, on a $10 million deal, the success fee would be $500,000 or 5 percent of the total transaction.  As you can see, the fee as a percentage of the total deal decreases as the translation gets larger.

Although these fees may seem high relative to the fees paid to the seller's attorneys and CPA, it is important to keep two things in mind.  First, as with any professional advisor, an investment banker is selling his time and expertise.  In our experience, it takes approximately 850 hours of an investment banker's professional time spread out over approximately 12 months to sell a middle market company successfully.  Given that most good investment bankers have MBAs, and either attorneys, CPAs, or CFAs by training, their time is valuable.  On top of that, keep in mind investment bankers, unlike a client's other advisors, do not get paid much unless the transaction is successful.  As a result, it is not uncommon for them to work with a client for 12 months or more, with the only guaranteed revenue coming from the small retainer received at the beginning of the engagement.

## Summary

Selling a business is simply too complicated and the stakes too high for any business owner to consider handling it on his or her own.  The additional after-tax proceeds an investment banker can deliver far outweigh the cost of using a professional advisor to sell the company.  If the company has revenues of $5 million or more, it is essential the business owner work with an investment banker who provides exit planning services rather than just transactional services. Most competent investment bankers can sell a company, but will the resulting transaction meet all the business owner's personal goals and objectives?  That's the question.  By working with an investment banker who is comfortable being part of a multi-disciplinary team, you ensure that your client, the business owner, is getting the best possible advice along the way and is able to accomplish his or her personal goals in the process.

# Chapter 21

# Surviving Due Diligence

After your client has signed the letter of intent (LOI) from a purchase, the transaction progresses from the marketing and negotiating phase to the due diligence phase. During this phase, the buyer is given access to much more detailed information about the company's operations, finances, customers, employees, and so on. This investigation is designed to confirm the information provided in the offering package and to help the buyer better understand the risks involved in a potential acquisition or investment.

Many business owners view the due diligence process as very intensive and exhausting, particularly if they are not aware of what to expect. It is often stressful as well because the business owner knows this is typically where deals fall apart—this is the final step before the buyer signs the binding purchase and sale agreement. A business owner, therefore, needs to be completely familiar with the due diligence process and prepared to fully cooperate with the buyer in order to ensure a smooth and successful transaction.

## What to Expect

At the outset of due diligence, the target's investment banker establishes a due diligence timeline spelling out all the information and steps required to lead to the signing of the definitive purchase and sale agreement. At the same time, the buyer provides the seller with a detailed list of information the seller wants, including a list of documents that need to be examined. This information and these documents typically fall into four broad categories:

1. **Strategic**

   Strategic due diligence focuses on the strategic fit between the two companies and whether that fit has the potential to deliver the kind of synergies and economies of scale the purchaser originally expected.

2. **Financial**

   Financial due diligence is intended to "prove up" the target's financial statements. In many cases, the seller's financial statements only have been compiled or reviewed, rather than audited. If that is the case, the buyer usually wants the financial statements audited by an outside accounting firm to make sure they are presented according to Generally Accepted Accounting Principles (GAAP).

**3. Sales, Operations, Marketing**

Due diligence in these areas is closely related to the three other areas of due diligence. Operational due diligence is intended to provide details on how a company does what it does, what makes it different, who makes things happen, and other internal "trade secrets." As a result, this information is generally considered to be very confidential because improper use of this information could have a significant adverse impact on the company's financial future should the deal fall through.

**4. Legal**

Legal due diligence is conducted to ensure there are no legal issues to create future problems for the buyer. This due diligence is intended to uncover any legal loose ends, potential liabilities, or potential claims that could be asserted against either the seller or the buyer. Legal due diligence also might include checking for any civil or criminal charges or convictions against the company, its owners, or its management team.

Figure 21-1 shows the breakdown for a comprehensive due diligence review. The overall due diligence process is usually divided into four basic components; strategic, financial, operational, and legal issues. Below each of these heading are examples of some of the issues reviewed.

| Strategic | Financial |
|---|---|
| • Strategy | • Accounting policies |
| • Culture | • Revenues |
| • Industry | • Expenses |
| • Synergies | • Forecasts |
| • Economies of Scale | • Capital structure |
| • Diversification | • Accounts receivable |
| • Tax benefits | • Assets |
| **Operational** | **Legal** |
| • Management | • Contracts |
| • Customers | • Leases |
| • Sourcing | • Environmental |
| • Inventory | • Title/Ownership |
| • R&D | • Litigation |
| • Employees | • Tax payments |
| • Processes | • Intellectual property |
| • Technology | • Regulations |
| | • Approvals |

Figure 21-1: Due Diligence Overview

## Preparing for Due Diligence

As we emphasize elsewhere in this book, the high-stakes nature of this final due diligence is all the more reason for a business owner to conduct a pre-transaction due diligence exercise.  By going through the pre-transaction due diligence process, the business owner is prepared and informed and greatly can facilitate the due diligence process for all parties.  This exercise can eliminate a great deal of the stress and anxiety that comes with the final due diligence process.

There are several issues business owners and their advisors should address in advance, in order to anticipate and prepare for the buyer's due diligence.

First, the business owner should make sure all corporate documents are in order.  This includes having complete and current bylaws and minutes of regular shareholder meetings, as well as copies of the certificate of incorporation and other foundational documents.

Second, the business owner should conduct a lien and judgment search to ensure there are no old, unreleased liens or judgments that have not been cleared.  This provides the owner time to clear up these problems without the stress of having a buyer looking over his shoulder or having to meet a buyer's deadline.  This information can be provided to the buyer, thereby streamlining the due diligence process.

Third, the seller should make arrangements to have interim financial statements prepared on a monthly basis since a transaction may close before year's end.  This provides both the seller and the buyer with current, up-to-date information to structure a fair and equitable deal.  Without this information a buyer may want to wait until year's end or establish a reserve or an escrow to cover any potential short fall in the company's financial performance.

Fourth, the company should conduct a check of all its major legal agreements and contracts including leases, operating agreements, employment agreements, non-compete agreements, joint venture agreements, purchasing or supply agreements, and so on.

Fifth, the company should ensure it has good title to all its tangible and intangible assets.  This means making sure assets are held in the correct names, that copyrights, trademarks, and patents are properly filed to protect intellectual property, and trade secrets are protected by non-compete agreements with key employees.

We recommend owners establish a war room or a due diligence cabinet to store copies of all important and relevant documents a buyer might want to examine during due diligence.  Keeping all these documents in one easy-to-access place can make the buyer's due diligence much easier, and greatly reduce the stress and anxiety a seller feels during the process.

## Summary

It is interesting to note as many as 50 percent of deals fall apart during the due diligence phase of the transaction. The most common reason is the buyer uncovers some material and previously undisclosed information that has adverse implications for the company. Surviving due diligence comes down to following four basic guidelines:

1.  Ensure there are no skeletons in the closet—Identify problems and potential problems before the buyer discovers them. Either fix them before the company goes to market or be prepared to disclose them to potential buyers.

2.  Open channels of communication—It is the seller's job to make sure all information is organized and readily available. Any bottlenecks in responding to a buyer's request for information will not only delay the due diligence process, but also taint the buyer's impression of the company and its management team.

3.  Get advisors involved early—Buyers always have legal and accounting questions, so it is important a business owner's advisors be able to answer these questions in a timely and professional manner. The buyer should be given full access to these trusted advisors so there is no delay in getting answers. This open team-based approach to disclosure, demonstrates confidence and professionalism to the buyer, which reflects well on the seller and moves the deal along.

4. Create a cooperative environment—The seller and his team of advisors should do everything possible to create a cooperative relationship with the buyer, rather than an adversarial one. Although it's easy to think of "them versus us" when you are in the middle of a deal, successful due diligence is about finding solutions to problems or issues that develop or are uncovered. This is particularly important if the business owner or his management team is staying on with the buyer after the sale.

Ultimately, the due diligence process is the first experience the buyer and seller have working together. Though the process may be intense and stressful for a seller, careful preparation and full cooperation can ensure that the due diligence process is successful.

# Chapter 22

# Managing the Process: Stragetic Reviews

Communication is the secret to success in exit planning. Communication also is one of the most difficult things to facilitate. If you think about it, the client needs to communicate effectively with up to seven different advisors about his or her exit planning goals and objectives, and then coordinate and implement the feedback received from each. In addition, each of these different advisors needs to effectively communicate with each of the other advisors on the client's exit planning team.

The fact that this communication is so difficult is the number one reason most business owners skip exit planning entirely. As a result, one of the key roles of the lead, exit planning advisor is to coordinate and control this communication so it is productive and efficient. As in any team-based sport, when all members of the team understand what they need to do, and get regular feedback and guidance from the coach, the team is more likely to excel. The same is true in exit planning.

One of the best ways to launch this communication initially, and then facilitate it on an ongoing basis, is through the use of Strategic Reviews. The concept behind the Strategic Review is simple. Strategic Reviews are meetings in which the clients and the members of the client's exit planning team are present and participate.

There are two types of strategic reviews, an Initial Strategic Review (ISR) and an Annual Strategic Review (ASR).

### Initial Strategic Review

At the Initial Strategic Review, as you might expect, the client and the lead exit planning advisor assemble the exit planning team so they can outline the scope of the project to everyone at the same time. The ISR is usually scheduled after the client and the lead advisor have completed the goal and objectives' articulation process. This enables the client to share these goals with all his or her advisors. It also enables the lead advisor to brief the other advisors on the overall timeline and deliverables expected from each advisor. One of the goals of the ISR is to reach an agreement between and among the client's advisors about who will do what and when. With all advisors present, you can establish a timeline to execute estate planning and legal documents, complete financial planning work, finish the business valuation, and receive tax projections.

## Annual Strategic Review

It is important to realize that although many business owners decide on and choose to implement an exit option immediately, for many others the exit planning process is a multi-year endeavor. As a result, it is important for these clients that you adopt a formal Annual Strategic Review (ASR) program. Following the Initial Strategic Review, we recommend that clients and their team of exit planning advisors meet periodically, usually annually, to review the performance of the business and any changes in the client's goals or situation, and to discuss possible or recommended changes to the client's exit plan.

The Annual Strategic Review should be scheduled about 45 days before the client's company's fiscal year-end. In advance of the ASR, the lead exit planning advisor provides the client and all other members of the exit planning team with an ASR Agenda (see below for example) and relevant supporting documents including the company's year-to-date financial statements. This allows all members of the team to review 11 months of financial data. This enables the investment banker to update the business valuation with current numbers, and the CPA to calculate projected income tax liabilities for the company and the owner.

About two weeks before the company's fiscal year end, the lead advisor should hold the ASR with the client and all the exit planning team members present. The primary purpose of the meeting is communication. It allows the client to understand his or her tax exposure as well as to learn about any tax or legal developments that occurred during the year which might affect either the business or the owner's exit plans. In addition, the ASR provides a unique and cost-effective way for clients to update all their advisors about what the client has accomplished during the year and what changes, if any, have occurred regarding the client's personal goals and objectives. This ensures the coordination of the client's legal, tax, estate, and financial objectives.

The ASR also is an important communications tool. We suggest after the client has brought the group up to speed on changes from the client's perspective, each advisor presents the group with a 10–15 minute summary of the status of the deliverables that were assigned to each advisor at the previous ISR or ASR. This helps each of the advisors learn about what the other advisors have been doing with respect to the exit plan during the previous 12 months. This helps ensure the coordination of all the different professionals working on the exit planning team. It also may prompt discussions or ideas about new, better ways to accomplish the client's goals.

The ASR also becomes a powerful motivational tool. As too often happens, clients and their advisors get busy or distracted and put off important, but not urgent tasks. Having the ASR scheduled a year in advance and having the clients and each advisor give a status report helps to motivate all concerned to accomplish the tasks on their lists.

In summary, the ASR is an important and unique way to elicit and exchange vital information between and among the client and all his or her advisors.

## The Strategic Review Agenda

The following is an overview of the topics that should be included in a Strategic Review Agenda.  The agendas for the initial and annual strategic reviews are and should be very similar.  The only difference between the two meetings is that the initial strategic review is the kick-off meeting for the group.  As a result, the agenda for the ISR typically includes time for introductions, followed by the lead advisor outlining how the exit planning process will work, describing what his or her role is, and establishing timetables and communication channels so each member of the group is on the same page.

1. **Introductions**

   The lead advisor opens the meeting and provides an opportunity for each of the other advisors to spend a few minutes introducing themselves to the group.  These introductions can be eliminated in subsequent annual strategic reviews after everyone knows each other.

2. **Overview of the Exit Planning Process**

   The lead advisor spends a few minutes discussing the exit planning process, describing the contributions sought from each team member, and giving an overview of the timetable for each major step in the process.  The team leader should conclude by emphasizing the importance of communication, how communication should be handled, and circulating an exit planning team contact information sheet to each team member.  This step can be eliminated from subsequent annual strategic reviews.

3. **Review of Business Performance**

   This is where the review process begins.  Understanding the current condition of the company and its future prospects is the basis for all subsequent discussions.  If revenues are up or down, it is important to understand why.  The same is true for earnings, assets, and liabilities.  If there have been significant changes in customer concentration or in backlogs, these changes also are important to understand.

   It also is important to take some time to look forward and predict where the company will be next year at this time.  Changes in capital requirements should be taken into account.

4. **Tax Review**

   After the CPA on the team has a good idea of what the company's earnings are likely to be for the year, he or she can project the likely taxes both the company and the owner will pay. This is an opportune time to bring up possible tax moves to be discussed more fully later in the meeting.

**5. Review of Business Valuation**

The investment banker updates the company's valuation using the year-to-date financial statements and presents the revised valuation to the client and the rest of the group. The investment banker should explain why the value has gone up or down and what current market conditions are like.

**6. Review of Business Contingency Plan**

The attorney on the team should update the client on the status of the owner's current business contingency plan and what changes, if any, need to be made.

**7. Review of Owner's Personal Goals**

This section of the ASR needs to address the fundamental reason for all this exit planning—helping to accomplish the client's goals. The owner's goals and objectives are the foundation upon which everything else is built. At the same time, it is important to realize that a client's goals are constantly changing. As a result, it is important to revisit the owner's goals periodically to make sure everyone is still on the same page and no adjustments need to be made. The owner should be prepared to discuss what he sees as the future for his business and what role he sees himself playing in the business going forward. This discussion also should include any changes in the owner's goals that might impact his personal, financial, estate, contingency, or exit plan. These might include an accelerated or extended time to exit, a desire to spend less time in the business or to purchase another business, an eagerness to support a new charity, an interest in a new hobby, the desire to build a vacation or retirement home, and so on.

**8. Review of Owner's Personal Situation**

The owners should brief the group about his or her personal situation, including a summary of any major health, family, personal, or financial issues relevant to the exit planning process. This could include things such as the birth of a grandchild, the divorce or illness of a spouse, the death of a business partner, and other changes.

**9. Protecting Current Value**

The attorney, financial advisor, benefits consultant, or other person responsible for developing the stay bonus and compensation programs for the clients should update the group on the current status of those efforts and make recommendations about changes, if any, that are required or prudent.

10. **Review of Estate Planning Considerations**

The client's estate planner should update the rest of the group on the status of the client's estate planning efforts.  When the estate plan is done, this usually takes little or no time unless the value of the company has changed dramatically, the tax laws have changed, or the owner has changed his wishes.  Nonetheless, a review of the estate plan each year allows the client to reaffirm those wishes and the other advisors to make sure their contributions dovetail with these estate planning objectives.

11. **Review of Exit Options**

The investment banker should update the group regarding progress toward the owner's exit option.  In addition, the investment banker should advise the group about any changes over the last 12 months that may impact the owner's chosen exit option.  These include things like a change in the owner's objectives, a change in the value of the business, a change in market conditions, and so on.

## Implementation

Although the idea behind the Strategic Reviews is pretty simple, implementing the idea can be quite the opposite.  Unfortunately, Strategic Reviews require coordinating a number of moving parts, which can make them very difficult to pull off.  On the other hand, without these meetings, coordinating all the different opinions that each professional brings to the exit planning process is even more difficult.  Let's look at an example.

Anthony Pappas, the client's insurance professional, recommends that the company purchase additional life insurance on the life of the owner.  This is recommended as a way to fund a buy-sell agreement and to provide some liquidity for the owner's family in the event of his death.  Although this is a pretty simple concept, implementing it in a team-based planning environment in which everyone has an opinion can take extensive time.  To make sure the company could afford the policy, the client's CPA wanted to do an analysis to understand its impact on the bottom line.  In addition, the attorney had some questions about whether the policy should be owned by the company or the owner's family and heirs, and what impact it would have on the client's overall estate plan.  Finally, the client wanted to make sure the premiums were paid in the most tax-effective manner possible.

Without a face-to-face meeting, in which all the advisors can discuss these concerns, coordinate fact finding, and reach a consensus in real time, implementing this relatively simple decision could have dragged on for weeks or even months, and could have been very costly for the client. Using the ASR format, the issue was discussed for 30 minutes by the exit planning team, recommendations were proposed, and a decision was made on the spot.

## Summary

There are three secrets to managing a successful, multi-disciplinary exit planning team. Communicate, communicate, and communicate! The best way to do this is to establish a formal system of communication relying on Strategic Reviews so the message is delivered to all advisors simultaneously, and all advisors have an equal chance to communicate with the client and the other members of the exit planning team. Using an Initial Strategic Review to launch an exit planning assignment is a great way to set the stage to help everyone understand how the process will work. Strictly adhering to an Annual Strategic Review, scheduled for 45 days before the end of the company's fiscal year, is the best way to continue this important exchange of information in an efficient and cost-effective manner.

# Chapter 23

# The ROI of Exit Planning

Return on investment or ROI is important to every business owner. Throughout this book we have emphasized that exit planning is a winning proposition for business owners. Now it is time to actually quantify the benefits or ROI of exit planning for business owners. Put simply, exit planning delivers stunning returns on investment for business owners.

The best way to make this point is with an example of a fairly typical exit planning engagement.

### Case Study: Return on Investment

Roger owned a successful, medical equipment rental business. He had tried unsuccessfully to sell his company for about a year before he started working with us. Roger had tried to sell his company to a key manager because Roger believed this would be the best way to accomplish his personal objectives.

Roger's personal goals were to maximize the value of his company so he could comfortably retire and pursue other interests. Roger felt a sale to this individual would maximize the value of the company because the key manager knew the business and its potential better than anybody else ever could. Roger also liked the idea of selling to someone he knew who was effectively part of his "extended family." He and the key manager agreed $6 million was a fair price. After pursuing this path unsuccessfully, Roger came to us for help.

When we began the formal exit planning process, we discovered Roger had no tax plan, no accountant, and no personal financial plan! In addition, he had not shared with his attorney or anybody other than his key manager that he was thinking of selling his company.

After working with Roger for about 30 days, we presented him with a formal exit plan. The plan showed Roger that he:

1. Had been pursuing the wrong exit option.
2. Undervalued his company by approximately $1 million.
3. Needed a personal financial plan to help him understand what he must net after taxes and fees in order to accomplish his personal goals.

4. Should sell to a third party, not his key employee.

5. Should use a controlled auction to maximize the selling price.

6. Should develop a strategy to minimize taxes at the time of sale.

7. Should conduct a pre-transaction due diligence prior to taking the company to market.

The first thing the exit plan showed Roger was that he needed to net $5.3 million from the sale after taxes in order to retire and support the same lifestyle he had before the sale. The plan showed Roger if he had sold to his key manager for $6 million, he would have received after-tax net proceeds of only $3.6 million. To Roger's shock, he discovered had he pursued this option, he would not have netted enough to comfortably fund his retirement.

The second thing the exit plan showed Roger was that he had been substantially undervaluing his company. The original $6 million value Roger and his manager were using was based on industry rules of thumb, not a formal valuation. The valuation to which Roger and his key manager agreed had actually been a little higher originally, but because the manager was unable to line up financing, he convinced Roger the price was too high.

A formal valuation revealed the company was actually worth approximately $7 million or $1 million more than Roger had been willing to accept. Nonetheless, the plan showed Roger that even with the additional $1 million in expected sales price, Roger still would not be able to meet his financial goals.

That discovery led to a series of additional recommendations.

First, the value enhancement section of the exit plan pointed out several things Roger could do to improve the market value of his company. These "fixes" were relatively inexpensive and could be implemented quickly.

Second, the exit plan showed Roger how important it was to focus on maximizing net proceeds, in addition to maximizing the sales price. This compelling case motivated Roger to begin working with his attorney and CPA to create a tax minimization strategy.

After beginning this process, Roger discovered he could reduce his tax bill by $500K at the time of sale, if he acted quickly to implement a proven IRS-approved tax structure. Unfortunately, if Roger had waited much longer, this tax structure and many of his other options would not have been available because they needed to be in place well in advance of a transaction.

> Third, the exit plan made a compelling case for protecting the value Roger's company already represented. This motivated Roger to have his attorney and CPA perform a pre-transaction due diligence on Roger's company to identify and address any issues that might derail a deal or affect the value of the company during the sales process. The attorney found a number of small issues that were easily fixed which would have distracted from an otherwise beautiful company.
>
> As an unexpected bonus, while Roger's accountant was recasting the company's financial statements to get them ready for the sales process, he discovered an error the company's bookkeeper made. The good news is by fixing it, the company was entitled to a $190K tax refund that could be applied for at the time of sale. This refund would be payable to Roger personally after the closing.

Fourteen months later, we sold the business for $7.2 million to a private equity group looking for an add-on to an existing portfolio company. A controlled auction process was used that solicited interest from more than 1,400 potential buyers. One thousand of these buyers were institutional buyers; the other four hundred were strategic or industry buyers. We sent out 61 offering memoranda to interested buyers who signed non-disclosure agreements. Six of these buyers submitted qualifying bids for Roger's company. Roger invited five of the six to visit his facility and meet with him. Three of these buyers ultimately submitted letters of intent or offers for the company. Roger chose the final buyer. The deal was closed within 18 months from start to finish. Roger received $7.2 million for his company at closing. He netted $5,600,000 after taxes.

At each step of the way, Roger made informed decisions based on sound advice from his advisors. This process resulted in Roger's feeling confident he had maximized the value of his business. In total, the client spent $25,000 in investment banking fees to develop his exit plan. He spent another $25,000 in legal and accounting fees to develop the tax strategy, handle the pre-transaction due diligence, and file for the tax refund.

The exit plan showed Roger how to receive $1.9 million *more* in after-tax proceeds than Roger expected based on his prior efforts. Perhaps more important, the plan showed Roger how close he had come to selling his company and not accomplishing his personal financial goals in the process.

The cost of developing Roger's exit plan was approximately $50,000 including legal, accounting, financial planning, and insurance fees. Looking at the cost of the planning process alone, Roger received a 38 to 1 return on his money in less than three months.

When Roger was ready to sell, he retained us to implement his exit plan and sell his company. When the transaction closed, he paid us a success fee of approximately $300,000, or 4.2 percent of the total transaction price.

In total, the combined cost of the exit planning and the investment banking process was $350,000. Even when you include the investment banking success fee, Roger received a 5.5 to 1 return on his money in less than 18 months. But the best return on Roger's investment was knowing he had done everything possible to ensure his family's financial security and that he and his family would now be able to retire without financial worries.

## Summary

Roger's situation is not unusual. The ROI analysis presented above does not reflect any increase in the fundamental value of Roger's business. In one engagement, we worked with a client to implement new sales practices, hire and train a new level of senior management, and improve profitability. That company's value improved from $6.0 million to $10 million in 24 months. These were truly exceptional results and will not be available for every company, but it shows the power and the promise of exit planning.

# Chapter 24

# Introducing Exit Planning Into Your Practice

Congratulations on making it this far! By now you know more about exit planning than the vast majority of people in your profession. You are well on your way to differentiating yourself, your practice, and your firm from your competitors.

But in order to truly differentiate yourself, you must explore how to integrate these exit planning principals into your professional practice. First, be aware exit planning does not and should not replace your existing services. Exit planning is a framework in which your existing services and products provide valuable solutions to business owners.

So before we examine exactly how to incorporate exit planning into your existing practice, let us revisit one of the fundamental premises of this book:

> There is a tremendous and growing need for competent exit planning professionals. More than 9 million baby boomer business owners will begin to exit their businesses over the next 15 years. When they do, they will need your help to receive the maximum amount of money possible in order to accomplish their personal, financial, and estate planning goals.

How can you actively meet this need and create a win-win situation for both you and your client?

Introducing exit planning into your practice does not require a huge investment or a dramatic change in the way you already do business. In fact, what is attractive about exit planning is that it can be so easily and seamlessly integrated into your existing practice.

Listed below are 10 basic steps to start you down the path to use exit planning as a powerful business development and practice enhancement tool.

### Step One: Target Your Efforts

Identify clients who meet the following criteria:

- The client is either a majority or minority shareholder in a privately held business.
- One or more of the owners is 45 or older.
- An entrepreneur who is just starting a new business.

These clients will become the core focus of your initial exit planning efforts. Although exit planning is appropriate for business owners of all ages, owners who are 45 years old or older tend to be more receptive to the importance of and need for a comprehensive exit plan.

If you decide you want to market your exit planning message to a broader audience of business owners, you should target private companies with revenues of $5 million to $200 million. A professional, personalized letter *followed up by a phone call* is still the best way to establish a relationship with these prospects.

### Step Two: Communicate Internally

Make it a policy to discuss exit planning and its importance at your firm's partner or staff meetings so your colleagues understand the issues and are able to identify potential exit planning opportunities when they arise.

### Step Three: Communicate with Clients and Prospects

Make a commitment to raise the topic of exit planning with your pre-screened clients and any prospects with whom you meet who fit the same criteria. See Chapter 4 for a more detailed discussion of some ice breakers. We suggest you develop a 10-second "elevator speech" outlining the importance of exit planning for the business owner and the role you play. This enables you to smoothly work what you do into conversations with clients and prospects virtually anywhere you meet them.

### Step Four: Discuss with Your Referral Sources

Raise the topic of exit planning with other professionals who may be valuable team members on future exit planning assignments. The collaborative nature of the exit planning process is an ideal vehicle for networking and establishing strong and active referral relationships with other professionals. It also presents a context in which collaborative selling and prospecting works very well since each professional on the exit planning team does not compete with, but complements, the services provided by the other team members.

### Step Five: Develop Marketing Collateral

Develop a short marketing piece about the importance of exit planning for business owners and the role you play in helping business owners tackle this difficult topic. Communications experts now say that in our information overloaded lives, printed brochures no longer get read. As a result, do not spend a lot of time or money developing a substantial multi-page brochure. A simple bi-fold or tri-fold brochure is all you need to get started. Make sure that your printed materials answer the question on every prospect or client's mind, "What's in it for me?" That's another way of saying do NOT use your brochure to educate your prospects about what exit planning is, tell them what exit planning can do for them. You should include your exit planning write up on your firm's website. The same information developed for your brochure should be used there for consistency.

**Step Six: Make it Part of Your Existing Communication Tools**

Include the topic of exit planning in your firm's newsletter, website, and other communications with clients. Use the same information in your brochure and on your website to ensure the consistency of your message.

**Step Seven: Develop New Marketing Programs/Events**

Develop an executive breakfast for your clients to update them on exit planning issues. Executive breakfasts can be as elaborate or as simple as you like. We typically recommend a 45-minute presentation format and include a complimentary buffet breakfast. Executive breakfasts can be held in your offices or in a private dining room of a local restaurant. You also may decide to develop a seminar program hosted in your offices or at a local hotel. Seminars can be an effective way to get the word out, but they are time consuming to organize and relatively expensive to host. We have found by co-hosting events with one or more other exit planning professionals, we can defray the cost and widen the audience. This approach also reinforces the multi-disciplinary team based approach that produces results for our clients.

**Step Eight: Reach Out to Existing and Former Clients**

Like a doctor checking in on a patient, create a regular follow-up program to make sure you raise the issue of exit planning with your business owner clients on an annual basis. Touch base with clients about a month before an exit planning event and send them an invitation to a breakfast or seminar a few weeks later. A personal call about a week before the event asking them to come is the best way to ensure you have a good turnout.

**Step Nine: Use Public Relations**

As you become more comfortable with the exit planning process, you may decide to develop a marketing or public relations program designed specifically around the concept of exit planning. The concept of exit planning is one that many trade associations and community networking groups will be interested in promoting to their business owner members. As a result, articles on this topic are generally well received and are published by trade associations and regional newsletters, newspapers, and magazines.

**Step Ten: Just Do It**

Like the Nike ad says, "Just do it." Once you begin the process you will find that one success leads to another. All it takes is asking your existing clients a few probing and insightful questions regarding their thoughts about exiting their business. You'll be surprised at the results.

## The Exit Planning Institute

If you are serious about introducing exit planning into your practice, you may want to consider joining the Exit Planning Institute and becoming a Certified Exit Planning Advisor. The Exit Planning Institute or EPI is the leading authority on exit planning with members in the Untied States, Canada, Great Britain, Australia, Vietnam and China. EPI awards the Certified Exit Planning Advisor or CEPA designation to professionals who complete EPI's in-depth exit planning program that includes a 5-day course, a series of homework assignments, and a 4 hour comprehensive exam.

Much like the CFP® and CFA® designations for financial professionals, the CEPA credential is evidence of a professional's in-depth knowledge and expertise in the field of exit planning. You can learn more at http://www.exit-planning-institute.org.

## Summary

By committing yourself to use an exit planning approach, you will find you differentiate yourself from the hundreds of other professionals against whom you compete for business. You also will find the number of business owners you get as clients will increase dramatically. If used diligently, an exit planning framework will help you generate more business per client than in the past. Finally, as an exit planning professional who actively brings in other advisors to help you develop and implement exit plans for your clients, you will see your referral network blossom and the number and quality of the referrals you receive increase significantly.

And, at the end of the day, your professional practice will be more personally satisfying as you help your clients struggle with one of the most important events in their lifetime and deliver results that will benefit them and their families for generations to come.

Good luck!

| Austin Family Business Program | Oregon State University, College of Business<br>201 Bexel Hall<br>Corvallis, OR 97331-2603<br>Phone: 800-859-7609 Fax: 541-737-5388<br>www.familybusinessonline.org<br>Dr. Mark T. Green, Director<br>familybuisness@busoregonstate.edu |
|---|---|
| Case Western Reserve University | The Partnership of Family Business<br>Weatherhead School of Management<br>10900 Euclid Avenue<br>Cleveland, OH 44106-7235<br>Phone: 216-368-2076  Fax: 216-368-4785<br>www.weatherhead.cwru.edu/entp/program.fb/cfm<br>Ernesto Poza, Professor for the Practice of Family Business, ErnestoPoza@case.edu |
| Centro de Empresas Familiares (CEFAM) ITESM. | Av. General Ramon Corona<br>2514. Co. Nuevo Mexico<br>CP 45201 Zapopan<br>Jalisco, Mexico<br>Phone 52 33 3669 3095  Fax: 52 33 3669 3093<br>www.gda.itesm.mx/cefam<br>Jaime Navarro, Professor, jaimen@itesm.mx |
| The Family Business Center | Elizabethtown College<br>One Alpha Drive<br>Elizabethtown, PA 17022-2298<br>Phone: 717-361-1275<br>www.etown.edu/family<br>Mary Beth Matteo, Director<br>Rosa Burmeister, Assistant Director, fbc@etown.edu |
| Family Business Center of Central Ohio | Ohio Dominican University<br>P.O. Box 3124<br>Dublin, OH 43016<br>Phone: 614-334-8916  Fax: 614-876-1409<br>www.familybusinesscenter.com<br>Marty Graff, Executive Director<br>Dick Emens, Chair of Advisory Board<br>demens@cwslaw.com |

| | |
|---|---|
| Family Business Council, California State University | California State University<br>P.O. Box 6848<br>Fullerton, CA 92834-6848<br>Phone: 714-278-4182  Fax: 714-278-3106<br>www.business.fullerton.edu/centers/fambusiness.com<br>Mike Trueblood, Director, mtrueblood@fullerton.edu |
| Family Business Forum at King's College | The William G. McGowan School of Business<br>133 North River Street<br>Wilkes-Barrre PA 18711<br>Phone: 570-208-5972  Fax: 570-208-5989<br>www.kings.edu/fbf<br>Patrice R. Persico, Director, fbf@kings.edu |
| Kellogg Graduate School of Management, Center for Family Enterprises | The Center for Family Enterprises<br>Jacobs Center, Room 5228<br>2001 Sheridan Road<br>Evanston, Il 60208<br>Phone: 847-467-7855.  www.kellogg.nwu.edu/familyenteerprises.com<br>John L. Ward, Co-Director johnward@kelloggnorthwestern.edu<br>Lloyd Shefsky, Co-Director<br>l-shefsky@kelloggnorthwestern.edu |
| Family Business Center, Loyola University Chicago | Loyola University Chicago<br>820 North Michigan Avenue<br>Chicago, IL 60611<br>Phone: 312-915-6490. Fax: 312-915-6495<br>www.sba.luc.edu/familybbusiness<br>Andrew D. Keyt, Executive Director<br>Suzanne M. Lane, Program Director, akeyt@luc.edu |
| Center for Family Business, Northeastern University | Northeastern University<br>101 Hayden Hall<br>Boston MA 02115-5000<br>Phone: 617-373-7031  Fax: 617-373-2056<br>www.cba.neu.edu/fambiz.com<br>Ted Clark, Executive Director, Ted.clark@neu.edu |
| South Dakota Family Business Initiative | The University of South Dakota School of Business<br>414 East Clark Street<br>Vermilion, SD 57069<br>Phone: 605-677-3157  Fax: 605-677-5427<br>Beth Adamson, Executive Director badamson@usd.edu<br>www.usd.edu/fambus.com |

| | |
|---|---|
| Tulane University Family Business Center | A.B. Freeman School of Business<br>New Orleans, LA 70118-5669<br>Phone: 504-862-8482  Fax: 504-862-8902<br>http://freeman.tulane.edu/lri/fbc<br>Rosalind G. Butler, Assistant Director Rosalind.Butler@Tulane.edu |
| University of Connecticut, Family Business Program | University of Connecticut<br>2100 Hillside Road<br>Unit 1041<br>Storrs, CT 06269-1041<br>Phone: 860-486-5678  Fax: 860-486-5678<br>www.business.uconn.edu/familybusiness<br>Priscilla M. Cale, Director<br>pcale@business.uconn.edu |
| University of Massachusetts, Amherst Family Business Center | University of Massachusetts<br>358 North Pleasant Street<br>Amherst, MA 01003<br>Phone: 413-545-1537  Fax: 413-545-3351<br>www.umass.edu/fambiz<br>Ira Bryck, Director<br>bryke@contined.umass.edu |
| University of Illinois, Chicago Family Business Council | University of Illinois<br>815 West Van Buren Street<br>Suite 321<br>Chicago, IL 60607<br>Phone: 312-413-5433  Fax: 312-996-9988<br>www.uic.edu/cba/fbc<br>Ernest Barrens, Director<br>barrens@uic.edu |
| University of Pittsburgh, Family Enterprise Center | University of Pittsburgh,<br>First Floor, Wesley W. Posvar Hall<br>230 South Bouquet Street<br>Pittsburgh, PA 15237<br>Phone: 412-648-1544  Fax: 412-648-1636<br>http://iee.katz.pitt.edu<br>Ann Dugan, Executive Director<br>adugan@skatz.pitt.edu |

| University of San Diego, Family Business Forum | University of San Diego<br>5998 Alcala Park<br>San Diego, CA 92110-2492<br>Phone: 619-260-4231  Fax: 619-260-5988<br>www.sandiego.edu/fbf<br>Jodi Waterhouse, Director<br>jodiw@sandiego.edu |
|---|---|
| The University of Toledo, Center for Family Business | The University of Toledo<br>MS103 St 1045<br>2801 West Bancoft Street<br>Toledo, OH 43606-3390<br>Phone: 419-530-4058  Fax: 419-530-8497<br>www.utfamilybusiness.org<br>Debbe Skutch, Director<br>dskutch@utnet.utoledo.edu |
| University of Wisconsin. Madison Family Business Center | University of Wisconsin<br>601 University Avenue<br>Fluno Center, #338<br>Madison, WI 53715-1035<br>Phone: 608-441-7338 Fax: 6 08-441-7337<br>http://www.uwexeced.com/fbc<br>Ann Kinkade, Director<br>akinkade@bus.wisc.edu |
| Wake Forest University, Family Business Center | Wake Forest University<br>3455 University Parkway<br>Winston-Salem, NC 27106<br>Phone: 336-758-5417  Fax: 336-758-4514<br>www.mba.wfu.edu/fbc<br>Tom Ogburn, Director<br>tom.ogburn@mba.wfu.edu |
| Wisconsin Family Business Forum, University of Wisconsin-Oshkosh | University of Wisconsin-Oshkosh<br>800 Algoma Boulevard<br>Oshkosh, WI 54901<br>Phone: 920-424-2257  Fax: 920-424-7413<br>www.uwosh.edu/wfbf/<br>Susan Schierstedt, Director<br>schierss@uwosh.edu |

**Acquisition**

Transfer of control of one corporation to another via merger, buyout or otherwise.

**Add-backs**

Extraordinary one-time expenses, such as the cost of moving the plant or owner's perquisites such as travel and entertaining that are added back to earnings to give a more realistic view of the company's earning power. Add-backs are subject to acute scrutiny by the buyer because business travel and business entertaining are usually a regular cost of doing business.

**Angel Investors**

An individual high-risk investor who likes to make investments in promising acquisitions. Angels often have valuable business experience and can be helpful as a member of the board of directors.

**Asset Sale**

A form of acquisition whereby the seller of a corporation agrees to sell all or certain assets and liabilities of a company to a purchaser. The corporate entity is not transferred.

**Assets Retained**

The specific assets an owner would retain after selling a business. Examples include items such as whole life insurance policies, personal automobiles, and excess cash and country club memberships.

**Auction**

The process for selling a business that involves soliciting a number of potential buyers and inviting them to offer bids for a business by a specified date. The competition between multiple buyers normally will push the purchase price upward.

**Basis**

Purchase price of a security, private stock or asset, including commissions and their expenses, used to determine gains and losses for tax purposes. Also called "cost" or "tax" basis.

**Benchmarking**

A business tool that identifies "best in class" business processes, which when implemented, will lead to higher performance through organizational and process improvements.

**Book Value**

A company's net worth: assets (cash, receivables, inventory, fixed assets, etc.) minus liabilities (accounts payable, accrued expenses, debt, etc.). Also refers to the value at which an asset is carried on a company's balance sheet.

**Business Cycle**

A long term pattern of alternating economic growth (recovery) and decline (recessions), characterized by rising (falling) employment, productivity and interest rates. Also called economic cycle.

**Buyout**

Purchase of a controlling interest of a company's stock.

**Buy-Sell Agreement**

A contractual arrangement between business owners or the owners and the business organization that controls who can buy a departing owner's share of the business and establishes what price will be paid for that share. Life insurance commonly funds the business purchase.

**Business Broker**

Typically, an individual or small firm that acts as the agent for either a buyer or seller of a small private company with revenues of less than $5 million. Also see intermediary.

**C Corporation**

An entity organized under state law with rights of conducting business. A corporation has unlimited life regardless of that of its owners and ceases to exist only if dissolved according to proper legal process. Liability of the owners is limited to the amount invested in the entity.

**CAPX**

The acronym for Capital Expenditures that are necessary within the next year.

**Capital Asset Pricing Model (CAPM)**

A financial model that determines the Cost of Capital for a firm based upon that firm's risk tolerance, the risk-free rate of return, and the expected return on the market in general.

**Capital Expenditures**

See CAPX.

**Capital Gain**

The increase in value of an asset. Company stock or assets sold at a profit produce a realized gain. Realized long- term gains are taxed at a maximum federal rate of 20%.

**Capital-gains tax**

Tax on profit from sale of an appreciated asset.

**Capitalization**

The conversion of future income into a present value by use of a capitalization factor usually expressed as a percentage such as return on investment (ROI).

**Capitalization (of a business)**

The sum of a corporation's long-term debt, stock, and retained earnings.

**Capitalization Rate**

The percentage rate used to determine the present value of a stream of future earnings. The rate is a subjective rate dependent upon the perceived risk associated with the business.

**Cash Equivalents**

Short-term investments due in a year or less. Similar to cash in liquidity and safety from market volatility.

**Cash Flow**

A company's cash receipts minus its cash payments; or as an equivalent, its net profit plus depreciation and amortization charges, less capital expenditures, plus or minus changes in working capital.

**Cash Flow Statement**

An analysis of all the changes that affect the cash account during an accounting period. These changes may be shown as either sources or uses of cash.

**Charitable Remainder Trust (CRT)**

A trust allowing a person to donate property or securities to charity, but continue to use the property and/or receive income from the securities while living. The annuity version pays a fixed dollar amount each year; the unit-trust form pays a variable dollar amount based on a fixed percentage of the fluctuating value of the assets given to the charity. A tax deduction is also allowed based on the value of the assets donated.

**Closing**

The formal process of legally completing the purchase of a company through the exchange of cash, promissory notes, and other compensation for asset titles, stock certificates, etc.

**Comparables Analysis**

A method of analyzing the value of a firm by reviewing similar recent transactions in the industry.

**Cost of Capital**

The interest rate of borrowing for a firm's debt and equity. The more risky a firm appears to investors, the higher the cost of capital.

**Deal Structure**

The form by which the purchase of a business is accomplished. It can include cash, notes, stock, consulting agreements, earn-out provisions, and covenants not to compete. The sale can take the form of an asset sale or a stock sale.

**Definitive Agreement**

The final agreement between the buyer and seller that lays out all the terms of the transaction in detail.

**Depreciation**

The amount that tangible assets decrease over the normal life cycle as designated by the parameters of the IRS.

**Discounted Cash Flow**

The valuation tool that looks at future/projected cash flows, and discounts them to present value. The discounting factor is in part determined by the Capital Assets Pricing Model.

**Due Diligence**

Refers normally to the acquirer's investigation into the business's claimed financial and operation performance so that the buyer is satisfied that all representations are accurate. Due diligence also can apply to the seller's review of the buyer.

**Earn-out**

A contingent payment for a business normally tied to future company performance. Performance is typically measured against sales or profits and payment is made once the measure meets or exceeds a set figure.

**EBIT**

The acronym for Earnings Before Interest and Taxes.

**EBITDA**

Earnings Before Interest, Taxes, Depreciation, and Amortization. An approximate measure of a company's operating cash flow based on data from the company's income statement. Calculated by looking at earnings before the deduction of interest expenses, taxes, depreciation, and amortization. This earnings measure is of particular interest in cases where companies have large amounts of fixed assets which are subject to heavy depreciation charges (such as manufacturing companies), or in the case where a company has a large amount of acquired intangible assets on its books, and is thus, subject to large amortization charges (such as a company that has purchased a brand or a company that has recently made a large acquisition). Since the distortion in accounting and financing effects on company earnings do not factor into EBITDA, it is a good way of comparing companies within and across industries. This measure also is of interest to a company's creditors, since EBITDA is essentially the income that a company has free for interest payments. In general, EBITDA is a useful measure only for large companies with significant assets, and/or for companies with a significant amount of debt financing. It is rarely a useful measure for evaluating a small company with no significant loans. Sometimes also called operational cash flow.

**EBITDA-CAPX**

EBITDA minus capital expenditures. A more realistic assessment of earnings than EBITDA.

**Employment Agreement**

An agreement in which a key employee agrees to continue to work at the company for a specified period of time, at a specified salary and other conditions.

| | |
|---|---|
| **Enterprise Value** | Market value of equity, plus interest-bearing debt. |
| **Equity** | The interest or value that an owner has in property over and above any indebtedness. |
| **Estate** | The total property owned by an individual prior to the distribution of that property under the terms of a will, trust, or inheritance laws.  An individual's estate includes all assets and liabilities. |
| **ESOP or Employee Stock Ownership Plan.** | A trust established by a corporate which acts as a tax-qualified, defined-contribution retirement plan by making the corporation's employees partial owners. Contributions are made by the sponsoring employer, and can grow tax-deferred, just as with an IRA or 401(k). But, unlike other retirement plans, the contributions must be invested in the company's stock. The benefits for the company include increased cash flow, tax savings, and increased productivity from highly motivated workers. The main benefit for the employees is the ability to share in the company's success. Due to the tax benefits, the administration of ESOPs is regulated, and numerous restrictions apply. Also called stock purchase plan. |
| **Estate Plan** | A plan that provides for the orderly control and management of one's assets with arrangements for the eventual transfer of those assets to one's chosen heirs, and with the least complication and cost possible. |

**Exit Plan**

A plan that addresses how a business owner will successfully transition the ownership of his/her business to others in order to facilitate the owner's retirement or exit.

**Fair Market Value**

The price at which a business passes from a willing seller to a willing buyer. It is assumed that both the buyer and seller are rational and have a reasonable knowledge of relevant facts.

**Free Cash Flow**

Cash available for distribution after taxes but before the effects of financing. Calculated as net income plus depreciation, less expenditures required for working capital and capital items, adjusted to remove effects of financing.

**GAAP**

Generally Accepted Accounting Principles are accounting standards established by the FASB (Financial Accounting Standards Board).

**Going Concern Value**

The gross value of a company as an operating business. This value may exceed or be at a discount from the liquidating value.

**Goodwill**

The amount by which the price paid for a company exceeds the company's estimated net worth at market value of its underlying assets and liabilities.

**Hart-Scott-Rodino Act**

An amendment to the Clayton Act that requires certain firms to file notice of a pending acquisition with the Federal Trade Commission and the Department of Justice in advance of any such transaction. The Act is only applicable to large transactions that pass three separate tests.

**Indemnification**

Exemption for the buyer from incurred penalties or liabilities after the closing from incomplete representations and warranties of the seller.

| | |
|---|---|
| **Initial Public Offering (IPO)** | The first offering of the common stock to the public by a closely held company. |
| **Installment Sale** | A transaction in which the sales price is paid in two or more installments over two or more years. If the sale meets certain requirements, a taxpayer can postpone reporting any gain on an installment until the tax year proceeds are actually received. |
| **Intangible Asset** | Nonphysical resources or rights to other assets. Patents, goodwill, permits, and computer programs are examples of intangible assets. |
| **Intermediary** | Typically, an individual or small firm that acts as the agent for either a buyer or seller of a small or middle market company. An intermediary typically functions as a finder and only introduces the two parties to each other, but does not provide value added services like business valuations, structuring advice, negotiating the deal, or coordinating due diligence. Also see business broker. |
| **Investment Banker** | An individual or institution which acts as an underwriter or agent for corporations and municipalities issuing securities. Most also maintain broker/dealer operations, maintain markets for previously issued securities, and offer advisory services to investors. Investment banks also have a large role in facilitating mergers and acquisitions, private equity placements, and corporate restructuring. Unlike traditional commercial banks, investment banks do not accept deposits from or provide loans to individuals. Middle market investment bankers typically represent private companies with revenues of between $10 and $500 million. Bulge bracket investment banks handle transactions involving large private companies ($300 million +) and public companies. |

**Key Man Insurance**

Insurance purchased by a business on the life of an employee whose services contribute substantially to the success of the business of the firm.

**Lehman Formula**

The industry standard commission rate, which is a sliding scale-5-4-3-2-1- percent on each successive million dollar purchase price.

**Letter of Intent**

A letter from one company to another acknowledging willingness and ability to enter into a transaction. A letter of intent is most often issued as acknowledgment of the fact that a merger between companies or an acquisition is being seriously considered. Sometimes, a letter of intent also may be issued by a lending institution to a potential borrower to indicate that it is interested in lending certain amounts of money at certain specified times. In exchange for signing a letter of intent, the shareholder would often qualify for reduced sales charges. A letter of intent is <u>not</u> a contract and <u>cannot be enforced</u>; it is simply a document stating serious intent to enter into a transaction.

**Leveraged Buyout (LBO)**

The purchase of a company that is financed primarily by debt.

**Liquidating Value**

The value of a company based on the market value of its assets, net of liabilities.

**Management Buyout (MBO)**

A leveraged buyout that is lead by a management team within the firm.

**M&A Advisor or Intermediary**

An agent of the business owner mandated with helping to arrange and negotiate a merger or acquisition. Typically, he/she focuses on larger transactions than business brokers. See investment banker.

**Merger**

The combination of two or more companies in which the resulting firm maintains the identity of the acquiring company.

**Mezzanine Financing**

Loans that are generally subordinate to senior secured debt but are superior to claims on equity. Normally, the terms involve interest-only payments and warrants.

**Middle-Market**

Private and public businesses with sales ranging from $5 to $100 million.

**NAICS**

See North American Industrial Classification System.

**Net Cash Flow**

Cash available for distribution after taxes and after the effects of financing. Calculated as net income plus depreciation less expenditures required for working, capital and capital items.

**Net Present Value**

A measure of a project's/firm's initial investment, and its projected future cash flows discounted at an appropriate weighted average cost of capital.

**Net Worth**

Also called "book value" of a business; the net worth is determined from the financial records by subtracting all current and long term liabilities from the total assets of a company. See book value.

**North American Industrial Classification System**

A newer classification system developed by the U.S. Department of Commerce and used to assign one or more industry categories to a business.

**No-Shop Clause**

An agreement between the prospective buyer and seller to discontinue the marketing of the business to other potential buyers for a specified period of time.

| | |
|---|---|
| **Notes** | A note evidencing an indebtedness including terms of payment. Notes can be either secured with pledges of real or personal property, company stock, or a personal guarantee, or can be unsecured for which no security has been pledged. |
| **Offering Memorandum** | A written publication describing a company in detail including its past financial history and future projections prepared for the purpose of selling that firm to potential buyers. |
| **Option** | The right, but not the obligation, to buy (for a call option) or sell (for a put option) a specific amount of a given stock, commodity, currency, etc., at a specified price during a specified period of time. |
| **Partnership** | A legal business association of two or more individuals co-owning a business. The partners share the profits. The two most common partnership structures are general and limited partnerships. |
| **P/E ratio** | See price-to-earnings ratio. |
| **Performance** | Usually, the return of an investment over a period of time, but in company financial evaluations, also can refer to the sales and/or profit history over a period of time. |
| **Present Value** | The value today of a future payment or stream of payments, discounted at some appropriate, compound interest (discount) rate. |
| **Price-to-earnings Ratio** | A company's market value divided by its earnings, either historical or forecasted. Also know as a company's "earnings multiple" or "P/E" ratio. |
| **Pro Forma Statements** | Hypothetical financial statements as they would appear, if some event such as increased sales or production were to occur. |

**Promissory Note**

A financing instrument that states the terms of the underlying obligation, is signed by its maker, and is negotiable. See also "Notes."

**Recap**

A sale transaction in which an owner(s) sells part of the equity of the business in order to take "some chips off the table," while still operating the business. The recap can entail a sale of any amount of company stock, but most involve change of control.

**Recapture**

The inclusion of a previously deducted or excluded amount in gross income or tax liability. Recapture may be applicable to accelerated depreciation, cost recovery, amortization, and various credits.

**Recast Earnings**

Earnings that have been recast by "adding back" certain unusual or excess expenses to determine the "true" earnings of a private company. Examples include owner compensation above market salaries and bonuses, owner perks, one-time expenses, and other discretionary expenses. Recasting allows meaningful comparisons with other investment opportunities.

**Representations & Warranties**

Indemnifications and covenants written into the purchase and sale agreement that provide factual information that is important to protect the buyer from future occurrences.

**Residual Value**

The estimated market value of a company at the end of certain number of years, usually 4 to 5 years.

**Retained Earnings**

Net profits kept to accumulate in a business after dividends are paid.

| | |
|---|---|
| **Return on Assets (ROA)** | A measure of a company's profitability, equal to a year's earnings divided by its total assets, expressed as a percentage. |
| **Return on Investment (ROI)** | A measure of a company's profitability, equal to a year's income divided by common stock and preferred stock equity, plus long term debt expressed as a percentage. |
| **Risk Premium** | The reward for holding a risky investment rather than a "riskless" one such as Treasury bonds. |
| **Risk/Reward Trade-Off** | The customary relationship between risk and return in which you must be willing to accept greater risk, if you want to pursue greater returns. |
| **ROA** | See return on assets. |
| **ROI** | See return on investment. |
| **Roll-up** | A transaction in which several individual businesses are combined to create a new and larger entity. |
| **S Corporation** | A sub-chapter S corporation is an entity under IRS regulations that provides the same liability limitations as a C corporation, but does not pay corporate taxes. Corporate income flows directly to the shareholders in proportion to their ownership and each shareholder is responsible for paying his/her tax liability. |
| **Standard Industrial Classification (SIC Code)** | A code developed by the U.S. Department of Commerce used to assign one or more industry categories to a business. A newer classification system called NAICS (North American Industrial Classification System) is currently being implemented. |

**Stock Sale**

A form of acquisition whereby all or a portion of the stock in a corporation is sold to the purchaser.

**Stockholder**

An owner of an incorporated business, the ownership being evidenced by stock certificates.

**Strategic Acquisition**

The purchase of a business that supplements the buyer's strengths or complements the buyer's weaknesses. This "extra" value often increases the value the buyer is willing to pay above a value strictly determined by financial return.

**Sweat Equity**

A slang term generally used to refer to the time and effort invested in the business by the owner.

**Synergy**

A situation whereby the combination of two or more entities results in a new entity that is worth more than the sum of the parts, i.e., 2 + 2 = 5.

**Tangible Asset**

Assets other than real estate that physically exist. Business Equipment and vehicles are tangible personal property. Assets such as stock certificates and franchises only represent value and are therefore intangible property.

**Tax Loss Carry-Forward**

A loss that can be carried forward for a number of years to offset future taxable income. Often can be utilized by the buyer in a merger or acquisition.

**Treasury Bond**

A negotiable, coupon-bearing debt obligation issued by the U.S. government and backed by its full faith and credit, having a maturity of more than seven years. Interest is paid semi-annually. Exempt from state and local taxes.

**Trust**

A tax entity created by a trust agreement. This entity distributes all or part of its income to beneficiaries as instructed by the trust agreement.

**Trustee**

The person named in a trust document who will manage the property owned by the trust and distribute any income according to the document. A trustee can be an individual or a corporate fiduciary.

**Variable Interest Rate**

An interest rate that moves at a pre-defined level above or below an index rate. A commonly used index is the bank prime rate.

**Valuation**

The formal process of estimating the worth of a business. Various valuation methods include capitalization of net earnings, present value of future earnings, asset based evaluations, and market comparisons.

**Venture Capital ("VC")**

A source of funding that looks to take an equity position with a firm at an early stage of the company's development. The VC most often will like to invest in companies that show promise of becoming public companies within 5 to 7 years of their investment.

**Working Capital**

The excess of current assets over current liabilities.

# Bibliography

## Books

Aronoff, Craig E. and Ward, John L. Family Business Succession: The Final Test of Greatness. Marietta, GA. Business Owner Resources.

Atchley, R.C. Social Forces and Aging (9th Ed.). Belmont, CA: Wadsworth. 2000.

Banta, Kim Ciccarelli and Dunton, Loren. Preserving Family Wealth and Peace of Mind. Chicago, IL. Probus Publishing, 1994.

Beckhand, Richard, Goldsmith, Marshall, and Hesselbein, Frances. The Leader of the Future, Ed. San Francisco, CA. Jossey-Bass. 1996.

Bensen, Benjamin, Crego Jr. Edwin T., Drucker, Ronald H.. Irwin, Dow Jones. Your Family Business. Homewood, IL. 1990.

Blackman, Irving L. Transferring the Privately Held Business. Chicago, IL. Blackman Kallick Bartelstien, 1994.

Brown, Bonnie M. and Frishkoff, Patricia A. Preparing...Just in Case. Corvallis, OR. Oregon State University, 1992.

Brown, John H. and Durnford, Joseph M. The Completely Revised How to Run Your Business so You Can Leave it in Style. Denver, CO: Business Enterprise Press, 1997.

Case, Randolph and PriceWaterhouseCoopers. Whose Business is it Anyway?: Smart Strategies for Ownership Succession. 2000.

Cohn, Mike. Passing the Torch: Succession, Retirement, and Estate Planning in Family Owned Businesses. New York, New York. McGraw-Hill, 1992.

Conndias, I.A. Family Ties & Aging. Thousand Oaks, CA: Sage. 2001.

Connolly, Graham and Jay, Christopher. The Private World of Family Business. Warriewood, NSW, Australia. Woodslane Fty. Ltd. 1996.

Creating Effective Boards for Private Enterprise, by John L. Ward; Jossey-Bass, San Francisco, CA.

Danco, Leon. Beyond Survival. Cleveland University Press, 1982.

Danco, Leon and Jonovic, Donald. Someday It'll All Be...Whose?; The Center for Family Business-University Press, Cleveland, OH: King Features Syndicates, Inc., 1990.

Davis, John A., Gersick, Kelin E., Lansburg, Ivan, and McCollum Hampton, Marion. Generation to Generation: Life Cycles of the Family Business. Boston, MA. Harvard Business School Press, 1996.

Deloitte and Touche. Business Succession Planning. Deloitte & Touche LLP. 2002.

Dreux IV, Dirk R. and Goodman, Joe M. Business Succession Planning and Beyond: A Multidisciplinary Approach to Representing the Family-Owned Business. Chicago, IL: American Bar Association, 1997.

Dychtwald, Ken, Ph.D. Age Power: How the 21st Century will be Ruled by the New Old. New York, New York: Tarcher/Putnam, 1999.

Dychtwald, Ken, Ph.D. The Age Wave: How the Most Important Trend of our Time Can Change Your Future. New York, New York: Bantam Books, 1990.

Grace,  Richard E. When Every Day is Saturday, The Retirement Guide for Boomers, San Jose, CA, Writer's Showcase. 2004.

Hawkey, John. Exit Strategy Planning: Grooming Your Business for Sale or Succession. Aldershot, Hampshire, UK: Gower Publishing, 2002.

Henning, Mike. Your Final Test for Success. Effingham, IL. Henning Family Business Center,1992.

Kets de Vries, Manfred. Family Business: Human Dilemmas in the Family Firm. Boston, MA. International Thomson Business Press, 1996.

"Passing the Torch," by Mike Cohn; McGraw-Hill, New York, New York.

Pratt, Shannon P., Reilly, Robert F., and Schweihs Robert P. Valuing a Business: The Analysis and Appraisal of Closely Held Companies. Edition 4. San Francisco, CA. McGraw-Hill, 2000.

Poza, Ernesto. Smart Growth: Critical Choices for Business Continuity and Prosperity. San Francisco, CA. Jossey-Bass, 1989.

Sonnenfeld, J. The Hero's Farewell: What Happens When CEOs Retire. Oxford University Press, 1988.

Syms, Marcy. Mind Your Own Business and Keep it in the Family. New York, New York. Mastermedia Ltd. 1992.

The Family Business Succession Handbook: A Practical Guide to Transferring Leadership and Ownership to the Next Generation. Philadelphia, PA: Family Business Publishing Co, 1997.

Vancil, R.F. Passing the Baton: Managing the Process of CEO Succession. Boston,

MA. Harvard Business School Press. 1987.

Ward, John L. <u>Creating Effective Boards for Private Enterprise</u>. San Francisco, CA. Jossey-Bass, 1991.

Ward, John L. <u>Keeping the Family Business Healthy: How to Plan for Continuing Growth, Profitability, and Family Leadership</u>. San Francisco, CA. Jossey-Bass, 1987.

## Studies

AIG Sun America and Harris Interactive. "Re-Visioning Retirement Survey."

Marquette University Center for Family Business. "Survey of Family Business Issues Report of Findings." Milwaukee, WI. 2005.

Mass Mutual Financial Group and Raymond Institute and the George & Robin Raymond Family Business Institute. <u>American Family Business Survey.</u> January 2003.

## Articles

### *Corporate Governance:*

"Boards of Privately Held Companies: Their Responsibilities and Structure," by John M. Nash; *Family Business Review*; Vol. 1, No.3 (1988); Jossey-Bass, San Francisco, CA.

"Selecting Outside Boards," by Gardner W. Heidrick; *Family Business Review*; Vol.1, No.3 (1988); Jossey-Bass, San Francisco, CA.

### *Financing:*

"Financing Family Business: Alternatives to Selling Out or Going Public," by Dirk R Dreux IV; *Family Business Review*; Vol. 3, No. 3 (1990); Jossey-Bass, San Francisco, CA.

### *Strategic Planning for Professional Management:*

"The Special Role of Strategic Planning for Family Businesses," by John L. Ward; *Family Business Review*; Vol. 1, No. 2 (1988); Jossey-Bass, San Francisco, CA.

### *Management/Ownership Succession:*

"Business Continuity Is the Prize of Succession," by Ernesto J. Poza; *Private Business Advisor*; Summer 1993; Dirk R. Dreux IV, Editor; U.S. Trust Company, New York, New York.

"Rough Family Justice: Equity in Family Business Succession Planning," by Glenn R. Ayres; *Family Business Review*; Vol. 3, No. 1 (1990); Jossey-Bass, San Francisco, CA.

"The Parting Patriarch of a Family Firm," by Jeffery A. Sonnenfeld and Padriac L. Spence; *Family Business Review*; Vol. 2, No. 4 (1989); Jossey-Bass, San Francisco, CA.

### Marketing to Middle Market Business Owners:

"Marketing Private Banking Services to Family Businesses," by Dirk R. Dreux IV and Bonnie M. Brown; *Journal of Bank Marketing*; Vol. 12, No. 3 (1994), p.26; MCB University Press.

"Targeting the Affluent Small Business Owner," by R.A. Prince and A. Schultz (1989b); *Journal of Bank Marketing*; Vol. 21 No. 11, pp.38-9; MCB University Press

"Targeting the Affluent Small Business Owner," by R.A. Prince; *Trusts & Estates*; Vol.129, No. 12 (1990), pp.39-46; Intertec Publishing Corporation, Atlanta, GA.

### Consulting to Middle Market Business:

"The Challenges of Multidisciplinary Consulting to Family-Owned Businesses," by Stephen Swartz; *Family Business Review*; Vol. 2, No. 4 (1989); Jossey-Bass, San Francisco, CA.

### Lawyers and Family Owned Businesses:

"Financing the Transaction," by Dirk R. Dreux IV, John Dadakis, Esq., Joe Goodman, Esq., and Richard Narva; *The Life Cycle of a Closely-Held Business*; American Bar Association Section of Real Property, Probate and Trust Law (May 1992); Chicago, IL.

"Lawyers, Families and Feelings: Representing the Family Relationship," by Gerald Le Van; *Private Business Advisor*; Fall 1991; Dirk R. Dreux IV, Editor; U.S. Trust Company, New York, New York.

CPSIA information can be obtained at www.ICGtesting.com
Printed in the USA
BVOW01*0515270913

332202BV00007B/499/P